# V

# ome

James Morwood

D1423510

WITHDRAWN

WITHDRAWN

3011780259021 2

CAMBRIDGE
UNIVERSITY PRESS

CAMBRIDGE UNIVERSITY PRESS
Cambridge, New York, Melbourne, Madrid, Cape Town, Singapore, São Paulo, Delhi

Cambridge University Press
The Edinburgh Building, Cambridge CB2 8RU, UK

www.cambridge.org
Information on this title: www.cambridge.org/9780521689441

© Cambridge University Press 2008

This publication is in copyright. Subject to statutory exception and to the provisions of relevant collective licensing agreements, no reproduction of any part may take place without the written permission of Cambridge University Press.

First published 2008

Printed in the United Kingdom at the University Press, Cambridge

*A catalogue record for this publication is available from the British Library*

ISBN   978-0-521-68944-1 paperback

ACKNOWLEDGEMENTS
We are grateful for permission to reproduce copyright photographs:

akg-images: p.57; akg-images/Erich Lessing: p.111(both); © 2002 The American Numismatic Society, all rights reserved: p.12; The Art Archive/Musée Archéologique, Naples/Alfredo Dagli Orti: p.150; The Art Archive/Musée Archéologique, Naples/Gianni Dagli Orti: pp.5, 21; The Art Archive/Museo Nazionale Taranto/Gianni Dagli Orti: p.10; The Art Archive/National Archaeological Museum, Athens/Gianni Dagli Orti: p.154; Snark/Art Resource, NY: p.92; © Museo Archaeologico Nazionale, Naples, Italy/The Bridgeman Art Library: p.23; © Galleria Borghese, Rome, Italy/Alinari/The Bridgeman Art Library: pp.36, 63; © Museo Capitolino, Rome/Italy/The Bridgeman Art Library: p.45; © Collection of the Earl of Leicester, Holkham Hall, Norfolk/The Bridgeman Art Library: p.16; © Louvre, Paris, France/The Bridgeman Art Library: p.76; © Louvre, Paris, France/Peter Willi/The Bridgeman Art Library: p.132; © Vatican Museums and Galleries, Vatican City, Italy/Lauros/Giraudon/The Bridgeman Art Library: p.56; bpk/Antikensammlung, SMB/Johannes Laurentius: p.86; Roma, Musei Capitolini, statue of Hercules (inv.MC.1265/S)/photo by James Morwood: p.125; Roma, Musei Capitolini, coin showing She-wolf feeding Romulus and Remus (inv Med.104), Archivio Fotografico dei Musei Capitolini: p.131; Courtesy of the Sovraintendenza of the Comune di Roma/photo by James Morwood: p.114; Juraj Kaman Photography, photographersdirect.com: p.30; James Morwood: pp.99, 112, 135; © NTPL/Paul Mulcahy: p.136; © 1990, Photo Scala, Florence – courtesy of the Ministero Beni e Att. Culturali: pp.46, 71; © 1990, Photo Scala, Florence: p.73.

Cover picture
*Virgil Reading the Aeneid to Livia, Octavia and Augustus, c.* 1812 (oil on canvas) by Jean Auguste Dominique Ingres (1780–1867) /Musée des Augustins, Toulouse, France/ The Bridgeman Art Library.

Picture Research by Sandie Huskinson-Rolfe of PHOTOSEEKERS

# Contents

# Preface

Virgil's great epic, the *Aeneid*, became an instant classic. Even before its publication, it had been accorded western literature's most famous flourish of advance publicity when Virgil's fellow poet Propertius wrote: 'Something greater than Homer's *Iliad* is being brought to birth.' When it appeared, it at once established itself as Rome's national epic. The earlier, shorter poems are in their different ways equally remarkable. In the *Eclogues* Virgil removed the pastoral genre from its never-never land and plunged it into the maelstrom of real-life suffering in the aftermath of civil war. His second poem, the *Georgics*, a farming manual which also confronts the harshness of man's experience in the natural and political world in which he lives, was described by John Dryden, one of the greatest of the English poets, as 'the best Poem of the best poet'. Virgil is to Latin literature what Homer is to Greek and Shakespeare is to English. His influence on subsequent western thought and literature far surpasses that of any other Roman writer.

Virgil's poetry will be for ever linked with the name of Augustus, his patron and the first Roman emperor. Much of his work can be seen as propagandist, justifying the ways of the emperor to man. However, many have felt that a more questioning voice is often to be heard sounding a note of challenge and even protest. As well as the supreme poet of Rome's greatness, he is its most profound poet of the suffering involved in the human experience. In a poem written for the nineteenth centenary of his death, Tennyson refers to him as 'majestic in [his] sadness at the doubtful doom of human kind'. There is indeed a universality about Virgil's poetry. It may be located amid the terrors and glories of late republican and Augustan Rome, but, as Ben Jonson wrote of Shakespeare, 'He was not of an age, but for all time'.

In putting this book together, I owe much to the help and encouragement of Eric Dugdale, my fellow series editor. My main debt, however, is to Keith Maclennan, himself an editor of Virgil, who commented on my manuscript in a critique informed by a deep love and knowledge of the poet. I am enormously grateful to him.

The line numbers in the margin of this book refer to the original Latin.

# Introduction

Publius Vergilius Maro, generally known in English as Virgil, was born on 15 October 70 BC in Andes, a village near Mantua in Cisalpine Gaul (now northern Italy). He was educated in Cremona and Milan before he came to Rome. At some stage of his life he was involved with the Epicurean community at Naples. He died at Brundisium, a harbour in south-east Italy, on 21 September 19 BC, and was buried in Naples. He is said to have composed his own epitaph on his deathbed:

> Mantua gave me birth, Calabria snatched me away;
> Now Naples holds me. I sang of pastures, fields and leaders

This simple account should be viewed with caution. Scarcely a single fact about Virgil's biography can be stated with certainty.

Much of his life was lived against a backdrop of intense political unrest. Rome was traditionally governed by groups of aristocratic families competing for power by means of more or less democratic elections. This is the system to which we give the name the 'Roman republic'. During the first century BC it broke down amid a remorseless succession of ever more violent struggles between leading figures, until towards the end of the century power became concentrated in the person of Julius Caesar's great-nephew and adopted son Octavian, who called himself Augustus and instituted the line of Roman emperors. Virgil's twenties witnessed the civil war between Julius Caesar and Pompey (49–48 BC). Caesar won, but was assassinated on the Ides (15th) of March 44 BC. Another civil war broke out between (on the one hand) Octavian, Caesar's heir, and Mark Antony, the murdered man's great friend, and (on the other) Brutus and Cassius, the two leading assassins. The latter were defeated at Philippi in northern Greece in 42 BC. But then Italy was flung into unrest yet again when Octavian seized large areas of land on which he could settle the veterans of his and Antony's victorious army. These confiscations provide the context for poems 1 and 9 of Virgil's *Eclogues*, his sequence of poems about 'pastures'.

In 43 BC Antony, Octavian and a third individual called Lepidus had seized power and given themselves a facade of constitutional respectability by calling themselves the 'committee of three for the re-establishment of government', an arrangement which historians call the 'second triumvirate'. This was one of the many nails driven into the coffin of the Roman republic but, though the three of them instituted a reign of terror, they did offer a measure of stability. However, the 30s BC proved to be years of constant tension between Octavian and Antony. Antony was in command of Roman territories in the eastern Mediterranean and found himself able to achieve success in his military plans only with the help of the Egyptian queen Cleopatra, in favour of whom he divorced his Roman wife Octavia, Octavian's sister. What was in effect another civil war flared up. It ended with Octavian's victories over Antony and Cleopatra at the battle of Actium in 31 BC and at Alexandria in the following year. The Roman republic was now, beyond gainsaying, a thing of the past.

In the 30s BC Virgil became a member of the poetic circle surrounding the great statesman and patron of the arts, Maecenas, and thus came into contact with Octavian, who was Maecenas' friend. In 29 BC he published the *Georgics*, the work about 'fields', a didactic poem about farming which also voices a passionate plea for political stability. (For the term 'didactic poem', see the introduction to the *Georgics*.)

The tension between optimism and pessimism in Virgil's work is an apt reflection of the times in which it was written. When Octavian changed his name to Augustus in 27 BC, he was making use of a word with strong religious associations, and in a remarkably successful exercise of political spin, he left behind his ruthless and blood-stained image, reinventing himself as the pious father of the fatherland, a title he actually assumed in 2 BC. He had certainly brought an end to the horrors of civil war and given Italy the stability for which Virgil longed. However, he had also become Rome's first emperor and freedom had been extinguished, though this may not have become fully evident until after Virgil's death. In the *Aeneid*, the great epic about 'leaders' to which Virgil devoted the last ten years of his life and which remained incomplete at his death – it was edited by his friends Varius Rufus and Plotius Tucca – the poet celebrates Augustus' achievements. But many have felt that another voice is sounding a very different, anti-Augustan message.

It is certainly possible to articulate a clear-cut response to the question of the poem's two voices, saying, for example, that at the time Virgil was writing the *Aeneid* it was still allowable to be frank and balanced about Augustus' regime without being thought to oppose him. But so deep is the pessimism that has often been identified at many stages of the poem that such an explanation can seem altogether inadequate in the face of the profound doubts about Augustanism that this pessimism raises. For those who feel like this and wonder how Virgil got away with writing such a poem under Augustus' autocracy, the twentieth century provides an interesting parallel. Up till 1979 it was taken for granted that the Russian composer Dmitri Shostakovich (1906–75) had created works which gave undiluted support to Soviet communism when it was under the control of the mass-murdering dictator Stalin. But in that year Solomon Volkov published a book called *Testimony* which claimed that the composer's public music, far from straightforwardly asserting Soviet ideals, was often informed with bitter sarcasm and thus deeply subversive. A battle has subsequently raged over Volkov's claims, but our experience of listening to Shostakovich has certainly been transformed. As we hear music that we used to consider nobly patriotic, we can find ourselves tugged in other, deeply disturbing directions. It may be that reading Virgil offers a similar experience. To the objection that the language of music is more subject to a range of interpretations than that of poetry, it can be answered that we are here talking not about Virgil's words but his tone.

Other tensions can be found in Virgil's work. He overtly lays claim to Epicureanism at *Georgics* 4.563–4, thus aligning himself with the philosophy of the Greek Epicurus (341–270 BC), who recommended withdrawal from the turmoil and confusion of the active life into the study of philosophy. At the same time, one can identify in his work a profoundly Stoic sensibility. The Stoic school, founded by Zeno of Cyprus (335–263 BC), preached that to be virtuous was the only good and not to be virtuous the only evil. Man should accept whatever happens to him with calm, giving way neither to intense joy nor to excessive grief. Thus he will come into harmony not only with the universal brotherhood of man but also with God. The two philosophies are irreconcilable, and the presence of both of them in Virgil's work offers the opportunity for thought-provoking contrasts.

Another striking paradox in Virgil's work arises from the fact that the writer of a great Roman epic was so deep-dyed in the Hellenistic poetic tradition. When we talk of Hellenistic culture, we refer to the art of the Greek world from 323 to 30 BC, a world dominated by the Greek-ruled kingdoms established in the wake of the conquests of Alexander the Great. Its epicentre was the Greek city of Alexandria. Indeed 'Alexandrian' is another name used to describe aspects of this culture. In poetry the Hellenistic ideal lay in elegance, the display of learning, and brevity. Callimachus (third century BC), the poet who was its archetypal embodiment, famously wrote that 'a big book is a big evil'. There was a self-conscious contrast with the grand, discursive, wide-ranging tradition of Homeric epic. Virgil can work wonderfully on a miniature scale. His telling of the story of Orpheus and Eurydice in *Georgics* 4 is a small-scale epic which is altogether true to the Hellenistic tradition, but it is superbly assimilated into the poem's larger design. And throughout the *Aeneid* he invokes both the spirit and the letter of the works of Homer. Virgil the pointillist could paint with broad brushstrokes too. To balance the two techniques in a masterly equipoise was not the least remarkable achievement of Rome's greatest poet.

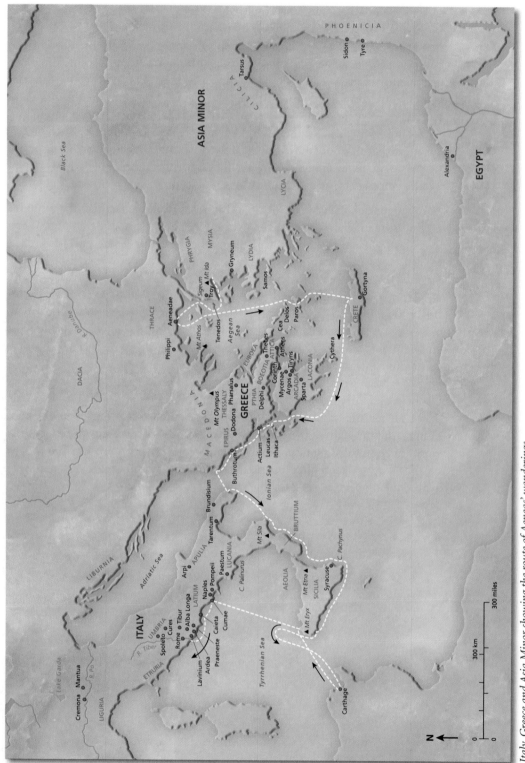

*Italy, Greece and Asia Minor showing the route of Aeneas' wanderings.*

# 1 Eclogues

The ten *Eclogues* (or pastoral poems) were written by Virgil at around the age of 30. His first poems to be published, they evoke the world of the pastoral poetry of the third-century Syracusan poet Theocritus, though they are, of course, written in Latin and not the Sicilian's Greek. Two of the *Eclogues* which we shall look at, 1 and 9, link the pastoral world of poetry with real – and for many, tragic – events. The civil war between Mark Antony and Octavian, the avengers of Julius Caesar, and his assassins ended when the assassins were defeated at Philippi in 42 BC. The victors agreed that land in Italy, including the area round Mantua where Virgil had been born, should be confiscated and settled by their veterans, who perhaps numbered 50,000. In the first of the *Eclogues*, Tityrus has had his farm restored to him by an unspecified young man in Rome, while Meliboeus has been forced out from his property.

*A wall painting from Pompeii showing a rustic shrine set in an idyllic pastoral landscape.*

## Eclogue 1

1.1–83 MELIBOEUS **Tityrus**, you lying there beneath the shade of a spreading beech practising your woodland music on a slender pipe, we are leaving the boundaries of our country and our sweet fields. We are being exiled from our country, while you, Tityrus, at your ease in the shade, **teach the woods to re-echo the name of beautiful Amaryllis.** 5

TITYRUS O Meliboeus, **a god** brought us this peaceful life. For that man will always be a god to me, a tender lamb from our flocks will often stain his altar. He it was who allowed my cows to graze, as you see, and me, their master, to play what I want on my rustic pipe. 10

MELIBOEUS For my part I do not begrudge you this. Rather I marvel at it. There is **such complete chaos everywhere throughout the countryside.** Look, I myself am driving my goats forward, sick at heart. This one here, Tityrus, I can scarcely drag along. For just now, here amid the thick hazel trees, she gave birth to twin kids, the hope of the flock, but **left them, alas! on the bare flint.** I remember that **this disaster** 15 was often foretold to us by **oaks struck by lightning** – but I was too foolish to take any notice. But still, tell me, Tityrus, who this god of yours is.

TITYRUS The city which they call Rome, Meliboeus, I thought in my folly was like this one of ours to which we shepherds are often accustomed to 20 drive the tender lambs. I used this yardstick: I knew that puppies were like dogs, kids like their dams. That was the way I used to compare great things with small. But this city towers above all others as far as cypresses often do amid the yielding shrubs. 25

MELIBOEUS And what was the great cause of your seeing Rome?

---

MELIBOEUS   the name means 'cattle-minder'. The names **Tityrus** and **Amaryllis** come from Theocritus. Compare line 68 of Milton's pastoral poem *Lycidas*: 'To sport with Amaryllis in the shade'.

**teach the woods to re-echo the name of beautiful Amaryllis**   Philip Hardie suggests that the echo may be 'the sign of nature's sympathy with men', while at the same time 'we are made aware that the magic of pastoral song may be such stuff as dreams are made on'.

**a god**   Tityrus refers to his benefactor with understandable hyperbole. He plans to sacrifice to him (1.7–8, 42–3).

**such complete chaos everywhere throughout the countryside**   the countryside has been turned upside down by the confiscations.

**left them, alas! on the bare flint**   either the kids were born dead or they were so weak that they could not be saved.

**this disaster**   that his farm would be confiscated.

**oaks struck by lightning**   Jupiter is the god of lightning and the oak is his own sacred tree. His striking of his own tree may have made these omens particularly threatening.

TITYRUS   **Freedom**. Though late in the day, she did at last look upon me in
          my paralysis after my beard became whiter as it fell beneath the
          scissors. Yes, she looked upon me and came to me after a long time,
          now that Amaryllis holds me in her power and Galatea has left me.   30
          For, I shall confess it, as long as Galatea ruled me, I had neither
          any hope of freedom nor any thought of **savings**. Although many
          a victim left my sheep stalls, and many a rich cheese was pressed
          for the ungrateful town, I never returned home with my right hand   35
          weighed down with money.

MELIBOEUS  I used to wonder, Amaryllis, why you used to call sadly on the
          gods, and **for whom you were letting the fruits hang on their
          trees**. Tityrus was away from here. The very pines, Tityrus, the very
          springs, these very orchards were calling you.

TITYRUS   What was I to do? I could neither get away from my slavery nor find   40
          gods to give me such present help **anywhere else**. **Here**, Meliboeus, I
          saw **that young man** for whom **our altars smoke twelve days every
          year**. Here that man was the first to respond to my petition: 'Feed
          your cattle as before, boys. Rear your bulls.'                        45

MELIBOEUS  Fortunate old man, so the lands will remain yours then, and they
          are large enough for you, although bare rock and the marsh with

---

**Freedom**   personified as a goddess. We now discover that Tityrus had been a slave. He has
now bought his freedom. His spendthrift partner Galatea had not allowed him to think
of spending his savings on this. His liaison with Amaryllis has instilled in him more thrifty
ways.

**savings**   the Latin word translated here ('peculium') in fact means something more precise.
A slave could not own property himself but could occupy a piece of land (*peculium*) on
sufferance from his master, surrendering to him a percentage of the profits on working it.
If he saved sufficient money, he could buy his freedom and gain full possession of the land.
Tityrus has done this, and so it would be a disaster for him if the land he was working was
confiscated.

**for whom you were letting the fruits hang on their trees**   is Amaryllis too grief-stricken in
Tityrus' absence to look after the estate? Or is she hoping that her partner can have fresh
fruit when he gets home?

**anywhere else**   According to Appian, crowds of threatened occupants came to the forum
and temples of Rome to protest, and the Romans had a lot of sympathy with them (*The
Civil Wars* 5.12).

**Here**   i.e. at Rome.

**that young man**   presumably Octavian, who was 21 at the time of the confiscations. On 1
January 42 BC the senate had confirmed the deification of his adoptive father Julius Caesar,
and Octavian was given the title 'son of a god' on coinage struck in the following years.

**our altars smoke twelve days every year**   Tityrus is preparing to make a monthly
offering.

its muddy rushes cover the whole pasture. No unfamiliar pasturage will assail **the sickly mothers in your flocks** and no damaging infection from a neighbour's flock will harm them. Fortunate old 50 man, here amid well-known rivers and **sacred springs** you will seek out the cool shade. On this side, as ever, the hedge on your neighbour's boundary will often soothe you to slumber with its soft whispers as **Hybla's bees** feed their fill on its willow blossom. On 55 that side beneath the lofty rock the pruner will sing to the breezes; and meanwhile your pets, the throaty wood-pigeons, and the turtle doves shall not cease from moaning from the towering elm.

TITYRUS Sooner, then, will the light-footed stags pasture in the air and the seas leave the fish uncovered on the shore, sooner, **wandering in** 60 **exile** over each other's territories, will the Parthian drink of **the Arar** or the German of the Tigris than that man's face could fade away from my heart.

MELIBOEUS But we shall go away from here, some to the thirsty Africans, some 65 of us will reach Scythia and **the Oaxes** that snatches up chalk as it flows, and the Britons, utterly cut off from the whole world. Ah, shall I ever, a long time hence, look upon the land of my fathers and the roof of my humble cottage heaped high with turf, look upon and marvel one day at my kingdom, **a few ears of corn**? Will some **godless** soldier hold this fallow land which I have cultivated so well, 70 some barbarian hold these crops? See where **civil war** has brought

---

**the sickly mothers in your flocks**   the she-goats are especially vulnerable immediately after giving birth.

**sacred springs**   each spring has its own divine nymph.

**Hybla's bees**   bees will play a significant part in Virgil's future work. Hybla, on the southern slopes of Mount Etna in Sicily, was famous for its honey. The idyllic landscape Meliboeus here describes is reminiscent of Theocritus (7.133–45 – bees in line 142). It is interesting that the evocation of the pastoral dream comes from the man about to be excluded from it. But is the dream a never-never land in any case?

**wandering in exile**   as Meliboeus and those like him must now do.

**the Arar**   the river Saône, which joins the Rhône at Lyons in eastern France.

**the Oaxes**   possibly a river in Mesopotamia.

**a few ears of corn**   the state to which Meliboeus feels that the new occupant will have reduced his farm.

**godless**   'impius', the Latin word used here, is to prove of major importance in Virgil's *Aeneid*.

**civil war**   literally 'discord', to be personified in one of the horrific shapes at the entrance to hell in *Aeneid* 6 (280).

our wretched citizens. It was for **them** that we sowed these fields. **Now, Meliboeus, graft your pears, plant your vines in rows.** On, my goats, once a happy flock, on! No more, as I lie in a mossy cave, 75 shall I watch you at a distance, poised on the edge of a bushy cliff; no songs shall I sing; I shall be your herdsman but you will not crop flowering **clover** and bitter willows.

TITYRUS      But for this night you could take your rest with me here on the green foliage. We have ripe fruits, tasty chestnuts and an abundance of 80 cheeses. Already now the roofs of the country houses are smoking in the distance and longer shadows are falling from the lofty mountains.

---

1   How expressive do you find Virgil's evocation of the countryside? How realistic does it seem to you to be?

2   Compare the characterization of Tityrus and Meliboeus. How do you feel about them both? Does Meliboeus' attitude change in the course of the poem? Do you find that Tityrus is offputtingly absorbed in his own good fortune? If so, does anything he says modify your impression?

3   How do you respond to the fact that Tityrus calls Octavian, a living human being, a god, to whom he will make sacrifices?

4   'By including such images of current events in his poems, the poet boldly transformed the pastoral genre' (Josiah Osgood, p. 112). Do you feel that the fact that it reflects actual historical events makes a difference to your appreciation of this poem?

---

## Eclogue 4

Before long the relationship between Mark Antony and Octavian had deteriorated to such an extent that another civil war looked imminent. Two men, both important figures in the literary world and hence known to Virgil, Maecenas, acting for Octavian, and Asinius Pollio, acting for Antony, brokered a treaty between them at Brundisium in September 40 BC.

To cement the peace, Antony married Octavian's sister Octavia. (Both their spouses had just died.) Virgil's fourth Eclogue celebrates this peace, asserting that a new golden age will begin with Pollio's consulship (40 BC) and

---

**them**   bitterly used to refer to the new occupants of the farm.

**Now, Meliboeus, graft your pears, plant your vines in rows**   what do you feel is Meliboeus' tone here?

**clover**   actually shrub trefoil, which has clover-like leaves and yellow flowers.

foretelling the birth of a Messiah-like boy. Among a number of suggestions proposed for **the identity of this figure**, which inevitably but implausibly include Jesus Christ, the most convincing is a hoped-for child of Antony and Octavia. (In fact, they were to have no sons.)

*Octavian. The original of this marble copy dates from the earliest years of his political career.*

4.1–25    **Sicilian Muses,** let us sing of somewhat greater things. It is not everyone that woodlands and the low-lying tamarisk bushes delight. If we sing of woods, let the woods be worthy of a **consul.**

Now there has come the final age of **Cumaean prophecy.** The great line of the    5 centuries is being born anew. Now even **the Virgin** returns, **the reign of Saturn** returns. Now a new generation is being sent down from the high heavens. Only

---

**the identity of this figure**   perhaps the poet left the identity of the boy in doubt quite deliberately. As Philip Hardie remarks, 'The *Eclogues* were written in the rapidly changing and unpredictable conditions of the second Triumvirate, and a poet with an eye to future fame but also with a desire to intervene in contemporary political debate could do worse than develop an allusive and polysemous manner.'

**Sicilian Muses**   a reference to the powers that inspired the Sicilian Theocritus, the inventor of pastoral poetry.

**consul**   i.e. Pollio, the consul for 40 BC.

**Cumaean prophecy**   the reference is to the Sibyl of Cumae, priestess of Apollo.

**the Virgin**   Justice or Astraea, the last of the immortals to leave the world when the behaviour of mankind became intolerable to her (see *Georgics* 2.473–4).

**the reign of Saturn**   Saturn, father of Jupiter, had presided over the first golden age.

do you, chaste **Lucina**, show favour to the birth of this boy, under whom **the iron age** will at last cease and a golden race rise in all the world. Your own **Apollo** is 10 ruling now.

It is in your consulship, Pollio, yes yours, that this glorious age will begin and the great months start to move forward. Under your leadership, if any traces of our **sin** remain, they will be erased and will free the earth from fear for ever. **He** will assume the life of the gods, see heroes mingled with gods and himself be seen by 15 them, and rule the world to which his father's qualities have brought peace.

But for you, boy, the uncultivated earth will pour forth as her first little gifts wandering ivy with **cyclamen** everywhere, and Egyptian lilies mixed with laughing 20 bear's-breech. Of their own accord goats will bring home their udders bulging with milk, and **the cattle will not fear huge lions**. Of its own accord your cradle will bloom with delightful flowers. The snake will perish too, and the plant which conceals its poison will perish. Assyrian **cardamom** will spring up everywhere. 25

> • How successfully do you feel Virgil conveys his vision of a new golden age?

## Eclogue 6

> At the beginning of his sixth Eclogue, Virgil excuses himself from singing of warfare as Alfenus Varus, a leading statesman and soldier, has asked him to. Echoing the refusal poem (*recusatio*) of the Alexandrian tradition (see Introduction, p. 3), he does not – at the moment – feel that his Muse is well suited to an epic subject.

---

**Lucina**   the goddess of childbirth, often identified with Diana.

**the iron age**   this was the final age of the poet Hesiod's cycle: gold, silver, bronze, heroic, iron.

**Apollo**   the brother of Diana, Apollo is the sponsor of the new age not only as the god of the Sibyl who foretold it, but also as the god of poetry, inspiring Virgil to sing about it.

**sin**   referring to the civil wars.

**He**   i.e. the boy.

**cyclamen**   we do not in fact know precisely to what plant Virgil is referring here. According to the elder Pliny, it had medicinal uses.

**the cattle will not fear huge lions**   compare Isaiah 11.6: 'The calf and the young lion will grow up together and a little child will lead them'; and the *Sibylline Oracles* 3.791–3: 'And the lion, devourer of flesh, will eat husks in the stall like an ox, and tiny children will lead them in chains.'

**cardamom**   a fragrant shrub.

**6.1–8** Thalea, my Muse, first deigned to sport in **Syracusan poetry** and did not blush to dwell in the woods. When I was starting to sing of kings and battles, **the god of Cynthus** tweaked my ear and gave me warning: 'A shepherd, **Tityrus**, **ought to feed his sheep to keep them fat but keep his song thin-spun.**' Now I 5 – for you will find poets aplenty who are eager to sing your praises, Varus, and to write about grim warfare – **will practise the rustic Muse on a slender reed.**

*This coin shows on one side a head of Octavian and on the reverse a legionary eagle, a plough and the surveyor's rod. The coin is a commemoration of the fulfilment of the promises to soldiers made by their generals. The veterans, who had soldiered hard in the generals' cause, would take a very different view of the process by which they were given land from that of the dispossessed victims. They had the law on their side, even if it was the dubious lex Titia of 43 BC, which gave power to the second triumvirate (see Introduction, p. 1).*

> • Can you think of any English-language poet who wrote both pastoral and epic poetry? If so, do you think that he or she was equally successful at both?

**Thalea**   this Muse is mentioned here for the first time in Latin poetry.

**Syracusan poetry**   Virgil again pays tribute to the pastoral Muse of the Syracusan Theocritus.

**the god of Cynthus**   i.e. Apollo, born on the island of Delos, whose mountain (or rather hill) is called Cynthus.

**Tityrus**   Virgil is addressed by the name of the lowly, ageing herdsman of Eclogue 1.

**ought to feed his sheep to keep them fat but keep his song thin-spun**   Virgil makes use of Callimachus (*Aitia* 1.1.22–3): 'Apollo said to me ... "Fatten the beast you offer to the gods, but keep your style lean"'.

**will practise the rustic Muse on a slender reed**   the poet looks back to *Eclogues* 1.1.

In Eclogue 1 the irruption of the confiscations into the pastoral world was not given a specific location. Eclogue 9 appears to be set near Mantua (lines 27–8), Virgil's birthplace. Neighbouring Cremona (it was about 37 miles away) had been chosen as an area for confiscation because of its fertility in wheat, olives, vines and pasturage, but it had proved too small to hold all the veterans assigned to it. The deficiency was made good by the forcible seizure of large parts of Mantuan territory.

## Eclogue 9

9.1–29

LYCIDAS    Where are you walking to, Moeris? Is it where the road leads, to the **city**?

MOERIS     We have lived to see ourselves come to this, that a stranger – something that we never feared – should possess our little farm and say, '**These lands are mine.** Off with you, old tenants.' Now, beaten  5 and grim – since Chance rules everything – **we are taking these kids on his behalf**, and may it turn out badly for him!

LYCIDAS    Certainly what *I* had heard was that from where the hills begin to retreat and slope from their summits in a gentle descent, right up to the water and the old beeches with their now-shattered tops, your friend **Menalcas** had saved everything with his songs.              10

MOERIS     Yes, you had heard that, and so the story went. But amid the weapons of war, Lycidas, our songs are only as effective as men say **Chaonian** doves are when **the eagle** comes. So, had not a crow on the left first  15 warned me from the hollow oak to cut short **this new litigation** some way or other, neither your Moeris here nor Menalcas himself would still be alive.

---

**city**   presumably Mantua (see 9.27–8).

**These lands are mine**   this may be technical legal language; after all, the new occupant was now the legal owner. But there is a directness about this and the next sentence that suggests a confrontation.

**we are taking these kids on his behalf**   i.e. to the city. It sounds as if Moeris may be working for the new owner.

**Menalcas**   the pastoral poet was hoping to gain back his and Moeris' former land through his poetry. The implication of Moeris' next speech is that the appeal has not proved successful.

**Chaonian**   Chaonia was an area in Epirus in north-west Greece where Dodona, famous for its dove-haunted oak trees, was situated.

**the eagle**   not only does the bird of prey make a strong contrast with the dove, it also brings into the poem the menacing military emblem: see the coin on p. 12.

**this new litigation**   it looks as if a quarrel had broken out with the new owner which could have resulted in the death of Moeris and Menalcas, had they not backed down.

LYCIDAS  Alas that anyone could fall victim to such wickedness! Alas, was the consolation of your music almost snatched from us, Menalcas, and you as well? Who would sing of the Nymphs? Who would scatter the ground with flowery grasses or cover the springs with green shade?  20 And who would sing the songs which I stole from you the other day when I eavesdropped as you were going off to see Amaryllis, my sweetheart? '**Tityrus**, until I return – the way is short – feed my goats and when you have fed them drive them to water, Tityrus, and while you drive them be careful not to run up against the he-goat  25 – he butts with his horn.'

MOERIS  But what about this, which he sang to **Varus** although it was not yet finished: 'Varus, only let Mantua survive for us, Mantua, alas! too near to wretched Cremona, and singing **swans** will bear your name aloft to the stars!'

---

1  Serious issues are dealt with in Eclogues 1 and 9. Are they blunted by the escapist setting of pastoral poetry?

2  Do you feel that poetry has any role to play at times of national crisis or disaster?

---

**Tityrus ...**  Virgil takes almost all of these verses of Menalcas from Theocritus 3.3–5. But the lines addressed to Varus that follow (9.27–9) are decidedly alien to the spirit of Theocritus' pastoral poetry. As Wendell Clausen remarks, the worst that can befall one of the Sicilian poet's herdsmen 'is defeat in a singing-match, a thorn-prick in the foot, or rejection in love'.

**Varus**  the dedicatee of Eclogue 6 (see above) and one of the land-commissioners overseeing the confiscations. An ancient commentator on Virgil who is usually referred to as Servius Danielis writes that 'because of the unfairness of Alfenus Varus, who managed the confiscations, nothing was left to the Mantuans but swampland'.

**swans**  Mantua was famous for these birds: compare *Georgics* 2.198–9.

# 2 Georgics

The years that followed the confiscations were to prove as dangerous and unsettled as those that had preceded them. Antony's marriage to Octavia broke down as he became more and more committed to Cleopatra, the queen of Egypt. The tensions between Octavian and Antony finally erupted in civil war. The former defeated the latter in the battle of Actium (off the west coast of Greece) in 31 BC and Antony killed himself the following year. After mopping-up operations in various areas, Octavian eventually returned to Italy in 29 BC. He was now the undisputed master of the Roman world.

On his way to Rome, Octavian spent a few days near Naples recovering from an illness. There is no reason to disbelieve **Donatus'** story that here Virgil read to him his new poem about farming, the *Georgics*. Virgil's beautiful reading voice tired easily and so Maecenas took turns with him. They spent four days reading the poem, presumably one of the four books on each day.

Virgil's new work was a didactic poem, i.e. it set out to teach. Its two great predecessors in the genre were Hesiod's *Works and Days* (see note on 2.176, 'a song of Ascra', p. 24) and Lucretius' *On the Nature of the Universe*, which dates from the middle of the first century BC and expounds the Epicurean philosophy in language of extraordinary power and intensity.

24

## Book 1

1.1–42   **What** makes the crops happy, at what time of the year it is right to turn the soil, **Maecenas**, and wed vines to elms, what efforts are needed for oxen, what care for keeping flocks, what great expertise for the thrifty bees, I shall now begin to sing. You, o **most radiant lights of the sky** who guide the year as it slips through   5
the heavens; **Liber** and kindly **Ceres**, as surely as it was by your gift that the earth

---

**Donatus**   an ancient biographer of Virgil.

**What … sing (1–5)**   Virgil here outlines the subjects of each of his four books: tillage (1), viticulture (2), rearing cattle (3) and bee-keeping (4).

**Maecenas**   Virgil's great patron and the dedicatee of this poem. He is addressed at the start of all four books.

**most radiant lights of the sky**   the sun and the moon.

**Liber**   a name for Bacchus, god of wine (and hence of the vine), meaning 'the one who frees'.

**Ceres**   goddess of wheat and fertility.

changed **the Chaonian acorn** for the nourishing corn-ear and blended **the draughts of Achelous** with the new-found grapes; and you **Fauns**, gods of the countryfolk 10 ever present to help – come together here, Fauns and **Dryad nymphs** – it is of your

*An illustration in a medieval manuscript of the* Georgics.

**the Chaonian acorn**   Chaonia was an area in Epirus in north-west Greece where Dodona, famous for its dove-haunted oak trees, was situated: cf. *Eclogues* 9.13.

**the draughts of Achelous**   i.e. water. Achelous is a river in western Greece, said to be the oldest of all rivers. Compare these lines from Richard Lovelace's (1618–57) *To Althea, from Prison*:

> When flowing cups run swiftly round
> With no allaying Thames …

**Fauns**   rustic deities often associated with Pan.

**Dryad nymphs**   tree-nymphs.

gifts that I sing. You also, o Neptune, for whom **the earth first produced a neighing horse** when struck by your great trident; and you, **guardian of the groves**, for whom **three hundred** snow-white bullocks graze on the rich thickets of **Cea**. And 15 you too, Pan, leaving **your native woods** and the glades of **Lycaeus**, you guardian of sheep, if you care for your own **Maenala**, be present, o **Tegean** one, and show me favour; **Minerva** too, inventress of the olive tree, and you, the **boy** who showed men the curving plough, and you, **Silvanus**, carrying a young uprooted cypress; 20 and all you gods and goddesses whose love it is to look after the fields, both you who nurture the young fruits which sow themselves naturally and you who send down abundant rain from the sky. Yes, and you, **Caesar**. We do not know which assemblies of the gods will later have you amongst them, whether you wish to 25 watch over cities and care for our lands, and the great globe will receive you as the giver of increase and the lord of the seasons, garlanding your brows with **your mother's myrtle**; or whether you come as god of the vast sea and sailors worship your divinity alone, while **Thule** at the edge of the world is your slave and **Tethys** 30 **buys you as her son-in-law** with a dowry of all her waves; or whether you add yourself as a new constellation to the sluggish months where a space is opening

---

**the earth first produced a neighing horse**   Neptune struck the earth with his trident in Thessaly or Attica and a horse sprang out.

**guardian of the groves**   Aristaeus, who is revealed in Book 4 as having taught men how to produce new swarms of bees.

**three hundred**   this term in fact stands for an indefinitely large number.

**Cea**   an island in the Aegean, also known as Ceos.

**your native woods**   in Arcadia in southern Greece. **Lycaeus** and **Maenala** (more commonly known as Maenalus) were high mountains in that region, and **Tegea** was a city there.

**Minerva**   called Athena in Greek, she became the patroness of Athens when she gave the city an olive tree.

**boy**   Triptolemus, to whom Ceres (Demeter in Greek) revealed the mysteries of agriculture in Eleusis.

**Silvanus**   a Roman country deity. He was the lover of the youth Cyparissus: hence the cypress tree.

**Caesar**   Octavian. We call him by this name to distinguish him from Julius Caesar, his adoptive father, but he would certainly have expected to be addressed as Caesar.

**your mother's myrtle**   myrtle was sacred to Venus, the goddess from whom the Julian line (to which Octavian belonged) claimed descent.

**Thule**   proverbial for the northernmost point of Ocean. It may refer to Iceland or Shetland or Britain.

**Tethys buys you as her son-in-law**   Tethys was the mother of the sea-nymphs. A marriage on the lines of the sea-goddess Thetis to Peleus is implied.

between **Erigone** and the grasping **Claws** – look, for you the burning Scorpion is now drawing back his arms and has left you more than a fair share of the sky. 35 Whatever you will be – for **Tartarus** does not hope for you to rule it and may such a terrible desire to be a king never come over you, although Greece marvels at the **Elysian fields** and **Proserpina** does not care to follow her mother who has called her back – grant me an easy journey, support my bold undertaking, and, pitying 40 with me the countryfolk who do not know the way, come forward and **even now** accustom yourself to being invoked in prayers.

---

1 What do you feel is the effect of the amassing of invocations to gods and heroes of the countryside in lines 1–23?

2 Here again, what do you feel about the invocation of the mortal Octavian as a god (24–42)? (You have already responded to this question in discussing Eclogue 1.) Is Virgil here playing the courtier? He could scarcely have intended that the passage be taken literally. Do you find it off-putting or even repellent, or do you think that it works as a literary device?

---

The first book of the *Georgics* ends with a passage which moves from a discussion of the signs which the sun can give the farmer to a powerful description of the omens that followed the assassination of Julius Caesar on the Ides (15th) of March 44 BC. After this comes a passionate plea to the gods of Rome to allow Octavian to come to the help of a world dislocated by warfare and sin. Here is this final movement of the first book.

1.461–514    In short, the sun will give you signs of what message the late evening has, from where the wind drives fine-weather clouds and what the rainy south is plotting. Who would dare to say that the sun is false? He and no other often warns us that dark riots are imminent and that treachery and hidden wars are coming to a head. 465

---

**Erigone**   i.e. Virgo, the constellation. Between Virgo and Scorpio comes Libra, the sign under which Octavian was born (on 23 September 63 BC).

**Claws**   the claws of Scorpio.

**Tartarus**   a name for the underworld.

**Elysian fields**   the land of the blessed, located in the underworld.

**Proserpina**   abducted by her uncle Pluto, king of the underworld, and found by her mother after a long search, Proserpina, according to this version, wishes to stay with him. The usual story is that she spends some months of each year in the underworld and some on earth.

**even now**   i.e. while still on earth.

He and no other pitied Rome after Julius Caesar had been killed, when **he covered his shining face in a violet gloom** and a **godless** age feared everlasting night. And yet at that time the earth also, the plains of the sea, accursed dogs and ill-omened 470 birds gave signs. How often did we see **Etna** gushing from its broken furnaces into the fields of the **Cyclopes**, rolling balls of fire and molten rocks! **Germany** heard the sound of arms all across the sky, and the Alps trembled with earthquakes 475 never suffered before. Then too a mighty voice was heard by many among the silent groves and wondrously pale ghosts were seen in the darkness of the night, and cattle spoke (unspeakable!), rivers stood still and the earth gaped open and ivory images shed tears of mourning in the temples and the brazen ones sweated. 480 **Eridanus**, king of rivers, swept forests along, spinning them in his mad swirl, and carried the cattle and their stalls all over the plains. And at the same time there was no respite from the appearance of threatening **filaments** in ill-omened entrails or from blood flowing in wells or from the sound of wolf-howls in the night echoing 485 through our lofty cities. At no other time did so many lightning flashes fall from a cloudless sky or dire comets blaze so often.

---

**he covered his shining face in a violet gloom**    there was an eclipse of the sun in November 44, months after Caesar's murder in March. The dreadful portents here described all postdate his death. They are seen as omens of the civil wars that were to come. A parallel passage in *Hamlet* (1.1.113–20), in which Shakespeare causes Horatio to talk of portents which came before the assassination, is worth quoting:

> In the most high and palmy state of Rome,
> A little ere the mightiest Julius fell,
> The graves stood tenantless, and the sheeted dead
> Did squeak and gibber in the Roman streets;
> As stars with trains of fire and dews of blood,
> Disasters in the sun; and the moist star,
> Upon whose influence Neptune's empire stands,
> Was sick almost to doomsday with eclipse …

**godless**    again, the Latin word 'impius': cf. *Eclogues* 1.70.

**Etna**    a volcano on Sicily beneath which the one-eyed giants, the **Cyclopes** (Greek plural of Cyclops), worked as blacksmiths. According to Servius, an eruption of this volcano before Caesar's death was noted by Livy in Book 116 (fragment 57).

**Germany**    Julius Caesar had fought here in a famous war, but Virgil's aim in his location for this portent may have been to universalize the time out of joint. It affected the whole western world, not just Rome.

**Eridanus**    the river Po.

**filaments**    veins of the larger organs which were thought to be significant if they were irregular in any way. When soothsayers cut open sacrificial victims and examined the layout of their entrails, any abnormality was a bad omen.

So it was that **Philippi saw Roman armies clash for a second time with Roman** 490
arms; and the gods did not think it monstrous to make **Emathia** and the broad
plains of **Haemus** rich twice over with our blood. Yes, and a time will come when
the farmer, toiling at the ground in that territory with his curving plough, will
discover javelins roughly eaten away by corrosion, or with his heavy hoe strike an 495
empty helmet and wonder at the huge bones in the graves he has dug out.

Gods of our country, divine heroes of our land, and you, **Romulus**, and you,
mother **Vesta**, who watch over **Tuscan** Tiber and Rome's Palatine hill, grant that 500
this young man at least may come to the help of our ruined age. Long enough
have we paid with our blood for **Laomedon's perjury at Troy**. For a long time
now, Caesar, the realm of heaven has begrudged us your presence and complains
that you care for triumphs among mortals; for right and wrong are overturned: 505
there are so many wars throughout the world; crimes show themselves in so many
ways; there is no proper respect for the plough; the fields go to waste where the
farmers have been taken away, and curved scythes are forged into straight swords.

---

**Philippi saw Roman armies clash for a second time**   Philippi was the site of the battle
in which Mark Antony and Octavian defeated the assassins of Julius Caesar in 42 BC. The
first time was at the battle of Pharsalus, in which Julius Caesar defeated Pompey, in 48
BC. Since the two sites are about 160 miles away from each other, the geography may
seem problematic, but ancient poets did not seem too worried about this sort of thing.
In the *Aeneid* Virgil talks about Tyre and Sidon as if they are the same place when in fact
they are some 22 miles apart. As T. E. Page notes, 'it was a remarkable fact that two such
battles … should have taken place so soon after one another both in the same Roman
province of Macedonia, and this fact so struck the Roman poets that they not infrequently
speak of the two battles as occurring in the same place': cf. Ovid, *Metamorphoses* 15.824.
'Two disastrous battles', as Josiah Osgood remarks, 'like two Roman armies, have been
run into one bloody blur' (p. 97). (There were in fact two battles of Philippi, separated
by about three weeks, and Virgil's lines could refer to them. This strikes me as an inferior
reading.)

**with Roman arms**   the fact that each side had matching weapons stresses the horror of
civil war.

**Emathia**   this name is used pretty vaguely for the area of Macedonia, which contained
both Philippi and Pharsalus and Mount **Haemus**.

**Romulus**   the founder of Rome. Though commanding enormous respect, he is an
ambivalent figure, having killed his brother while founding the city.

**Vesta**   the goddess of the hearth.

**Tuscan**   the Tiber was often called Tuscan since it flowed from Etruria (cf. Tuscany).

**Laomedon's perjury at Troy**   Laomedon, an early king of Troy (from where, according
to mythology, the future Romans had come), had cheated Apollo and Neptune of their
payment for building the walls of Troy. This is seen as a kind of 'original sin' for the
Romans and the idea that their civil wars could be attributed to it is traditional.

Here **Euphrates** calls to war, there **Germany**; neighbouring cities break the pacts  510
between them and take up arms; **unholy Mars** rages throughout the world: as
when the chariots pour out of the starting gate, speed on lap after lap, and the
charioteer, vainly pulling at the reins, is carried along by the horses and the chariot
does not heed the curb.

*A wall painting from Pompeii
showing a chariot race. The drivers
wear tight-fitting leather helmets
and a harness of leather thongs on
their bodies and legs for protection
in the event of a crash.*

1   What is the effect of Virgil's description of the portents following the death
    of Julius Caesar? You may wish to compare his account with some portents
    listed for this time by a late writer, Julius Obsequens:
    • There were frequent earthquakes.
    • Lightning struck dockyards and many other places.
    • A meteor was seen in the sky going towards the west.
    • The howling of dogs was heard at night in front of the house of the
      Pontifex Maximus (the High Priest).
    • The Po flooded, and when it went back within its banks, it left a great
      number of snakes.

2   How does Virgil convey the horror of civil war in lines 489–97? How are
    warfare and agriculture set in contrast with each other in this passage?

3   How sincerely expressed do you find the poet's appeal in lines 498–504?

**Euphrates**   a river in Assyria, which flows through Baghdad. The reference is too
imprecise to allow us to date the military activity referred to (as with **Germany**). The
mention of these distant areas, in the north and east, helps to convey the impression
that the whole world has gone war-mad. Presumably this passage was written before
the battle of Actium (31 BC) which seemed likely to usher in a time of comparative peace
– and indeed did.

**unholy Mars**   Mars is, of course, the god of war. The Latin word that I have translated
'unholy' is 'impius': cf. line 468 ('godless').

**4** How effectively do lines 505–11 convey a world out of control? Compare W. B. Yeats's poem, *The Second Coming*:

> Turning and turning in the widening gyre
> The falcon cannot hear the falconer;
> Things fall apart; the centre cannot hold;
> Mere anarchy is loosed upon the world,
> The blood-dimmed tide is loosed, and everywhere
> The ceremony of innocence is drowned;
> The best lack all conviction, while the worst
> Are full of passionate intensity …

**5** What is the poet aiming to convey by the simile with which he ends the book (512–14)?

## Book 2

In a famous passage in the second book of the *Georgics*, the poet celebrates his native land. This section is generally known as 'the praises of Italy' (*laudes Italiae*).

**2.136–76** But neither **Media**'s groves, that richest of terrains, nor the beautiful Ganges nor the **Hermus**, muddied with gold-dust, can vie with the glories of Italy – not Bactra nor India, nor all of **Panchaia**, rich with incense-bearing sands. **This land was not ploughed by bulls** breathing fire from their nostrils for the 140 sowing of the teeth of the monstrous dragon, nor did it bristle with a harvest of warriors with crowding helmets and spears, but it was filled with teeming crops and **the Massic liquid of Bacchus**. Here there dwell olives and happy herds. From 145 here comes the warhorse prancing proudly over the plain, from here, **Clitumnus**, come bulls, the snowy herd and noblest of victims, which have often bathed in your sacred waters and gone to escort Roman triumphs to the temples of the gods.

---

**Media**  i.e. Persia.

**Hermus**  a river in Lydia. Traditionally it was its tributary Pactolus which was the golden river.

**Panchaia**  a semi-mythical island near Arabia.

**This land was not ploughed by bulls**  in his quest for the golden fleece, which was to be found in Colchis (to the east of the Black Sea), Jason had to yoke fire-breathing bulls, sow dragon's teeth and kill the armed warriors who sprang up from the teeth once they were sown.

**the Massic liquid of Bacchus**  a Campanian wine from the slopes of Monte Massico.

**Clitumnus**  a spring in Umbria near Spoleto, famous for its clear, abundant water and for its white cattle.

Here spring never ceases and summer extends to months not her own. Cows calve 150
twice a year, twice a year the trees bear fruit. But here there are no raging tigers, no
savage brood of the lion, no deadly nightshade to deceive the wretches who pick it.
Nor does **the scaly snake** snatch his huge coils over the ground or gather himself
into a spiral with so mighty a movement.

*A wall painting from Pompeii.*

Add so many outstanding cities built with so much toil, **so many towns piled on** 155
**top of sheer rocks** by human hand, and rivers gliding beneath ancient walls. Or
should I speak of **the seas which wash Italy's upper and lower shores**? Or of her
vast lakes? Of you, **Larius**, and you, **Benacus**, swelling with a thunder of waves 160
worthy of the ocean? Or should I speak of her harbours and **the barrier built**
**across the Lucrine lake** and the sea howling in indignation where the **Julian** wave
echoes from afar as the sea is pushed back and the tide of the Tyrrhenian sea is let
in to the waters of Avernus?

This land also has streams of silver and mines of copper to show in her veins, and 165
her rivers flow with an abundance of gold. She has produced a fine breed of men,

**the scaly snake**   the point here is that, though snakes exist in Italy, they are not as large
as elsewhere.

**so many towns piled on top of sheer rocks**   'These lines draw an unforgettable picture
of one of this country's most characteristic features, her hill towns … In these ancient
settlements, human labor has perfected the natural landscape. We are reminded here that
building is as much an Italian as Roman skill, an achievement to be marveled at in places
such as Anxur, Tibur, and Praeneste' (Josiah Osgood, p. 366).

**the seas which wash Italy's upper and lower shores**   the Adriatic and the Tyrrhenian sea
respectively.

**Larius**   now known as Lake Como.

**Benacus**   now known as Lake Garda.

**the barrier built across the Lucrine lake**   the reference is to the military works carried out
near Naples by Octavian's trusted general Agrippa in 37 BC. Lake Avernus was joined with
the Lucrine lake by a canal, and a breakwater was built on the coast. In this recent triumph
of Italian engineering, the desolate Lake Avernus was transformed into a busy new port.

**Julian**   because Octavian, Julius Caesar's adopted son, was ultimately responsible for the
work.

the **Marsi** and the able-bodied **Sabini** and the **Ligures**, inured to misfortune, and the **Volsci** with their short darts. She has produced the **Decii**, the **Marii** and the great **Camilli** and those tough warriors, the **Scipios**, and you, greatest **Caesar**, 170 who, now victorious on the furthest shores of Asia, turn away the unwarlike Indian from the hills of Rome.

Hail, **land of Saturn**, great mother of crops, great mother of men. For you I attempt a subject and a skill of ancient glory, daring to unlock **the sacred springs**, 175 and I sing **a song of Ascra** through **Roman towns**.

---

1 What is your first impression of this passage? How effective is its praise of Italy?

2 Scholars are divided on how these lines should be read. Because a number of details in it are not literally true, it has been seen as a 'Virgilian lie'. For example, to say that spring lasts throughout the year (line 149) is in conflict with a premise of the poem, and the nature of the real world, that the normal cycle of seasons operates in Italy. And in so far as it was believed that animals bore young and trees bore fruit twice a year (line 150), this was not restricted to Italy. Does it matter? In any case, is exaggeration not an acceptable feature of this kind of rhetorical set piece? What do you think?

3 If this picture evokes the golden age, there is ample evidence that hard work has been involved, even so. Where is it to be found?

4 Do you feel that the military and technological features of this passage sit well with its innocent, paradisal aspects?

---

**Marsi, Sabini, Ligures, Volsci**   Italian tribes, once in conflict with Rome, but now fully absorbed into a unified Italy.

**Decii, Marii, Camilli, Scipios**   Rome was saved by the Decii from the Latins, by Marius from the Cimbri, by Camillus from the Gauls and by the Scipios from Carthage. There were three famous Decii who held the consulship in successive generations in the fourth and third centuries BC, but the plurals for Marius and Camillus are generalizing: 'such men as Camillus...'.

**Caesar**   if, as seems likely, this passage dates from 30 BC, Octavian was successfully fighting against eastern peoples at the time. But the idea that he fought with anyone as eastern as the Indians is entirely hyperbolical.

**land of Saturn**   Saturn ruled in Latium in Italy during the golden age.

**the sacred springs**   sources of poetic inspiration.

**a song of Ascra**   Virgil's ultimate model in the *Georgics* was Hesiod's *Works and Days*, a Greek didactic poem about agriculture. Hesiod, who was the founding father of the genre, came from Ascra in Boeotia in central Greece. His work dates from around 700 BC.

**Roman towns**   why *Roman* towns? Does Virgil simply mean 'Italian towns', or is he suggesting that, while the geography may be Italian, the *civilization* is Roman?

Later in Book 2, Virgil sets the life of the farmer against that of the city dweller, to the former's complete advantage.

2.458–74   O happy farmers, all too happy if they come to realize their blessings. For them, far from the clash of arms, **the most equitable Earth** pours forth unasked **an**   460
**easy sustenance** from the soil. If they have no house built high with huge portals, spewing forth from every nook and cranny a vast wave of **morning clients,** if they do not gape at doors inlaid with beautiful tortoiseshell or at hangings tricked out with gold and at bronzes from Corinth, and their wool is white, not stained with   465
Assyrian dye, and they do not **degrade the clear olive oil they use with aromatic casia** – even so they enjoy sleep free from care and a life that knows nothing of deceit, wealthy in all sorts of ways – even so they have peace on broad acres, they have caves and **living lakes** and cold valleys and the lowing of oxen, and soft   470
sleep beneath the trees. There they have **woodland glades** and the haunts of wild beasts. The young men are inured to toil and conditioned to scanty resources. There is worship of the gods, and fathers are held in reverence. It was among them that **Justice left her last footprint as she departed from the earth.**

---

**the most equitable Earth**   'this is a summary of the great theme of the *Georgics*; the earth is fair to those who work it, repaying their efforts' (Deryck Williams).

**an easy sustenance**   yet we have been told (1.121–2) that father Jupiter himself did not wish the way of farming to be easy.

**morning clients**   clients would visit their patron, a man to whom they had attached themselves in the hope of advancing their careers and getting money and/or free food, in the morning. The custom was satirized by Juvenal (5.19–20) and Martial (4.8.1). The joke here is that the clients are described as leaving the house, not entering it. The patron appears to have kicked them out as quickly as possible.

**degrade ... with aromatic casia**   olive oil, normally employed for washing or cooking, would be degraded by being used in a perfume.

**living lakes**   i.e. natural lakes, not artificial ones.

**woodland glades**   to hunt in.

**Justice left her last footprint as she departed from the earth**   Justice (also called Astraea) was the last of the immortals to leave the world when the behaviour of mankind became intolerable to her (see *Eclogues* 4.6).

1 What is the tone of the descriptions of city and country life? Clearly they are strongly polarized. Does this make them unconvincing?

2 Christopher Nappa comments that the blessings of a peaceful life and an easy livelihood are in stark contradiction to the nearly backbreaking toil of farm life described in the poem hitherto, but remarks that 'the farmers will be happy if they understand not farming but what their own particular [blessings] are' (p. 100). He adds that 'attitude plays a great role in determining the tenor of human life'. Do you find his comments helpful in your response to this passage?

## Book 3

A fine passage in Book 3, which deals with the rearing of cattle, describes the disastrous effect of sexual passion on bulls.

**3.209–41** But no care builds up animals' stamina more than keeping sexual desire and the 210 stings of hidden passion away from them, whether a person prefers dealing with cattle or horses. Therefore men **banish** bulls **to lonely pastures** at a distance beyond the barrier of a mountain and across broad rivers, or they keep them shut up inside near well-stocked mangers. For the sight of the female gradually drains 215 their strength and inflames them, and indeed, with her sweet enchantments, she does not allow them to remember woods or pasture, and often she drives her proud **lovers** to fight it out with each other with their horns. On the great mountain of **Sila** a beautiful heifer grazes. **They** join battle with great violence, now one of 220 them attacking, now the other, striking wound after wound, black blood bathes their bodies, and their horns take the impact as they face their battling opponent with a mighty bellowing. The woods re-echo and **the sky from end to end**. And it is not usual for the warriors to herd together, but the conquered one goes off and 225 lives in exile in unknown regions far away with many a groan over his shame and

---

**banish**    in Latin the verb is political in its force (*relego* = I send into exile). This is the first hint of the personification that pervades the passage.

**to lonely pastures**    the language of the Latin love elegy. Lonely locations are the resort of the unhappy lover.

**lovers**    the language of love elegy continues.

**Sila**    in Bruttium.

**They**    neither here nor later on in the passage is the word for 'bull' or any other animal word employed. The personification is very strong.

**the sky from end to end**    the fight on Mount Sila gains cosmic reverberations.

the blows inflicted by his proud victor as well as over **the love he has lost without the satisfaction of revenge**, and turning his gaze upon his stall, he has departed from his ancestral kingdom. And so he takes every care to train up his strength and all night long **he lies on an uncovered bed** among hard rocks, feeding on prickly leaves and sharp rushes, and he tests himself and learns **to throw** his anger into his horns as he crashes against the trunk of a tree, and challenges the wind with blows and paws the flying sand as he rehearses for **battle**. Afterwards, when his strength has been mustered and his might restored, he advances to the fight and charges headlong upon his enemy, who has forgotten him: as when a wave begins to whiten in the middle of the sea, it curves its course from far out in the deep and rolling to the shore, makes a terrible sound upon the rocks, and, no less huge than a mountain, topples down; but the wave boils up in eddies from the bottom and flings black sand on high.

230

235

240

---

1  What do you feel to be the effects of the personification and the evocation of love poetry in this passage?

2  'There are obvious political resonances here, and it is tempting to view the passage as a full-scale allegory of the Roman civil wars with rival generals fighting for Italy ... We need not go so far as this, however, to see several political messages relevant to Octavian and to Vergil's audience. The first, perhaps, is that uncontrolled passion for anything will lead to violence – notably there is no one in the passage to regulate access to the heifer. More important, however, is the intimation that rivals are not neutralized simply because they are defeated' (Christopher Nappa, pp. 136–7). Can you think of any further political resonances? Is it possible to see Cleopatra as part of the equation?

3  The simile in 3.237–41 is based on one in Homer, *Iliad* 5.422–8, to describe the fearful advance of the Greek forces against the Trojans. What is Virgil aiming at in his use of the simile? Remember that we do not discover which bull won the second fight.

---

**the love he has lost without the satisfaction of revenge**   the personification continues with further use of the language of love poetry.

**he lies on an uncovered bed**   this is a very odd thing to say about a bull. He is made to seem like an ultra-tough general – Hannibal, say, who in Livy's description was often seen sleeping on the ground (though covered by a coarse military cloak; Livy 24.1.7). The personification certainly draws attention to itself here.

**to throw ... battle**   Virgil uses these words virtually unchanged to describe Turnus preparing to fight with Aeneas at *Aeneid* 12.104–6.

## Book 4

Virgil's evocation of country life in the *Georgics* is supremely expressive, and his description of agricultural procedures, selective though it may be, is basically accurate. Mistakes tend to be inherited from the writers on farming who were his sources (M. S. Spurr, 164–87). This is truly a poem about the country. At the same time it has allegorical, symbolic overtones, and this is particularly evident in Book 4, **where his description of the society of bees has much to tell us about human society.** They are personified from the start.

4.1–7   Next I shall deal with the heavenly gifts of **honey sent from the air**. Look upon this part of my work too, Maecenas, with favour. To bring you wonder, I shall tell you of the pageant of a tiny world, and the great-hearted generals, and the way of ₅ life and ideals of their whole race in order, and their peoples and their battles. **The theme of my work is a slight one**, but far from slight is the glory, if the adverse powers permit one, and **Apollo** listens when invoked.

---

**where his description … human society**   Shakespeare's *Henry V* (1.2.187–204) offers a comparable description of the society of bees as an analogy for human society:

> For so work the honey bees,
> Creatures that by a rule in nature teach
> The act of order to a peopled kingdom.
> They have a king, and officers of sorts,
> Where some like magistrates correct at home,
> Others like merchants venture trade abroad,
> Others like soldiers, armèd in their stings,
> Make boot upon the summer's velvet buds,
> Which pillage they with merry march bring home
> To the tent royal of their emperor,
> Who, busied in his majesties, surveys
> The singing masons building roofs of gold,
> The civil citizens kneading up the honey,
> The poor mechanic porters crowding in
> Their heavy burdens at his narrow gate,
> The sad-eyed justice with his surly hum
> Delivering o'er to executors pale
> The lazy yawning drone.

**honey sent from the air**   Aristotle believed that, while the bees made wax, honey fell from the air (*History of Animals*, 553b29).

**The theme of my work is a slight one … Apollo**   the god of poetry. For the idea here, compare Alexander Pope's imitation (*The Rape of the Lock*, 1.5–6):

> Slight is the subject, but not so the praise,
> If she inspire and he approve my lays.

'She' is Belinda, whose lock of hair was stolen, and 'he' is John Caryll, a dedicatee of this part of the poem.

In a passage where the thought of Rome's civil wars cannot be far away, Virgil describes the swarming of bees, presenting the phenomenon as a battle.

4.67–87    But if they go out for battle – for strife has often fallen on the two **kings** in a great upheaval – and you may at once foretell from far away the passions of the crowd and the way their hearts quiver with martial spirit. For **that warlike ring of harsh-** 70 **sounding brass** upbraids the laggards and a noise is heard like the broken blasts of trumpets. Then they swarm together, trembling with excitement, their wings flash, and **they sharpen their stings with their beaks**, make their arms ready, and swarm in masses around their king, yes, by the royal tent itself, and they call out 75 to the enemy with great cries. Therefore, when a clear spring day has arrived and they have found an open plain, they sally forth from the gates. The two sides clash. A sound arises in the high air. They mingle together and are massed in one great ball and fall down headlong. Hail from the sky is no thicker, acorns do not rain 80 so densely from the shaken holm-oak. As for the kings themselves, their wings marking them out in the thick of the fighting, a great heart beats in their tiny breasts, and they struggle on, refusing to yield until the fierce victor has forced 85 one side or the other to turn its back and flee. These passions and these mighty conflicts will be controlled and vanish if you throw a little dust.

> 1   Trace the instances of personification in these two passages from the start of Book 4. How effective are they?
>
> 2   How persuaded are you that an analogy is being drawn with Rome's civil wars?
>
> 3   What do you feel is the tone of the final sentence? Is there humour here? Deryck Williams says that 'these lines are very calm and serene after the excitement of the activity described in the previous lines'. Do you agree?

**But if they go out for battle …**    the sentence is never completed.

**kings**    the common belief in the ancient world was that the leader of the bees was male. The Dutch naturalist Jan Swammerdam discovered the truth about the queen bee by means of the microscope in the seventeenth century. The masculine personification suits Virgil's possible purpose of evoking the civil wars in this passage.

**that warlike ring of harsh-sounding brass**    a metaphor for the agitated noise of the bees.

**they sharpen their stings with their beaks**    in point of fact, when the bee strokes its abdomen with its mandibles it is cleaning itself. But the description is well observed.

> Moving on to gardens, Virgil describes an old man near Tarentum who has found happiness on his small plot of land.

4.116–46 And for my part, **if I were not going to furl my sails** and turn my prow in haste to the land as the final end of my labours now approaches, **I would perhaps be singing of** the cultivation which decks out rich gardens and of **the rose-beds of twice-blooming Paestum**, and of how the endive rejoices in the streams which 120 it drinks, and the green banks in their celery, and of how the cucumber twists through the grass and swells into a paunch; and I would not have failed to mention the late-flowering narcissus or the tendril of the twisting acanthus and the pale ivies and the myrtles that love the shore.

*One of the famous Greek temples from the sixth or fifth centuries BC amid the blossoms of Paestum.*

**if I were not going to furl my sails** Virgil makes the point that he cannot deal fully with gardens since he is coming towards the end of the length he has planned for his poem.

**I would perhaps be singing of** a rhetorical device called *praeteritio* by which the writer mentions the subject while saying that he is not going to deal with it. What is the effect of the use of this device here?

**the rose-beds of twice-blooming Paestum** this beautiful site on the coast some 55 miles south of Naples, now famous for its wonderfully preserved Greek temples and its tomb paintings, was proverbial for its twice-flowering roses. This may not be hyperbole since some roses, including the autumn damask rose, do blossom twice a year.

For I remember that I saw, beneath the towers of **the Oebalian citadel,** where the 125
**black** river Galaesus waters the golden crops, **a Corycian old man,** who had a few
acres of left-over land, a plot not rich enough **for ploughing oxen** nor suitable
for a flock nor favourable for the vine. Nevertheless, on this land he planted a 130
few vegetables among the scrub and white **lilies** round about, and **vervain** and
the slender poppy, and in his proud imagination he matched the wealth of kings,
and returning home **late at night** he would load his table with a feast he had not
bought. In the spring he was the first to pick roses, the first to pick apples in the
autumn, and when the grim winter was still cracking the rocks with cold and 135
curbing the flow of the rivers with ice, he was already plucking the flowers of
the soft hyacinth, taunting the summer and the lingering **west winds** for their
slowness.

As a result he was the first to have plenty of bees which had produced young, and
a large swarm, and the first to compact the foaming honey **after squeezing out** 140
**the combs.** His lime-trees and his **pines** were very luxuriant, and all the fruit with
which the fertile tree had dressed itself in its early bloom, it retained in autumn
fully ripened. He also transplanted elms into rows when it was late in the season,
pear trees which had hardened out, blackthorns already bearing sloes, and the 145
plane-tree which offers shade to **drinkers.**

---

**the Oebalian citadel**    i.e. Tarentum, founded by colonists from Sparta in southern
Greece, of which Oebalus was a legendary king. This round-about expression, which
involves a display of learning on the part of the poet and demands a knowledgeable
response on the part of the listener or reader, is characteristic of the poetry of this period.
We refer to such expressions as 'Alexandrian', after the city in Egypt that was the focal
point of Hellenistic poetry (see Introduction, p. 3). My feeling is that Virgil is careful never
to push such exhibitions of learning too far. He is not a showy poet, I think, in this sense
or in any other. You may disagree.

**black**    R. A. B. Mynors suggests that this may mean 'deep and clear'.

**a Corycian old man**    Corycus was a city in Cilicia (in modern Turkey) and Pompey settled
some Cilician pirates in Calabria in south-east Italy, where Tarentum is. (Modern Calabria
is in south-west Italy.) Our gardener may be one of these. Alternatively, there is a Corycian
cave above Delphi, the great sanctuary of Apollo in Greece, in which case the old man has
associations with the god of poetry.

**for ploughing oxen**    i.e. to produce crops.

**lilies, vervain**    these plants were not merely ornamental. The lily was used to make
ointment and oil and the vervain has medicinal uses.

**late at night**    i.e. when he had finished his day's work on his plot.

**west winds**    the Zephyrs, the winds of spring.

**after squeezing out the combs**    so that it would congeal as pure honey.

**pines**    or laurustinus shrubs, in an alternative version of the Latin.

**drinkers**    the shady plane-tree was a regular feature of a pleasant spot, well suited to
wine drinkers (Horace, *Odes* 2.11.13–17).

1   What difference does it make that Virgil presents his account of the Corycian gardener as a personal reminiscence: 'I remember that I saw ...' (125)?

2   Commentators agree that the passage is impossibly idealized or simply fictitious in the claims it makes for the old man's achievement in this environment. Do you agree with this assessment? If so, what do you feel may have been Virgil's purpose here?

Virgil goes on to describe the qualities which **Jupiter has given to bees.**

4.153–209    They **alone** have children in common, live communally in the dwellings of their city and lead their lives under mighty laws. They alone know a specific fatherland    155
and home, and, thinking of the winter to come, **they work away** in the summer and place what they have obtained **in the common store.** For some watch over the collecting of food and are busy in the fields by a fixed agreement; some, inside the enclosure of their home, lay down **the teardrops** of the narcissus and sticky **gum**    160
**from tree bark as the first foundation for their comb**, and they hang up clinging wax; **others** lead forth the next generation, the hope of the race, now that they are adult; others pack purest honey and stretch the cells with the liquid nectar. There    165
are those to whom **the lot** has assigned **guard duty at the gates**, and **by rota** they **keep watch** on the rains and clouds of the sky, or receive the loads from those coming in, or, **forming a column, keep** the drones, an idle bunch, **away** from the enclosure. The work is ablaze, and the fragrant honey smells of **thyme. Just like**    170
**the Cyclopes** when they speedily make their thunderbolts from molten lumps of metal; some suck in and blow out the air with their ox-hide bellows; others plunge the hissing bronze in water; Etna groans under the anvils placed on its

---

**Jupiter has given to bees**   as a reward for their part in saving him from being devoured by his father Saturn in his infancy (149–52).

**alone**   i.e. alone of non-human creatures.

**they work away ... in the common store**   in a very ant-like manner. Compare the simile describing the Trojans at *Aeneid* 4.402–3.

**the teardrops**   i.e. the secretion.

**gum ... the first foundation for their comb**   the comb-building does in reality start with a thin foundation of 'glue', propolis or bee-glue.

**others ... thyme**   lines 162–9 recur almost identically (but without 165–6) in the simile describing the building activities of the Carthaginians at *Aeneid* 1.431–6.

**the lot, guard duty at the gates, by rota, keep watch, forming a column, keep ... away**   a plethora of military imagery here plays its part in the pervasive personification in this passage.

**Just like the Cyclopes ...**   see note on 1.471 (p. 19, Etna).

floor. With great force they vie with each other as they raise their arms in rhythm, 175
and they twist the iron with their grappling tongs – in just this way, **if one may
compare small things with great**, does an inborn love of possession inspire the
**Cecropian** bees, each in his own sphere of activity.

The aged have charge over the towns, both the building of hives and the fashioning
of intricate houses. But the young come back exhausted late at night, their legs 180
loaded with thyme. They feed now here, now there on arbutus, on grey willows,
on casia and the ruddy crocus, and the rich lime tree and dark blue hyacinth. All
of them rest from labour at the same time, all work at the same time. Early in the 185
morning they rush from the gates – no loitering anywhere – and again when the
evening star has warned them to leave off their feeding in the fields, then they
make for their homes, then they look after their bodies. A sound arises as **they
mutter around the edges of their home and its doorways**. Afterwards, when they
have settled down in their bedrooms, silence reigns on into the night and the sleep 190
each one has earned takes hold of their exhausted limbs.

**Even so**, when rain threatens they do not go far from their stalls, or trust the sky
when eastern winds arrive, but **they get their water** close by in safety beneath the
walls of their city and they see if they can manage brief **sorties**, and **they lift up** 195
**little stones** just as unsteady skiffs take on ballast when the sea surges.

You will be surprised that this particular custom has contented the bees – that **they
do not indulge in sexual intercourse** or, languishing, relax their bodies in love or
bring forth offspring with birth pangs, but **by themselves** they gather their young 200
from the leaves and from the pleasant grasses with their mouths, by themselves

---

**if one may compare small things with great**   what effect do you feel that Virgil may
have achieved by doing this?

**Cecropian**   i.e. Athenian. Cecrops was an early king of the city. The honey from Mount
Hymettus near Athens was proverbial. Another fairly discreet Alexandrianism (see note
on 4.125).

**they mutter around the edges of their home and its doorways**   T. E. Page comments
that 'this beautiful phrase [is] descriptive equally of the bees and of an evening gossip
on the doorstep'.

**Even so**   the linking expression in the Latin conveys the idea of a correction of what has
just been said: i.e., 'do not think that this energy knows no limits'.

**they get their water, sorties**   more military language.

**they lift up little stones**   this is, of course, untrue, but the idea of bees carrying little
stones as ballast is found in Aristotle, *History of Animals* 626b24.

**they do not indulge in sexual intercourse**   again untrue, though the theory is raised
by Aristotle in a discussion of how bees are generated (*History of Animals* 553a16–25).
In actual fact, the sexual intercourse of bees takes place in flight. Virgil's bees avoid the
upheavals caused by sex in herds which we read about in 3.209–41.

**by themselves**   i.e. without the help of males.

they produce their king and their little **citizens** and refashion their courts and their kingdoms of wax. Often too, as they wander amid hard rocks, they wear away their wings, and voluntarily give their lives under **their burden**, so great is 205 their love of flowers and the glory of producing honey. Therefore, although the limit of a short life awaits the individual bees – for it does not last beyond the seventh summer – even so the race remains immortal, for many years the fortune of the house stands firm, and generation on generation can be counted.

> • Some scholars have seen in Virgil's bees a model for human society. In 1954 H. Dahlmann wrote, 'We are dealing with a framework which is simply and absolutely paradigmatic, which corresponds to the absolutely valid, rational, and right' (p. 13). In 1979 Jasper Griffin expressed reservations about trying to imagine Virgil 'recommending to his contemporaries as an absolute model a society like this: impersonal, collective … without art' (p. 96). And indeed without sex. Where do you stand in this debate?

The second half of the fourth and last Georgic arises from a discussion of how, if you lose your bees, they can be renewed by killing a calf and treating the carcase in such a way that bees are born from it. This process, known as *bugonia*, has no basis in reality but was widely regarded as scientific in ancient times. In Virgil's account, it is revealed to the shepherd Aristaeus, who has lost his bees, by the sea-shepherd Proteus. The latter explains that Aristaeus is being punished because of his involvement in the death of Orpheus' wife Euridice, and he tells their story.

4.453–527    It is not the case that no divinity's anger harries you. You are paying for a great crime. Pitiable Orpheus rouses against you **this punishment which you have by** 455 **no means deserved**, punishment which would be exacted did not fate forbid it, and he rages violently for **the wife** who was torn from him. It was she who, **in her bid to escape you** by headlong flight along the river, did not see, poor girl about

---

**citizens**   the Latin word used here is 'Quirites', a name given specifically to the citizens of Rome.

**their burden**   the weight of the pollen they are carrying can cause them to dash themselves against rocks.

**this punishment which you have by no means deserved**   because, though Aristaeus had caused Euridice's death, he had not intended it.

**the wife**   we do not discover her name until 30 lines later.

**in her bid to escape you**   Aristaeus seems to have been chasing another man's wife. In that respect he is certainly guilty. Virgil seems to have invented this aspect of the Orpheus story.

to die, a monstrous serpent at her feet, hugging the banks in the deep grass. **But** 460
**the chorus** of her playmates, the Dryads, filled the tops of the mountains with
their cries. The peaks of **Rhodope** wept, lofty **Pangaeum** and the warlike land of
**Rhesus** and **the Getae** and the river **Hebrus** and Athenian **Orithyia**.

**Orpheus himself**, comforting his heartache with his hollow tortoise-shell lyre,
would sing of **you, sweet wife**, sing of you to himself on the lonely shore, of you 465
as the day came, of you as it departed. He even entered **the jaws of Taenarus**, the
high portal of **Dis**, and the grove which is shrouded in dark terror, and actually
approached the abode of the dead and the fearful king and **those hearts** that 470
do not know how to soften at human prayers. But, moved by his singing, the
insubstantial shades, the phantoms of those shut off from the light, were moving
towards him from where they dwelt in the depths of **Erebus, as many as** the
thousands of birds which shelter under the leaves when evening or a winter
shower drives them from the **mountains, women** and men, and shapes of great- 475
hearted heroes whose lives were over, and unwedded girls, and young men placed
on the pyre before the eyes of their **parents**, but around them the black mud and

---

**But the chorus …** we are given no account of Euridice's death. We move straight on to
the reactions to it. Why do you think Virgil handles the story in this way?

**Rhodope, Pangaeum** mountain ranges in Thrace.

**Rhesus** the Homeric king of Thrace, who died at Troy.

**the Getae** a northern tribe.

**Hebrus** a Thracian river.

**Orithyia** an Attic princess who had married Boreas, the north wind, evoking this
northern region.

**Orpheus himself** he is not in fact named in the Latin at this point.

**you, sweet wife** Virgil employs a device called apostrophe whereby the deliverer of
a third-person narrative turns to a character and addresses them in the second person.
There is a sense of poignant immediacy, reinforced by the repetition of the word 'you'.

**the jaws of Taenarus** one of the entries to the underworld was reputed to be at
Taenarus, the southern tip of Laconia in southern Greece.

**Dis** or Pluto, king of the underworld.

**those hearts** I take it that the hearts are those of the spirits of the underworld.

**Erebus** the underworld.

**as many as … mountains** the simile is given a different turn at *Aeneid* 6.311–12. How
does it work in its context here?

**women … parents** these lines are repeated at *Aeneid* 6.306–8. They are based on Homer,
*Odyssey* 11.38–9 (Odysseus above the underworld) but the final line, with its intense
pathos, about the reversal of the natural order when parents outlive their children, is
Virgil's own.

ugly reeds of **Cocytus and the unlovely** **marsh** with its sluggish water bind them in and **the river Styx** which flows nine times around them **holds them fast.** Nay, innermost **Tartarus,** the very abode of Death, and **the Eumenides** with black snakes entwined in their hair were astounded and **Cerberus** gaped and his triple jaws fell silent, and the circle of **Ixion's** wheel was halted **by the wind.** 480

And now, as he retraced his steps, he had avoided every mishap and his **restored** Euridice was coming to the breezes of the upper world – **for Proserpina had imposed this condition** – when a sudden madness seized the heedless lover, a madness that should have won pardon if the underworld knew how to pardon! He stopped, and, just on the very verge of the light, forgetting himself, alas! and defeated in his will, he looked back at his own Euridice. At that moment, 485 490

*This statue showing Pluto abducting Proserpina with Cerberus, the three-headed dog of the underworld, at his feet is an early masterpiece by Gian Lorenzo Bernini (1598–1680).*

---

**Cocytus** the river of wailing in the underworld.

**and the unlovely marsh ... holds them fast** with a small variation, these lines reappear at *Aeneid* 6.438–9.

**the river Styx** presumably 'the unlovely marsh'. Styx is the river of hate.

**Tartarus** the pit of hell.

**the Eumenides** the Furies, grim avengers of blood-guilt.

**Cerberus** the three-headed dog which guards the entrance to hell.

**Ixion** he was attached to a revolving wheel in punishment for his attempt to seduce Juno.

**by the wind** i.e. because the wind stopped.

**restored ... for Proserpina had imposed this condition** again, the vital event, the restoration of Euridice to Orpheus, is passed over, though it is evoked in these words. The story is well known. Proserpina, the wife of Dis, had told Orpheus that he must not look back at his wife.

**all his efforts were poured away** and his pact with the merciless tyrant was broken, and three times a thunderclap was heard over the pools of **Avernus**. 'What **frenzy**,' she said, 'what so great frenzy has destroyed both me and you, Orpheus? **Look,** 495 **once again the cruel fates are calling me back** and sleep hides my swimming eyes. And now farewell. Surrounded by vast night, I am carried off, stretching my weak hands to you, alas! no longer your wife.'

She spoke, and suddenly she fled from his eyes in the other direction, **like smoke** 500 **vanishing** into the insubstantial breezes, and she did not see him vainly **clutching at shadows** and wishing to say so much more; and **the ferryman of Orcus** did not allow him to cross the barrier of the marsh again.

What was he to do? Where could he turn to after his wife had been snatched from him twice? With what tears could he move the underworld? What gods could he 505 appeal to? For her part she was voyaging in the Stygian skiff, now cold.

They say that he wept alone for seven whole months one after the other beneath a towering crag by the waters of the lonely **Strymon** and that he sang of these events beneath the cold stars, charming tigers and moving oak-trees with his song 510 – just as the nightingale grieves beneath the poplar's shade lamenting the loss of her young which the hard ploughman has pulled unfledged from the nest he was watching; but she weeps all night and, perched on a branch, she renews her pitiful 515 song and fills the region far and wide with her sad complaints. No love, no wedding song changed his heart. Alone he wandered over the **Hyperborean** ice along the

---

**all his efforts were poured away**   literally, 'all his labour was poured away'. Richard Thomas remarks: 'words crucial to the poem, and indicating one of the main connections between Orpheus and the participants of the agricultural *Georgics*; Orpheus, paradigm for the man who controls not only nature, but even the powers of the Underworld, finds his own *labor* [labour] destroyed by a momentary lapse – a lapse caused by *amor* [love], one of the very forces of nature which destroyed man's work in Book 3.'

**Avernus**   the lake at an entry to the underworld.

**frenzy**   the Latin word used here, 'furor', will prove a fundamental concept in the *Aeneid*.

**Look, once again the cruel fates are calling me back**   she is receding as she speaks. She has receded still further by line 506 where she is going back across the Styx.

**like smoke vanishing … clutching at shadows**   adapted from Homer, *Iliad* 23.99–101, where Achilles tries to embrace the ghost of Patroclus: 'So he spoke and he reached out with his dear hands but did not take hold of him, but the spirit departed like smoke beneath the ground, squeaking and gibbering.' The motif will be developed at *Aeneid* 2.790–4 and 6.699–702, as Aeneas tries to clasp first the apparition of Creusa and then the shade of Anchises.

**the ferryman of Orcus**   Charon. Orcus is the underworld.

**Strymon**   a river in Thrace.

**Hyperborean**   of the far north.

snowy **Tanais** and the fields never empty of frosts, lamenting lost Euridice and
the pointless gifts of Dis. During the rites of the gods and **the night-time revels
of Bacchus,** the mothers of the **Cicones,** spurned because of this devotion, tore  520
the young man in pieces and scattered his body over the broad fields. Even then,
when **Oeagrian** Hebrus carried away the head torn from his snow-white neck, his  525
disembodied voice and his frozen tongue kept calling 'Euridice, ah poor Euridice'
as life departed. 'Euridice' the banks re-echoed all along the river.

---

1   Jasper Griffin has pointed out that in antiquity bees and honey were
    constantly associated with poetry and poets. Yet, as he observes, this
    association is nowhere activated in the *Georgics*. Orpheus, the famous
    bard who features in the poem, is torn to pieces. It seems that the world
    of the *Georgics* can find no place for him. Yet his story is told with such
    unforgettable pathos that we cannot simply erase him from our thoughts.
    Why do you think it is told at such poignant length as the poem nears its
    conclusion?

2   What is the effect of the simile of the nightingale in lines 511–15? At first
    sight it may seem surprising that, in a poem about farming, a ploughman
    should be relegated to a simile. Why do you think that Virgil may have done
    this?

3   How do you respond to the eventual fate of Orpheus? Does it strike you as
    horrific, bizarre, appropriate – or what?

4   Two key moments of the story, the death of Euridice and her restoration to
    her husband, are passed over in Proteus' telling of it. Why do you think this
    may be?

---

Tanais   the river Don, which flows past the Crimea into the Black Sea.

**the night-time revels of Bacchus**   the followers of the god Bacchus were reputed to
practise *sparagmos* (the tearing of their victims to pieces) when in a state of frenzy.

Cicones   a people of southern Thrace. What they do to Orpheus recalls the grisly fate of
Pentheus in Euripides' play, *Bacchae*.

Oeagrian   Oeagrus was the king of Thrace and father of Orpheus.

Aristaeus follows Proteus' instructions about generating new bees and the poem proper ends with the creation of new life. The last lines of this final book, however, are an autobiographical epilogue, of the kind that is called a *sphragis* (a seal), because the poet is putting his personal imprint on his work.

**4.559–66**  This is what I sang about the cultivation of fields, of cattle and of trees, while  560
great **Caesar himself thundered by the deep Euphrates** and, as the victor,
**dispensed laws to willing nations** and set out on the path to **Olympus**. At that
time **Parthenope** nurtured me as I blossomed in the pursuits of ignoble ease, the
poet who sang shepherd's songs and in the boldness of my youth sang of you,  565
**Tityrus, beneath the shade of a spreading beech tree.**

---

1  It seems likely that the activities of Octavian and of Virgil have been
drastically polarized in this *sphragis*. Philip Hardie suggests that there
is genuine playfulness here in the contrast 'between Caesar Octavian
thundering in war in the remote east on his imperial mission, and the poet
Virgil indulging himself in his poetic games in the sequestered leisure of the
Greek city of Naples' (p. 48). Why do you feel that Virgil ends his poem by
pointing to this contrast?

2  From what you have read of the *Georgics*, would you say that the poem was
more optimistic than pessimistic? Give your reasons for your view.

---

**Caesar himself thundered …**  as Philip Hardie remarks, this 'final image of Octavian
"thundering" in battle in the distant east is a suitable advertisement of the full-dress
epic on Octavian's legendary ancestor that is to follow [the *Aeneid*]'. Hardie points to
the centrality of Octavian in the poem: 'The opening invocation of Octavian is mirrored
at the end of book 1 by the anxious prayer that Octavian should bring salvation to Rome
and end the civil wars triggered by the murder of Julius Caesar (lines 498–504); positive
images of Octavian successfully pursuing the foreign wars that will ensure the settled
peace at home cap the *laudes Italiae* [the praises of Italy] at 2.170–2 and conclude the
whole poem at 4.560–2' (p. 28).

**by the deep Euphrates**  the reference is to Octavian's eastern campaigns. The writing is
propagandist, not reflecting the reality of the situation: see note on 2.172 (p. 24).

**dispensed laws to willing nations**  this looks forward to Anchises' famous declaration
at *Aeneid* 6.851–3.

**Olympus**  the mountain in north-east Greece where the gods lived.

**Parthenope**  Naples. Parthenope is the name of one of the Sirens (nymphs whose singing
lured mariners to their death) who was supposedly buried in the city.

**Tityrus, beneath the shade of a spreading beech tree**  the poet refers back to the
opening line of his first Eclogue (see p. 6) and thus to the *Eclogues* as a whole.

# 3 The Trojans come to Carthage

## Introduction to the *Aeneid*

In Virgil's Latin the first words of the *Aeneid* are 'arms and the man'. They serve as a kind of manifesto for the poet's intent. 'Arms' looks back to Homer's *Iliad*, the first work of western literature, which has as its subject the fighting around Troy in which Aeneas, the hero of Virgil's poem, plays a small but significant role. The second half of the *Aeneid* similarly treats of warfare – in that poem the struggles of the Trojans to carve out a foothold in Italy for themselves and their descendants, the Romans. 'Man' is the opening word of Homer's *Odyssey*, the first half of which tells of the adventures of Odysseus (Ulysses in the English version of his Latin name) as he travels from the Trojan war to his home on the island of Ithaca. The man of Virgil's poem is of course Aeneas, and its first six books, essentially the story of the hero's journey to Italy, are clearly designed to call the *Odyssey* to mind. By invoking the two great Homeric works, the Roman poet sets his poem in the grand epic tradition.

However, the differences between the two poems are as illuminating as the correspondences. Odysseus, for example, is travelling back to his fatherland, while Aeneas' city of Troy lies in ruins and he must travel towards a future clouded in uncertainty to create the circumstances that will lead to the foundation of a new city and an empire which he will never see. Odysseus loses all his men and arrives at Ithaca alone, but Aeneas is a leader in a new mould, with a profound sense of social responsibility; he only briefly forgets his duty to his family, his men and the gods. While Odysseus is zestfully inventive in confronting the dangers that he encounters, Aeneas is doggedly determined. The climactic moment of the *Odyssey* focuses on the stability of its hero's marriage. In addition, he is able to part with the women he meets along the way on friendly terms. Aeneas loses his wife amid the ruins of Troy, engages in a disastrous love affair with Dido, and contracts a blood-stained dynastic marriage with a woman he has never met. One could go on. The interplay between the Homeric poems and the *Aeneid* is endlessly illuminating and the best way to understand Virgil's epic is to read those of his great predecessor.

Near the beginning of Book 7 of the *Aeneid* Virgil makes it clear that in his view he is embarking on a higher level of poetry in the second half of his poem (7.44–5). I hope that readers will not deduce from the fact that I have devoted four chapters to the first six books and only two to the six that follow that I do not share the poet's opinion. The problem was that, in selecting from the *Aeneid*, it is of enormous importance to give generous expression to the poet's treatment of the victims of Rome. For this purpose, Dido is simply irresistible and she, of course, belongs to the poem's first half. Much more could have been made of Turnus and Camilla in the final six books and had I devoted the available space to their tragedies, so powerfully communicated by the poet, the balance would have been even. I hope that readers will feel able to keep an open mind in their evaluation of the Italian books.

## Book 1

1.1–33    I sing of **arms and the man** who was the first to come, a refugee by fate, from the shores of Troy to Italy and the coast of **Lavinium** – much harassed both on land and on sea by the violence of the gods because of the unremitting **anger** of savage **Juno**, and suffering much in war as well, until **he could found a city** and bring **his** 5 **gods** to Latium. This was the origin of the Latin race, the elders of Alba Longa and **the walls of lofty Rome**.

Tell me, **Muse**, the causes of her anger – through what affront to her divinity, what grounds for sorrow, did the queen of the gods drive a man famous for his **piety** to 10 endure so many hardships, to face so many labours. Can the gods in heaven nurse such great anger?

---

**arms and the man**   'arms' looks back to Homer's *Iliad*, a poem of warfare; 'man' is the first word of the *Odyssey*. See the introductory summary to the *Aeneid*, p. 40.

**Lavinium**   Aeneas' first settlement in Latium (the part of modern Lazio south of the Tiber) in Italy.

**anger**   anger is thematic in the poem, as it was in the *Iliad*, a poem about the anger of Achilles.

**Juno**   the queen of the gods, wife of Jupiter.

**he could found a city**   city-building is thematic in the poem.

**his gods**   Hector's ghost entrusted the gods of Troy to Aeneas on the night that the city fell (2.293–7).

**the walls of lofty Rome**   the city-building theme now finds expression in the first of the poem's up-motifs (moments when upward movement or elevation is communicated).

**Muse**   Homer had invoked the Muse at the beginning of his epics. Virgil follows suit, as Milton will in a different world in *Paradise Lost*.

**piety**   the Latin word 'pietas' translated here in fact covers a far wider spectrum of meaning than 'piety' but no other English word works as well. A key concept in the poem, it signifies doing one's duty to one's gods, one's city and one's family as well as conveying such qualities as nobility and moral fibre. It is Aeneas' defining quality, though he does not always live up to it.

There was **an ancient city**, inhabited by settlers from Tyre, called Carthage, facing distant Italy where the Tiber runs into the sea, a place of great wealth and great ruggedness in the pursuit of war; and it is said that Juno loved this land uniquely, more than all others; she esteemed it even more than **Samos**. Here was her armour, here her chariot, this was the city that even then she nurtured, intending that it should have sovereignty over the peoples of the world if only the fates would allow it. But in fact she had heard that a race of Trojan blood was being established, which would **one day overthrow the Tyrian citadel**: that from that blood a people of widespread dominion and pride in war would come to destroy Libya: that is what **the fates** ordained. She feared this and remembered **the old war** which she had earlier fought at Troy for her dear **Argos**. In addition, her bitter resentment and the causes for her anger had not yet been forgotten: stored deep down in her heart there remained **the judgement of Paris** and the wrong done to her in the scorning of her beauty, her hatred for the Trojan race, and **the privileges of stolen Ganymede**. **Inflamed** by these things, she kept the Trojan remnants – those left over by the Greeks and brutal **Achilles** – far from Latium; and for many a year they wandered, driven by the fates, all over the seas. **So great was the toil** involved in founding the Roman race.

15

20

25

30

**an ancient city**   the city of Carthage is still being built when Aeneas arrives at the site. Thus it is ancient not for Aeneas but for the poet and his audience. At many points in the poem Virgil makes use of such 'double time', viewing events both as they occur in the narrative and as they appear in the context of Augustan Rome.

**Samos**   an island in the Aegean on which there was a famous temple to Juno.

**one day overthrow the Tyrian citadel**   in the Carthaginian (Punic) wars between Rome and Carthage of the third and second centuries BC. They ended with the total destruction of Carthage in 146 BC. Thus this ordinance of the fates (line 22) had already been fulfilled by the time Virgil wrote his poem.

**the fates**   the three fates were Clotho, Atropos and Lachesis. What is fated in the *Aeneid* will happen, but it can be delayed or modified. At 8.398–9 Vulcan tells Venus that he could have made the Trojan war last for another ten years; neither the fates nor Jupiter would have stopped him.

**the old war**   the Trojan war, which now, after seven years, seems to have taken place a long time ago. In it Juno had been unequivocally on the side of the Greeks.

**Argos**   a leading Greek city.

**the judgement of Paris**   the Trojan prince Paris was given the invidious task of awarding the prize for beauty to one of the goddesses Juno, Athena (Minerva) and Venus. When he declared Venus the winner, Juno's wrath knew no bounds.

**the privileges of stolen Ganymede**   falling for the beauty of Ganymede, another Trojan prince, Jupiter had him brought up to Olympus by his eagle to serve as his cup-bearer.

**Inflamed**   fire is often associated with frenzied passion in the poem.

**Achilles**   the greatest of the Greek warriors.

**So great was the toil**   the effort and human cost which have to be expended in the founding of Rome and the Roman race are thematic. In the *Aeneid* Virgil acknowledges the greatness of the Roman achievement but is very much alive to the suffering it involves.

After some seven years of travel, the Trojans are sailing from Sicily to Italy on the last stage of their journey to their destined home. Juno sees them and determines to stop them. She bribes Aeolus, the king of the winds, to stir up a terrible storm to wreck the Trojan fleet. This he does, though the damage the storm causes in fact turns out later to be largely illusory. We first see Aeneas, the hero of the poem, in the midst of what he takes to be an utterly devastating storm.

1.92–101    **Immediately Aeneas' limbs slacken in the cold**: he groans and, stretching out his hands palms upwards to the stars, he cries out: 'O three and four times blessed, you whose fortune it was to die before the eyes of your fathers under the lofty  95 walls of Troy! O **son of Tydeus**, bravest of the **Danaan** race! Why could I not have fallen at your hand and poured out my life-spirit on the plains of Troy, where **Hector** lies, slain by Achilles' spear, where huge **Sarpedon** lies, where **Simois** has  100 seized and rolls beneath its waves the shields and helmets and brave bodies of so many men!'

The sea-god Neptune realizes what is going on behind his back and appears on his chariot to calm the storm. Virgil conveys what is happening in a famous simile, the first in the poem.

**Immediately Aeneas' limbs slacken in the cold**   this is what I believe the Latin here means. It is usual to translate it as (e.g.) 'Immediately Aeneas' limbs were numbed in cold fear' (Deryck Williams), though David West in his Penguin edition has, unexceptionably: 'A sudden chill went through Aeneas and his limbs grew weak.' There is no evidence that Aeneas is afraid. He wishes that he had died a heroic death at Troy rather than drowning anonymously at sea (where, in any case, he would be unlikely to find burial and so gain admission to the underworld). This is an important matter since here we have our first impression of the poem's central character. The passage is based on a similar speech, similarly introduced, by Odysseus at *Odyssey* 5.297–312 and there is no mention of fear in the Greek hero. He makes the point that, if he had been killed at Troy, the Greeks would have spread his fame, 'but now it is by a miserable death [at sea] that it was my fate to be cut off' (311–12). Do you share my view on this matter?

**son of Tydeus**   Diomedes. Aeneas escaped death at his hands when he was rescued by the goddess Aphrodite (i.e. Venus) (Homer, *Iliad* 5.311–17).

**Danaan**   Greek.

**Hector**   the leading Trojan warrior, a son of Priam, the king of Troy.

**Sarpedon**   the leader of the Lycians (allies of the Trojans) killed by Patroclus, though Zeus, his father, wanted to save him.

**Simois**   a river of Troy.

**1.148–56**    **Just as often occurs** when disorder has arisen among the people of a great nation and the base mob rage with angry passion and already the firebrands and the 150 rocks are flying (frenzy puts weapons in their hands), then if their eyes happen to fall on a man revered for his piety and his services to the state, they fall silent and stand still listening with full attention: he rules their passions and soothes their hearts **with his words** – so did all the roaring of the sea fall quiet, after the father, 155 looking out over the waves and riding beneath a clear sky, drove his horses and gave free rein to his willing chariot as he flew onwards.

> Aeneas and his fleet are driven to the coast of North Africa. Here, despite his internal anguish, he raises his men's spirits and they eat seven stags which he has shot. They are saddened by the apparent loss of 13 of their 20 ships.
>
> Now Aeneas' mother, the goddess Venus, approaches her father Jupiter as he surveys the world, and implores him to end Aeneas' sufferings. Talking of what he has experienced so far, she asks Jupiter bitterly if this is the reward for piety (1.253). Jupiter replies reassuringly.

**1.254–96**    Smiling on her with the countenance with which he makes the stormy weather 255 sunny, the father of men and gods lightly kissed his daughter's lips and spoke these words: 'Lay aside your fears, lady of **Cythera**. Your descendants' fates remain unchanged. You will see the city of Lavinium with its promised walls, and **you will take great-hearted Aeneas aloft to the stars of heaven**. No argument has 260 changed my mind. You will see your son – for since this anxiety gnaws at your heart, I shall speak at some length, **unrolling the book of fate** and bringing its

---

**Just as often occurs … with his words**   similes are characteristic of the Homeric epics and have been a feature of the genre ever since. The one developed here most obviously relates to the situation to which it is being offered as a likeness, Neptune calming the frenzy of the sea. But at the same time it articulates concepts that are very important in the poem as a whole. Frenzy (*furor*) and piety (*pietas*) are set against each other. (Here piety wins.) Both concepts are vividly conveyed by concrete comparisons, frenzy by the out-of-control mob, piety by the elder statesman. What do you feel about Virgil's presentation of the common people here?

Another factor worth noting is that by causing the storm, Juno has unleashed frenzy onto the world. She is often seen as representing in the poem 'the slings and arrows of outrageous fortune' (*Hamlet* 3.1.60).

A further interesting feature of the *Aeneid* is that every time one encounters the word 'arms', one is likely to find the word 'man' fairly close by, and vice versa.

**Cythera**   an island just south of Greece which was a seat of the worship of Venus.

**you will take great-hearted Aeneas aloft to the stars of heaven**   Aeneas will become a god.

**unrolling the book of fate**   Jupiter is not in charge of fate. He seems to be responsible for its execution.

secrets to light – as he fights a great war in Italy and **crushes proud nations and sets up institutions and city walls for them**, until the third summer sees him reigning in Latium and three winters pass after his conquest of the Rutuli. But the boy Ascanius, who now receives the second name Iulus (he was **Ilus** while the state of Ilium stood firm in royal power), will rule for thirty great cycles of years rolling by, and he shall move the kingdom from its seat at Lavinium and build the strongly fortified city of **Alba Longa**. Here there will be kings of **the race of Hector** for a full span of **three hundred years**, until **Ilia**, a royal priestess pregnant

*The famous she-wolf of Rome, an Etruscan bronze dating from the late sixth or early fifth century BC. The statue is known as the Capitoline wolf because it used to stand on the Capitol of Rome.*

---

**crushes proud nations and sets up institutions and city walls for them**   a statement of the Roman mission to conquer and then to civilize, most famously asserted at 6.852–3.

**Ilus**   a name he inherited from the father of Laomedon, the founder of Ilium (Troy). Virgil is fond of such etymologies. The name Iulus looks forward to the family of the Julii, to which Julius Caesar and Octavian/Augustus belonged. Since Iulus' grandmother was Venus, they could lay claim to divine ancestry (cf. line 288).

**Alba Longa**   on the site of the modern Castel Gandolfo (where the Pope has his summer residence) 12 miles south-east of Rome.

**the race of Hector**   i.e. the Trojans, whose greatest hero Hector was.

**three hundred years**   Virgil's numbers have a pleasing symmetry. Aeneas rules for three years, Iulus for 30 years, and Alba Longa lasts for 300. The poet alters the standard 400-year period to fit into his number scheme.

**Ilia**   alternatively known as Rhea Silvia.

by Mars, shall give birth to two sons. Then **Romulus, rejoicing in the tawny covering of the she-wolf nursing him,** will take over the rule of the Roman race and will build the walls of Mars and will call his people Romans after his own name. 275

'For them I set no bounds in space or time: I have given them rule without end. And what is more, savage Juno, who now troubles the sea, the earth and the sky **out of her fear,** will change her views for the better and will join with me in cherishing the Romans, lords of the world, a people wearing **the toga.** This is what has been decided. 280

*A statue of one of the leading men of the Italian hill town of Perugia, dating from about 80 BC. He is dressed in a toga. The broad border on the toga marks him out as a member of the local aristocracy.*

**Romulus**   founder of Rome. Jupiter in this speech unfolds the history of Rome with superb assurance. But he can only do this by making some drastic omissions. At this point, for example, there is no mention of the fact that Romulus killed his twin brother Remus while building the city's foundations. This act of fratricide was seen as a symbol of the beginning of Rome's civil wars.

**rejoicing in the tawny covering of the she-wolf nursing him**   according to legend, the twins were abandoned to die. They were found and nursed by a she-wolf. The famous Etruscan she-wolf suckling Romulus and Remus in the illustration on p. 45 was originally created without the boys. (The ones in the picture date from about AD 1509.) But we know that statuettes of the boys were placed beneath her from before 300 BC, and in any case the wolf is usually portrayed, e.g. on coins, with the boys beneath her. I prefer to read the Latin in the way that suggests that Romulus was under the teats of the she-wolf than to follow the standard translation, e.g. 'delighting in the red-brown skin of a wolf-nurse' (Roland Austin), i.e. wearing his nurse's hide as a piece of clothing.

**out of her fear**   if this is the right translation, presumably it refers to Juno's fear for her beloved city of Carthage. The alternative meaning of the Latin would be that the elements are afraid of Juno.

**the toga**   the toga was the garment of civilian wear and the mark of a free-born Roman.

'There shall come a time as the years roll by when the house of **Assaracus** will reduce **Pthia** and famous **Mycenae** to slavery and rule over conquered Argos. 285 There shall be born a Trojan of noble lineage, **Caesar**, who shall bound his empire by **Ocean**, his glory by the stars, a Julius, a name passed down from great Iulus. In time to come, have no fear, you will receive him in heaven, laden with spoils from the East. **He also** will be invoked in prayers. Then wars will cease and the 290 savage centuries will soften; grey-haired Faith, and **Vesta**, and **Quirinus** with his brother Remus will be law-givers; **the gates of War**, terrible in their close-wrought frame of iron, shall be shut; and impious Frenzy will sit inside on a pile of savage 295 arms, his hands tied behind his back with a hundred knots of bronze, bellowing hideously from his bloody mouth.'

---

1  In lines 263–4 Jupiter says that Aeneas will crush proud nations and set up institutions and city walls for them. What are the benefits of Roman civilization outlined in this speech? What drawbacks may there be?

2  This passage conveys a great sense of confidence in Roman greatness. What is the basis for this confidence? Do you find a similar sense of cultural superiority to be prevalent today in various parts of the world, and, if so, how do you respond to it?

3  Can you think of any significant benefits of living in a colony of a great empire in modern times?

4  Can Frenzy be locked up permanently?

---

**Assaracus**  great-grandfather of Aeneas.

**Pthia**  the country of Achilles. Jupiter is looking forward to the Romans' defeat of Greece, a revenge for their ancestors' defeat in the Trojan war. The country became part of the Roman empire in 146 BC.

**Mycenae**  the city of Agamemnon, the Greek commander-in-chief at Troy.

**Caesar**  since this Caesar is given the name Julius two lines later, at first glance one would naturally assume that he is Julius Caesar rather than Octavian/Augustus, his adopted son. But since the assassination of Julius Caesar was followed by 13 years of civil war, he scarcely seems to fit the context here. And the reference to the spoils of the east fits the son, who had defeated considerable eastern forces at the battle of Actium (31 BC), far better than the father. In any case, Octavian became Julius when he was adopted.

**Ocean**  the river of Ocean was thought to flow around the edge of a platter-shaped earth.

**He also**  i.e. as well as Aeneas. See lines 259–60 above.

**Vesta**  goddess of the hearth. Along with Faith, she represents the permanence of old Roman values.

**Quirinus**  the name given to Romulus when he became a god.

**the gates of War**  the closing of the gates of War in the temple of Janus signified peace throughout the Roman world. They were closed in 29 BC, for the first time since 235, and then again in 25. Virgil was at work on the *Aeneid* from 29 to 19 BC. The gates make a dramatic reappearance in the poem at 7.607–10, 620–2 (not in this selection).

Venus now goes down to earth and meets her son who is exploring the empty country with his trusty companion Achates. She is disguised as a Tyrian huntress and he does not recognize her, though he asserts tactfully that she is undoubtedly of divine origin. She tells him about the place he has come to.

1.338–68    'What you see is the kingdom of Carthage, a Tyrian people and the city of **Agenor**, but the territory around belongs to the Libyans, a race unconquerable in war. Dido is in command. She set out from the city of Tyre in flight from her    340
brother. It is a long story of crime, a complicated one, but I shall go over the main outline of what happened. She had a husband called Sychaeus, the richest of the Phoenicians **in gold** and loved with great passion by the unhappy woman. Her father had given her to him **when she was still a virgin** and had joined them in    345
her first marriage ceremony. But her brother was in possession of the kingdom, Pygmalion, a monster of crime beyond any other. Frenzy came between the two men. Caring nothing about his sister's love and blinded with lust for gold, the    350
impious Pygmalion took Sychaeus off his guard **at the altars** and stabbed him. There were no witnesses and he concealed his actions for a long time, making up many false stories in his wickedness and deceiving the love-sick wife with empty hope. But the ghost of her **unburied** husband came to her in a dream. Lifting up to her a face strangely pale, **he laid bare** the altars where the cruel deed had been    355
done and his breast pierced by the iron, and revealed all of the dark villainy of the house. Then he urged her to flee and leave her fatherland with all haste and showed her ancient treasures hidden underground to help her on her journey, a mass of silver and gold known to no one. Moved by this, Dido started to prepare    360
her escape and to collect companions. Those who either savagely hated or bitterly feared the tyrant gathered together. They commandeered ships which happened to be at the ready and loaded them with gold. The wealth of greedy Pygmalion

---

**Agenor**   an ancestral king of Phoenicia, where Tyre was situated.

**in gold**   the manuscripts all say 'in land', but gold is so important in the narrative that editors mainly prefer to understand it here.

**when she was still a virgin**   this tells us emphatically that Sychaeus was Dido's first love. Her tragedy proves to be her failure to remain a one-man woman.

**at the altars**   the impiety of Pygmalion, appalling enough in his violation of family ties by killing his sister's husband, is lent further emphasis by the fact that he did the deed while Sychaeus was engaged in a religious rite.

**unburied**   we discover almost incidentally a further instance of Pygmalion's impiety. By failing to bury Sychaeus, he has denied his spirit entry to the underworld.

**he laid bare**   i.e. he brought before her eyes in the dream.

was carried over the sea. **A woman was the leader.** They came to the place where 365
you will now see huge walls and the rising citadel of new Carthage, and they
bought as much land as they could surround with a bull's hide, calling it **Byrsa**
after the transaction.'

---

1 Trace Dido's emotions and actions throughout this passage. What are your
feelings towards her?

2 Why do you think that Virgil makes Pygmalion such an out-and-out villain?

3 The way this narrative is handled has attracted admiration. Why do you
think this is so?

4 Dido and Aeneas are alike in important ways. In your view, does likeness of
character make for lasting relationships between men and women?

---

Venus covers Aeneas and Achates in a mist so that no one can see them and
they walk on towards the site of Carthage. They view it as they walk towards
it.

1.419–63    And now they were climbing the hill which looms large over the city and looks  420
down on the citadel facing it. Aeneas **wonders** at the vast bulk of the buildings,
**once just huts**, he wonders at the gates and the din and the paved streets. The
Tyrians press on with the work with burning enthusiasm, some of them building
walls and labouring at constructing a citadel and rolling up great stones by hand,
others choosing a site for a building and **enclosing it with a furrow**. They are  425

---

**A woman was the leader**   the Latin here is splendidly crisp: 'dux femina facti' (a woman
the leader of the action). Dido and Aeneas have much in common. They have both lost
their partners in marriage. Both of them have fled from a city where there is no future for
them after being warned by a ghost in a dream. They both show outstanding leadership.
Aeneas wishes to found a new city while Dido is already building hers. It is not surprising
that they are attracted to each other.

**Byrsa**   'bull's hide' in Greek. Dido bought as much land as a bull's hide could hold. Then
she cut a hide into one very long thin strip, which of course could contain a huge area. In
ancient mythology heroes are often credited with cunning strategies such as this.

**wonders**   in this passage I have kept Virgil's historic present tenses. Frequently I slip
them discreetly into the past because they tend not to work well in English, but here
there are so many of them that they cause no problem in translation. On the contrary,
they help to bring vividly before our eyes the scene that Aeneas sees, and give vitality to
his strong reaction.

**once just huts**   the word used for 'huts' is a Carthaginian one. Is Virgil using it to
contrast the original inhabitants of the site (i.e. Libyans) with the civilizing Phoenician
immigrants?

**enclosing it with a furrow**   i.e. marking out the foundations.

deciding upon laws, and choosing magistrates and a revered **senate**. Here some are digging **a harbour**, here others are laying the deep foundations of **a theatre** and quarrying huge **columns** from the rock, lofty adornments for the stage to be. **Like the busy activity** which seizes the bees through the flowery meadows at     430 the start of summer, when they lead forth the new generation now full-grown, or pack the oozing honey and stretch the cells with sweet nectar, or receive the loads from those coming in, or, forming a column, keep the drones, an idle bunch, away     435 from the enclosure. The work is ablaze, and the fragrant honey smells of **thyme**. 'O fortunate ones,' said Aeneas, '*your* walls are already rising!' And **he looks up** at the tops of the city's buildings. Veiled miraculously in a mist, he enters and walks through the middle of the men and is seen by no one.     440

In the middle of the city was a grove, very rich in shade, the place where in the beginning **the Carthaginians**, tossed by waves and raging winds, dug up **the token which royal Juno had told them of**, the head of a spirited horse: for thus, she declared, would the race be outstanding in war and prosperous in its way of     445 life through the ages. Here Dido of **Sidon** was building a huge temple for Juno, rich with offerings and the presence of the goddess. Bronze was its threshold, set high upon a flight of steps, bronze-jointed its beams, and bronze the door which grated on its hinge. **It was in this grove** that a strange sight first met his eyes and     450 softened his fears, here first Aeneas found the courage to hope for safety and to

---

**senate, a harbour, a theatre, columns**   Carthage had a senate from about 400 BC and its harbour was artificial (i.e. it was dug out like the one here). But the theatre with its ornamental columns sounds distinctly Roman, suggesting the theatre of Pompey (55 BC). Virgil seems to be presenting Aeneas with a picture of the creation not specifically of Carthage, but of an ideal Roman city.

**Like the busy activity ... thyme**   this passage is based on *Georgics* 4.162–9: see p. 32. But Virgil has made some significant changes, most notably the sunny setting at the start of summer. What difference, if any, do you feel that this makes to the impression you have of the bees in the *Georgics*?

**he looks up**   he was looking down at line 420. He has gone down the hill while observing the building going on.

**the Carthaginians**   i.e. the Carthaginians of the future.

**the token which royal Juno had told them of**   when Dido and her people fled from Tyre, Juno told them to found their city at a place where they would dig up the head of a war horse. This is a typical foundation myth, perhaps modelled on the story in Varro about the human skull found on the Capitol which gave the hill its name: the Latin for head is *caput* (*De lingua Latina* 5.41).

**Sidon**   Virgil uses the names Tyre and Sidon without discrimination. The cities are in fact some 22 miles apart.

**It was in this grove**   there is a disconcerting sense of menace in the fact that Aeneas should begin to find comfort in Juno's temple set in her grove. She continues to be implacably opposed to him until near the end of the poem. The pictures he later describes are, in any case, almost all illustrations of episodes that were disastrous for the Trojans (466–93).

have better trust in his fortunes, shattered as they were. For while he was looking around at everything from beneath the huge temple **as he waited for the queen**, while he wondered at the city's prosperity and the harmonious handiwork of the 455 various craftsmen and the hard work they had put into their building, he saw the battles at Troy **pictured in succession** and the war whose fame had already spread through the whole world, **the sons of Atreus** and Priam, and Achilles, fierce towards the Greek leaders and the Trojan. He stopped and said through his tears, 'What place, Achates, what region on earth is not full of the story of our toil? 460 Look, there is Priam! Here too there are due rewards for honour, **there are tears for the human lot**, and mortal sufferings touch the heart. Fear no more. The fact that we are known here will give you some hope for the future.'

Dido now appears.

1.494–508    While Trojan Aeneas was looking at these wondrous sights, while he was rapt and 495 motionless, fixed in one intent gaze, the queen, the surpassingly beautiful Dido, came to the temple, with a great company of young men thronging about her. **Just as** on the banks of **the Eurotas** or over the ridges of **Cynthus** Diana leads the dance, while a thousand mountain nymphs crowd behind her to right and left; 500 she carries a quiver on her shoulder and is taller than all the goddesses as she goes: joy thrills the silent heart of **Latona** – such was Dido, in such a way did she move

**as he waited for the queen**   'a movingly imaginative touch: he feels that the queen must come … to this holy place; his thoughts are already with Dido' (Roland Austin).

**pictured in succession**   there was a series of illustrations. Are they on the metopes of the temple (the rectangular blocks between the triglyphs at the bottom of the entablature)? These are often carved with scenes of two individuals in combat. Or they may be on the doors, like the pictures at the temple of Apollo at Cumae (6.20–30).

**the sons of Atreus**   Agamemnon and Menelaus, the Greek commanders-in-chief at the Trojan war. Achilles quarrelled with Agamemnon and withdrew from the fighting, with disastrous results for the Greeks.

**there are tears for the human lot**   the Latin translated here ('sunt lacrimae rerum', literally, 'there are tears over things') has often been taken out of context to convey the supposedly Virgilian idea that life is a vale of tears. In fact it means something very different, that people are sympathetic. The memorably brief encapsulation of the moving thought ensures its status as great poetry.

**Just as … Latona**   the simile is based on Homer, *Odyssey* 6.102–8. It is a joyous one, but it is worth remarking that Diana carries a quiver. She is the goddess of hunting and Dido will be the victim of a hunt. Latona is Diana's mother, and it has been well remarked (by Deryck Williams) that the final line, in which we are told that joy thrills her heart, 'conveys the effect which Dido has on those watching her, particularly Aeneas'.

**the Eurotas**   the river of Sparta.

**Cynthus**   the mountain on Delos, where Diana and her twin Apollo were born.

joyously through the middle of her people, urging on their work on the kingdom in the making. Then at the goddess' doors, beneath the centre of the temple's vault, high on her throne **with her armed escort**, she took her seat. She was giving laws and rules of conduct to the men, and was apportioning their tasks in equal shares or assigning it by lot … 505

1 Why is Aeneas heartened by seeing pictures of the Trojan war, in which his people suffered such disastrous losses, on a temple in Africa?

2 What is the message that Aeneas' words to Achates convey about the nature of humanity?

3 What does the simile used of Dido at her first appearance tell us about her? The simile represents Diana surrounded by nymphs while Dido is surrounded by a retinue of young men. How appropriate do you think it was considered for a woman to be a leader?

4 What is Dido doing when we first see her? How do you think this is likely to fit in with the themes of the poem?

Suddenly the Trojans whom Aeneas has believed lost in the storm appear. Dido gives them a generous welcome. She says that she will help them on their way or, if they wish, include them in her kingdom on equal terms with the Carthaginians. The cloud surrounding Aeneas disperses and he appears and expresses his undying gratitude to the queen.

All is going very well, but Venus now interferes in order to make sure that Dido stays warmly disposed to Aeneas. She substitutes her son Cupid, the boy god of love, for Aeneas' son Ascanius (whom she whisks away to Cyprus) so that he can inflame Dido with love for Aeneas. At a great banquet which Dido gives for the Trojans and the Carthaginians that night, the queen fondles the god in her lap and falls passionately in love with Aeneas. Book 1 ends when she asks him to tell the story of the fall of Troy and his seven years of wandering.

---

**with her armed escort**   arms and the woman! But note 'men' in the next line (507).

# 4 The fall of Troy

## Book 2

Book 2 starts with Aeneas telling his story.

2.1–56    They all fell silent and fixed their eyes on him in rapt attention. Then from his raised couch **father** Aeneas began thus:

The grief that you bid me renew, o queen, is too deep for words, the story of how the Greeks overthrew the wealth of Troy and the kingdom for which men mourn, and of the terrible things which I saw myself and in which I played a great part. 5 Which of the **Myrmidons** or **Dolopians**, which soldier of **hard-hearted Ulysses** could refrain from tears in the telling of such a tale? And already dewy night is speeding from the sky and the falling stars counsel sleep. But if you desire so 10 passionately to learn of our misfortunes and to hear a brief account of the final agony of Troy, even though my mind recoiled in pain and shudders to recall it, I shall make the attempt.

Now broken by war and frustrated by the fates **as so many years slipped by,** the leaders of the Greeks built **by the divine art of Pallas** a horse the size of a 15 mountain, interweaving its ribs with planks of fir. They pretended it was a votive offering for their return: this was the story that went round. **They chose their best men by lot** and stealthily shut them within its dark sides, cramming the vast 20 cavern of its **womb** with armed soldiers.

---

**father**   what do you feel is the effect of this description of Aeneas? There is no such epithet in Homer, which gives its use by Virgil an added emphasis.

**Myrmidons**   Greeks, Achilles' men.

**Dolopians**   Greeks, the men of Achilles' son, Pyrrhus.

**hard-hearted Ulysses**   it is little wonder that a Trojan should speak of this Greek hero's cruel heart. Ulysses had thought up the idea of the Trojan horse. The question makes the point that, if the war was so terrible that even harsh Greeks would weep to describe it, to do so will be even more traumatic for one of the defeated Trojans.

**as so many years slipped by**   the Trojan war lasted ten years.

**by the divine art of Pallas**   while the horse was Ulysses' idea, Epeos made it with the help of the goddess Pallas (also known as Athena and Minerva). She was the goddess of wisdom and of handicrafts.

**They chose their best men by lot**   choosing by lot allowed the fates to pick the best.

**womb**   the idea of the horse being pregnant with arms (and thus death) is traditional and is exploited further by Virgil (2.238, 6.516).

There lies in sight of Troy a very famous island called Tenedos, rich and prosperous as long as Priam's kingdom lasted, **now** just a bay and a treacherous anchorage for ships. They sailed off there and hid themselves on the lonely shore. We thought 25 they had gone and had sailed on the wind for Mycenae. So all of Troy freed itself from its long sorrow. The gates were opened. It was a joy to go and see the Greek camp, the deserted shore and all the places the enemy had left. Here the band of the Dolopians had their camp, here savage Achilles, here the fleet was stationed, 30 here they used to fight in battle. Some gazed in amazement at the deadly gift to the virgin goddess **Minerva** and wondered at the huge size of the horse. Thymoetes was the first to urge that it should be dragged inside the walls and placed on the citadel; either it was his treachery or maybe the fate of Troy was already tending that way. But Capys and those of better judgement were suspicious that the gift 35 was a Greek trap, and told us to throw it headlong into the sea or to light a fire underneath it and burn it or to pierce and drill the hollow recesses of its womb. The people were torn between these strong convictions and did not know what to do.

Then, in front of everyone else, with a great crowd following him, **Laocoon** 40 ran down blazing from the top of the citadel and cried from a distance, 'O my wretched countrymen, what is this terrible madness? Do you really believe that the enemy have sailed away? Do you seriously think that the Greeks give any gifts which are free of trickery? Is this all you've learned about Ulysses? Either Achaeans are lurking, hidden inside this wood, or this has been built as **an engine** 45 **of war** against our walls, to look into our homes and come down on the city from above, or else there is some deception about it that we cannot spot. Do not trust the horse, Trojans. Whatever it is, **I am afraid of the Greeks, even when they are bearing gifts.**'

---

**now**   when is 'now'?

**Minerva**   a later writer says that the horse had an inscription on it naming Minerva as the dedicatee.

**Laocoon**   a son of Priam and priest of Apollo. He falls within the category of prophets such as Cassandra and Teiresias (in Greek tragedy) who are fated to be ignored.

**an engine of war**   siege machinery was not a feature of the warfare of the Homeric age but it was a key factor in Rome's military success. Such anachronisms do not worry Virgil.

**I am afraid of the Greeks, even when they are bearing gifts**   the meaning seems to be that Laocoon fears the Greeks even when they are (apparently) performing a religious act, i.e. making an offering to Minerva. The Latin translated here ('timeo Danaos et dona ferentes') is used proverbially even today in a somewhat different sense: 'I fear the Greeks, especially when they bear gifts', i.e. 'if they are giving presents, they must be up to something!'

**So saying,** he hurled his huge spear with all his might into the side of the beast  50
and the arching structure of its belly. It stood there quivering and as the horse's
womb was struck, the cavernous hollows boomed and **moaned.** If the fates of
the gods, if **our own minds** had not been against us, he would have driven us to  55
violate the hiding-place of the Argives with steel, and Troy would be standing
now, and **you, lofty citadel of Priam,** would still survive.

---

1   How does Aeneas convey the relief of the Trojans after the apparent
    departure of the Greeks?
2   We know that Laocoon is right. How convincing do you find his words?

---

Some Trojan shepherds now bring along a Greek called Sinon, who has let
himself be captured so that he can persuade the Trojans to take the wooden
horse into the city. He weaves a virtuoso web of lies, claiming that he was
about to be killed by the Greeks but managed to escape. The Trojans believe
him and feel pity for him. They accept his assurance that the horse is indeed a
religious offering and that, if they take it into Troy, it is certain that the Greeks
will be defeated.

2.199–249    At this point another thing happened to shake the unhappy people, of greater  200
import and much more terrifying, confusing us in our unforeseeing souls.
Laocoon, **chosen by lot to be priest of Neptune,** was sacrificing a huge bull at
the solemn altars. But look! **From Tenedos** over the calm deep, two serpents with
huge coils – I shudder as I speak – **breast** the sea and make for the shore side by  205
side. Their bellies rise amid the billows and their blood-red crests overtop the
waves. With the rest of their bodies they cut the waters behind and arch their
enormous length in coils. A sound rises as the water foams. And now they were

---

**So saying ... moaned**   the description here conveys both sight and sound (in the Latin)
very effectively.

**our own minds**   alternatively the 'mind', 'intention' of the gods. Either translation makes
good sense. I prefer the first. Laocoon will be destroyed. The Trojans misunderstand what
has happened to him, and their failure of judgement leads to their doom.

**you, lofty citadel of Priam**   this fine apostrophe (Aeneas addresses not his audience, but
a city in his story) gains in pathos from the fact that Troy no longer exists. There is no
point in talking to it.

**chosen by lot to be priest of Neptune**   the priest of Neptune, god of the sea, had been
killed and Laocoon was selected to take over. There is a horrible irony in what happens
now. Neptune's new priest is killed by creatures from the sea.

**From Tenedos**   anticipating the voyage of the Greek fleet from there that night.

**breast**   I have preserved the historic presents in this passage.

on the very point of landing, and, **their blazing eyes** shot with blood and fire, 210
they licked their hissing mouths with **flickering tongues**. Our blood draining at
the sight, we scatter. In sure formation they make for Laocoon. And first the two
serpents enfold the small bodies of his two sons, twining round them and feeding 215
on their wretched limbs with their fangs. Then, when he comes to help them
spear in hand, they snatch hold of him too and bind him tight in their huge coils.
And now, twice enfolding his waist, twice entwining their scaly bodies round his
neck, they tower above him with their heads and lofty necks. The whole time 220
he struggles to prise the coils open with his hands, his priestly ribbons soaked
with gore and black poison; the whole time he raises horrible cries to the heavens
**like the bellowing** when a wounded bull has escaped from the altar and shaken
the ill-aimed axe **from its neck**. But the two serpents slide away, making their 225

*Laocoon and his sons. When this
sculpture, dating from about 50 BC,
was discovered on one of the hills of
Rome in AD 1506, famous sculptors
such as Michelangelo flocked to see it.*

**their blazing eyes … flickering tongues**   this is very well observed. As the serpents get
closer, more frightening detail becomes visible. Virgil anticipates the use of this technique
in cinema.

**like the bellowing … from its neck**   Laocoon was sacrificing a bull but has now become
a victim. Unlike Laocoon the bull in the simile is escaping. In view of these *un*likenesses,
how well do you feel that the simile works?

escape to the citadel of **cruel Pallas** where she has her lofty shrine, and they shelter under the goddess's feet and the circle of her shield.

Then indeed a strange terror makes its way through our trembling hearts and they say that Laocoon has deservedly paid for his crime since he violated the sacred 230 timber by hurling his accursed spear-point into the horse's back. 'We must take the image to **the temple**,' they shout, 'and pray to the goddess's divinity.'

We breach the walls and lay bare the buildings of our city. Everybody buckles 235 down to the work, putting rollers under the horse's feet and tying hemp ropes tightly on its neck. The engine of fate, pregnant with arms, scales our walls. Boys and unmarried girls sing holy songs around it and take joy in touching the cable with their hands. Up it goes, and it glides menacingly into the middle of the city. 240

O my fatherland, O Ilium, home of the gods, and you walls of the people of **Dardanus**, famous in war! Four times, at the very threshold of the gate, it stopped, and four times the arms sounded in its womb! But we press on heedlessly, blinded by frenzy, and stand the ill-omened monster on our sacred citadel. Even at that 245

*The Trojan horse. Part of a relief on a funerary urn of about 670 BC. The horse is mounted on wheels. The Greek warriors are clearly visible, some of them even holding their armour out of the apertures!*

**cruel Pallas**  Pallas has her temple on the citadel of Troy but she is an unremitting enemy of the Trojans. In a memorable moment in Book 6 of the *Iliad* (line 311) she rejects a prayer from the women of Troy.

**the temple**  i.e. the temple of Minerva (Pallas) to whom the horse has apparently been dedicated.

**Dardanus**  an ancestor of Priam.

moment **Cassandra** opens her lips to foretell what is fated, lips that the Trojans never believed: so a god commanded. That would be our final day but in our wretched folly we adorn the shrines of the gods with festive foliage throughout the city.

---

1 How do you respond to the description of the death of Laocoon and his children? Is it horrific, chilling, bizarre, overdone, vividly dramatic, melodramatic – or what? What effect do you think Virgil was aiming at here?

2 What tones of voice would you assume if you were reading Aeneas' speech from line 234 to line 249 ('We breach the walls … throughout the city')?

3 What expressions of the poem's up-motif (see note on 1.7, p. 41) are there in this passage?

---

That night the Greeks sail back from Tenedos and the warriors in the horse kill the Trojan sentries and let the enemy into the city, whose inhabitants are 'buried in sleep and wine'.

2.268–317    It was the time when sleep, that most grateful gift of the gods, first steals over **weary mortals**. Look! In a dream Hector seemed to stand before my very eyes,  270
weeping floods of tears in terrible sadness, looking as he did in days gone by **when he was dragged behind the chariot**, black with blood and dust, his swollen feet pierced with thongs. Ah me, what a sight he was! How greatly changed from the Hector who returned **wearing the spoils of Achilles** or **hurled Trojan fire onto**  275
**the Greek ships**! – with matted beard, hair clotted with blood, and those wounds

---

**Cassandra**   because she rejected his advances, the god of prophecy Apollo (the god of line 247) doomed her never to have her prophecies believed.

**weary mortals**   literally, 'sick mortals' or 'mortals sick at heart'. Virgil has taken the phrase over from Homer, using it at *Georgics* 1.237 and *Aeneid* 10.274 and 12.850. For Roland Austin it suggests 'the frailness of mortality in contrast to the serene strength of the gods'.

**when he was dragged behind the chariot**   after killing Hector, Achilles pierced his tendons, attached him to the back of his chariot and dragged him to the Greek camp (Homer, *Iliad* 22.395–404). The tradition that he dragged the body round the walls of Troy is post-Homeric. Even to the Romans, who humiliated their conquered enemies by parading them, such mutilation of the dead would appear extreme.

**wearing the spoils of Achilles**   with Apollo's help, Hector killed Patroclus, who was dressed in Achilles' armour (described in *Iliad* 16). In this way Hector acquired it.

**hurled Trojan fire onto the Greek ships**   the attack on the Greek ships referred to here is described in *Iliad* 15. In *Iliad* 22 the Greeks taunt the dead Hector with the words, 'Hector is far easier to handle now than when he burned the ships with blazing fire' (lines 373–4).

– so many of them – that he received around the walls of his fathers. I dreamed that I was weeping myself and was the first to speak, addressing the man with sad words: 'O light of Troy, o surest hope of the Trojans, **what has delayed you for so long?** From what shores do you come, Hector, so long awaited? With what eyes do we look upon you in our weariness after so many deaths of your people, after all the different toils of our men and our city! What has so shamefully disfigured that face that was once so serene? Why do I see these wounds?'

He did not reply, paying no heed to my futile questions, but heaving deep groans from the bottom of his heart, he said, 'Alas! Flee, son of the goddess, and escape **from these flames.** The enemy holds our walls. Troy is tumbling from her topmost heights. Enough has been given **to the fatherland and to Priam.** If anyone's right hand could have saved Troy, this hand of mine would have saved it. It is to you that Troy entrusts her sacred things and her household gods. Take them to share your fate, for them seek out a great city – which you will finally establish after wandering all over the sea.' So he spoke and with his own hands he brought out from the inner shrine the image of powerful **Vesta** with ribbons on her head and the undying fire.

Meanwhile the city was everywhere in a turmoil of anguish, and although the house of my father Anchises was set back in a remote spot and screened by trees, the sounds became more and more clear and the dreadful din of warfare grew closer. I shake myself free of sleep and climb up onto the topmost part of the roof and stand there listening intently: **as when a field of grain** catches fire as the south winds rage or a mountain river, churning in spate, flattens the fields, flattens

**what has delayed you for so long?**    Austin comments: 'Virgil gets the atmosphere of a dream with much subtlety. Aeneas has forgotten Hector's death, and at first he does not take in the significance of his ghastly appearance; he thinks only that Hector has been away, and asks him, so naturally, why he has been so long in coming.' Do you share Austin's view?

**from these flames**    the flames that are at present engulfing Troy have penetrated to Aeneas' dream.

**to the fatherland and to Priam**    in his Loeb translation, H. R. Fairclough renders this 'to king and country', capturing well the note of piety and patriotism sounded here.

**Vesta**    see note on 1.292, p. 47.

**as when a field of grain ... incomprehension**    the simile may have been suggested by Homer but is fundamentally Virgil's own. As Austin writes, it 'is very carefully worked out in its applicability to Aeneas: he is compared to a shepherd (as he was, of his Trojans), horrified (as he was) at catching from a high rock (Aeneas was on the roof of the house) the roar of flames or of a flood (such as was now swallowing Troy), barely realizing (like Aeneas, fresh from sleep) that his world of crops and ploughland was being swept away (as Aeneas' world was being swept to ruin).' What do you feel is the emotional effect of the simile?

**the happy crops and the labours of oxen** and drags great trees along in its headlong rush – the shepherd takes in the sound from the top of a rock and is dazed in **incomprehension**. In that moment the truth becomes clear, and the trickery of the Greeks is plain to see. Now the spacious house of Deiphobus has 310 crashed to destruction as fire overcame it. Now Ucalegon's house is ablaze. The broad straits of **Sigeum** reflect the flames. The shouting of men and the blare of trumpets rise to the skies. Mindlessly I take up arms; yet there was little purpose in arms. But my spirit is afire to mass together a group of fighting comrades and 315 to run with them to the citadel. Frenzy and anger drive my thoughts headlong, and it occurs to me that it is a fine thing to die in arms.

---

1  How effective do you find the dream sequence?

2  Aeneas will flee from the city. He could thus be seen as playing the coward's part. To what extent is he justified in doing so by Hector's instructions?

3  Trace Aeneas' emotions throughout this passage. What do you think about his final determination to take up arms and fight? Should he be doing this?

4  Comment on how the directions of up and down are used to convey meaning in this passage.

---

Aeneas discovers that Troy is lost – the priest Panthus tells him that 'we Trojans are no more, Ilium is no more' (line 325) – and goes into battle. Much terrible fighting ensues. Eventually Aeneas climbs onto the roof of Priam's palace but cannot stop the Greeks pouring in, among them Pyrrhus, the son of Achilles. The aged Priam has sought sanctuary at the altar. When Polites, one of his sons, is killed by Pyrrhus before his eyes, he angrily denounces the Greek.

2.544–58  [Priam] feebly flung his harmless spear, which immediately **recoiled from the** 545 **clanging bronze** and hung uselessly from the surface of the shield's boss. Pyrrhus said to him, 'You shall report this **then** and go as my messenger to my father, **Peleus' son**. Be sure to tell him of the dismal deeds of his son **Neoptolemus** who

---

**the happy crops and the labours of oxen**   from *Georgics* 1.325, where a deluge of rain sweeps them away. What do the agricultural images of the simile contribute to its effect? How does it contribute to the themes of the poem?

**Sigeum**   a promontory near Troy: it looks towards Tenedos.

**recoiled from the clanging bronze**   i.e. the spear cannot penetrate the bronze of the shield but just pierces the covering of the bronze enough to hang there by its point.

**then**   Pyrrhus responds to Priam's charge that he is an unworthy son of a great father.

**Peleus' son**   Achilles.

**Neoptolemus**   the Greek name for Pyrrhus. It works well here because it means 'young fighter' and emphasizes Neoptolemus' sarcastic gibe about his own degeneracy.

shames his father's name! Now die.' As he said this, he dragged him, **trembling** 550
and slithering in his son's streaming blood, to the altar itself and winding his hair
in his left hand, he raised his flashing sword in his right and buried it up to the hilt
in his side.

Such was the end of Priam's destiny. Such was the death that befell him by fate 555
– seeing Troy in flames and **Pergama in ruins**, when once he had been the proud
ruler of Asia, of so many peoples and lands. He lies, **a huge torso** upon the shore,
**a head severed from the shoulders**, a body without a name.

1 Comment on the ways in which the poet directs loathing at Pyrrhus in this
 passage.
2 What is the effect of lines 554–8 ('Such was the end … without a name')?
 See the note below for the possible political significance of the final
 sentence of this passage ('a head severed from the shoulders'). What does it
 add emotionally?

Aeneas' mother Venus appears to him and rebukes him for his anger and
frenzy. She tells him that he must think of his family. She grants him an
apocalyptic vision of the destruction of Troy.

**trembling** with age, not fear, according to the ancient commentator Servius.

**Pergama in ruins** Pergama (a plural word) was the citadel of Troy. The word I have
translated 'in ruins' means, more literally, having 'slipped/fallen down': a strong expression
of the down-motif.

**a huge torso** an unexpected description of the body of the frail old man. 'Huge' is
presumably a heroizing epithet, looking back to Priam's former prowess.

**a head severed from the shoulders** how has the body got to the beach? There was
an alternative version of the story (followed by the second-century BC author Pacuvius,
according to Servius) which says that Priam was killed at the tomb of Achilles and dragged
to the promontory of Sigeum. Then his head was carried around on a pole.

Why did Virgil introduce this detail from another version? After his defeat by Julius Caesar
at the battle of Pharsalus (48 BC), Gnaeus Pompey fled to Egypt and was treacherously
killed there on a boat near the coast. His head was cut off and the rest of his body was
thrown naked out of the boat. It was soon cremated on the shore. When Caesar was
presented with Pompey's head, he turned away appalled (Plutarch, *Life of Pompey* 80).
It seems likely that Virgil intends his readers to think of this traumatic episode in the civil
wars. For Virgil to equate Pompey with the sympathetic Priam may seem surprising in
view of the fact that he was the opponent of Julius Caesar, the adoptive father of the
poet's great patron Augustus. But Virgil does not seem reluctant to raise difficult, even
potentially dangerous, political issues in his poetry.

**2.604–33**  'Behold – for I shall snatch away all the cloud which now veils your vision, dimming  605
your mortal sight and surrounding you with its dank darkness. You must fear no
commands of your mother nor refuse to obey her orders. Here where you see
shattered buildings and huge stones torn away from stones and billowing smoke
mixed with dust, **Neptune** with his great trident has levered up the foundations,  610
is shaking the walls and uprooting the whole city from its base. Here most savage
**Juno** is the first to hold **the Scaean gates** while, girt with steel, she frenziedly calls  615
up columns in reinforcement from the ships. Now – look behind you – **Tritonian
Pallas** has taken her position on top of the citadel, flashing out from a storm-
cloud, a savage figure with her **Gorgon shield**. **The father himself** supplies the
Greeks with courage and the strength to win. It is he who is rousing the gods
against the arms of Troy. Escape with all speed, my son, and put an end to your
toil. I shall not part company with you for a moment until I bring you safely to  620
your father's threshold.'

She spoke and hid herself in the thick shadows of night. Terrible shapes appeared
before me, and the mighty divinities whose power opposes Troy.

Then indeed all of Ilium seemed to me to sink into flames and Neptune's Troy to  625
topple from her foundations. And just as when an ancient ash on the mountain
heights has been hacked with blow after blow of the iron axe and the farmers
vie with one another to bring it down, every moment it threatens to fall and,
as its leafy boughs tremble and its top is shaken, it nods, until little by little it is  630
overcome with wounds, groans one last deep groan, is torn away from the ridge
and crashes all its length on the ground.

I go down and with the goddess leading me, find a clear path amid fires and foes.
Arms part and flames draw back, letting me through.

> 1   What impression does this apocalyptic vision make (*a*) on you and (*b*) on
>     Aeneas? What does he learn from it, both practically and psychologically?
>
> 2   Discuss the ash tree simile (lines 626–31). What function does it play at this
>     stage of the poem?

**Neptune**   he hated Troy because he and Apollo had not been paid by Laomedon as
agreed when they built the walls of the city (compare *Georgics* 1.502).

**Juno**   her reasons for hatred of Troy were given in Book 1 (lines 25–8).

**the Scaean gates**   the gates of Troy.

**Tritonian Pallas**   Pallas/Athena/Minerva is the chief goddess of the Greeks. She had been
scorned by Paris in the divine beauty contest. The epithet is traditional but obscure.

**Gorgon shield**   on Pallas' shield was depicted the head of the Gorgon Medusa, slain by
Perseus.

**The father himself**   i.e. Jupiter. In the *Iliad* he holds the scales that decide whether the
fighting will go in the Greeks' or the Trojans' favour (8.69–72).

Aeneas arrives back home, but his father Anchises (whose thinking in this book and the next is almost always wrong-headed) refuses to depart. Aeneas determines to rush out against the Greeks again and his wife Creusa pleads with him not to leave them. But then a tongue of flame suddenly plays around their son Iulus' head, and this omen is soon followed by another, a shooting star with a fiery tail flying across the sky and coming to earth on Mount Ida, the mountain range behind Troy. Anchises now agrees to go and Aeneas gives his household their instructions.

2.707–29

'Come then, dear father, put yourself on my shoulders. I shall support you on them and this labour will not be a heavy one for me. However things fall out, we are together in danger and we shall be together in safety. Let little Iulus 710

accompany me, and let my wife follow my steps at a distance. **You servants**, pay attention to what I say. When you go out of the city, there is a mound with an ancient temple of Ceres, deserted now, and an old cypress nearby preserved for many years by the 715 reverence of our fathers. We shall come to that same place from different directions. You father, **take the sacred things and the household gods of our fatherland in your hands**. It is wrong for me to handle them – I have just been shedding blood in the fierce fighting – until I wash 720 myself in running water.'

*Aeneas escaping from Troy. Gian Lorenzo Bernini (AD 1598–1680) was only 15 when he sculpted this marble group with his father Pietro in 1613. Anchises carries an image of the goddess Vesta while Ascanius holds the sacred fire.*

**You servants**   the pious Aeneas takes responsibility for his whole household, not simply his immediate family. He will find himself with the responsibility for a nation.

**take the sacred things and the household gods ... in your hands**   Aeneas is now supremely self-possessed. He remembers what the ghost of Hector had told him at the beginning of this cataclysmic night (2.293–5).

So I spoke, and I threw a tawny lion's skin over my broad shoulders and my neck and stooped to take up my burden. Little Iulus clasped his hand in mine and followed his father **with shorter steps**. Behind came my wife. We went on our 725 way amid the shadows. I was the man who a moment ago had been unmoved by showers of missiles or Greeks facing me in a concentrated mass, but now every breath of wind frightened me, every sound alarmed me, so on edge was I, **fearing equally for my companion and my burden**.

> • In what ways does the statue in the picture illustrate the piety of Aeneas? Is this piety totally admirable?

> As they approach the gates, a sudden flurry of activity results in Aeneas losing Creusa. He leaves his father and his companions and rushes back into the city to find her.

2.768–804    I even dared to cry out loudly in the shadows. I filled the streets with my shouting, in my anguish calling out the name Creusa again and again and again – but to no 770 avail. As I endlessly rushed through the buildings of the city searching for her, the **unhappy** phantom of Creusa, her very ghost, appeared before my eyes, **her body larger than in life**. I was dumbfounded, my hair stood on end and my voice stuck in my throat. Then it seemed that she spoke to me and dispelled my torment with 775 these words:

'O my dear husband, why do you choose to give way to such mad grief? **These things are not happening without the gods willing them**; it is not the law of heaven that you take Creusa from here to accompany you, and the great ruler of high Olympus does not allow it. A long exile awaits you, and a vast expanse of 780 sea which you must plough. You will come to the land of **Hesperia** where the

---

**with shorter steps** this detail has understandably won much admiration from commentators. Iulus will have to scurry along to keep up with his striding father.

**fearing equally for my companion and my burden** is there something ominous about the way that Aeneas' wife Creusa is not included among the objects of his fears?

**unhappy** the ancient commentator Servius observes that this comment refers to Aeneas' own emotions about her, not to her own, and indeed she appears supremely calm and accepting.

**her body larger than in life** ghosts were believed to be of superhuman size. Compare Dido at 4.654.

**These things are not happening without the gods willing them** this is a key lesson that Aeneas learns in this book.

**Hesperia** the western land, i.e. Italy. At this stage Aeneas knows nothing about Italy. Creusa's words, like most oracles, are vague.

**Lydian** Tiber flows with its smooth onward march through the rich fields **of a noble people**. There a happy fortune will be your lot, a kingdom too and **a royal wife**. Cease to weep for your beloved Creusa. I shall not look upon the proud 785 homes of the Myrmidons or Dolopians or go to be the slave of Greek **matrons**, I a woman of **Dardanus'** line, the wife of the son of the goddess Venus. But **the great mother of the gods** holds me back on these shores. And now farewell, and **cherish your love for the son we share**.'

When she had said these things, she left me weeping there with so many things to 790 say and faded away into thin air. **Three times** then I tried to put my arms round her neck; three times the phantom, clasped in vain, escaped my grasp, like to the weightless winds, liker still to winging sleep. So it was that night was at last over 795 and I revisited my comrades.

And here I discovered to my amazement that a huge number of new companions had streamed in, a band of mothers and men gathered for exile, a pitiable crowd. They had come together from everywhere, ready in spirit and resources for me to lead them over the sea to whatever land I wanted. And now **the morning star** 800 **was rising** above the topmost ridges of Ida ushering in the day, the Greeks were in control of the gates, and there was no hope of any help. **I gave way**, and **raising up my father**, I made for the mountains.

---

**Lydian**  because the Etruscans, through whose land the river flows, were thought to have come from Lydia in Asia Minor (in modern Turkey).

**of a noble people**  literally, 'of men'. There is no trace of the accompanying word (or idea of) 'arms'. Creusa is silent about the devastating battles that Aeneas and his men will have to fight by the Tiber.

**a royal wife**  Creusa tacitly gives her blessing to Aeneas' future Italian marriage.

**matrons**  i.e. senior women, mothers of families.

**Dardanus**  a Trojan king. Creusa lays proud claim to membership of the royal line of Troy: she was Priam's daughter. The degradation that awaits the captive women – and which Creusa will avoid – is an important feature of Homer's *Iliad* and of Euripides' plays about the Trojan war.

**the great mother of the gods**  Cybele, whose main area of worship was the Troad (the region of Troy).

**cherish your love for the son we share**  Austin asks, 'How could Dido, as she listened, think that [Aeneas] could ever forget Creusa?' This may be a sentimental judgement – apart from this passage there is no evidence in the poem to show that he does think of her again – but it is certainly true that Dido hears these lines.

**Three times**  these deeply poignant lines (792–4) look back to Euridice at *Georgics* 4.499–502 (see note, p. 37) and forward to Anchises (6.700–2).

**the morning star was rising**  Troy has fallen, but a new day dawns. The book ends with two fine expressions of the up-motif, this and **raising up my father**. The morning star is the planet of Aeneas' mother Venus.

**I gave way**  i.e. to inevitable fate.

1   What are your feelings about Creusa here? What do the touches of personal emotion in her speech tell us about her?

2   At lines 431–3 Aeneas declares: 'Ashes of Troy and flames which ended my people's lives, I call you to witness that, in your doom, I shrank from no fighting and no dangers from the Greeks, and if I had been fated to die, I would have earned my death with my deeds [i.e. I would have died heroically].' Do you accept Aeneas' own verdict that he was not a coward? What new values has he had to learn in this book?

3   What difference does it make that Aeneas and not the poet Virgil is telling this story?

## Book 3

**The refugees build a fleet and set sail.**

3.13–48   At a distance there lies a land of **Mars** (the Thracians plough it), a country of vast plains once ruled by **fierce Lycurgus**, of old a place friendly to Troy with allied 15 gods – as long as Fortune was with her. Here I sailed and laid out **my first walls** on the curving shore, coining the name Aeneadae for my people after my own name; but the fates were ill disposed to this undertaking.

I was performing sacred rites to my mother, **the daughter of Dione**, and the gods who give their favour to work newly begun, and I was sacrificing a sleek bull to the 20 high king of the gods upon the shore. It happened that there was a mound nearby on the top of which grew cornel bushes and a bristling thicket of myrtle shoots. I went over to it, and tried to pull up the green undergrowth from the soil in order 25 to cover the altar with leafy branches. But I saw a ghastly portent, wondrous to describe. For from the first tree torn with broken roots from the ground, there trickled drops of black blood which stained the earth with gore. A chill of horror made my body shake, and my blood curdled, frozen with dread. And then again 30 I went to pull up a tough shoot from a second tree, trying to discover the cause, however deeply hidden. From the bark of this tree too the black blood flowed. With my mind in a turmoil I began to pray to the country nymphs and to father

**Mars**   Ares, the Greek equivalent of the Roman god Mars, had very strong associations with Thrace.

**fierce Lycurgus**   he resisted the introduction of the worship of Dionysus into Thrace.

**my first walls**   Aeneas makes false starts on four cities in the course of the poem. The theme of city-building has negative connotations in Book 3.

**the daughter of Dione**   Venus was the daughter of this child of Oceanus and Tethys.

**Gradivus**, who rules over the **Getic** fields, that they would grant a favourable issue 35
to what I had seen and lighten the omen. But after I had attacked a third lot of
shrubs with greater intensity and struggled on my knees against the resisting sand
(should I speak or be silent?) a piteous groan was heard from the bottom of the 40
mound and an answering cry came to my ears:

'Why are you tearing my poor body apart, Aeneas? Be merciful to me now that I
am buried, do not pollute your pious hands. I am no stranger to you. Troy gave
me birth. And it is no tree from which this blood oozes. Ah! Flee this cruel land,
flee from this shore of greed. For I am **Polydorus**. Here **an iron crop of weapons** 45
**transfixed me**, covered my body, and grew up with pointed shafts.'

At this, doubt and fear assailed me. I was dumbfounded, **my hair stood on end**
**and my voice stuck in my throat**.

---

- Deryck Williams asks the question, why has Virgil included this account of
  the legend of Polydorus? He gives this answer: 'It is intended to make us
  feel that the long voyage which ends in the foundation of Rome begins in
  tragedy, horror and despair. It is an episode of primitive folk-lore, and in it
  Aeneas receives his first omen of the voyage, a grim and unhappy one. It
  serves to emphasize the atmosphere of gloom and sorrow in which Aeneas,
  still a "ghost of Troy" rather than yet "father of Rome", sets out from his
  destroyed homeland.' If this is so, how effectively is horror evoked by this
  episode?

---

The Trojans leave Thrace and sail on through a series of *Odyssey*-like
adventures, even having an encounter with the Cyclops Polyphemus whom
Odysseus had blinded. At one stage they come to Leucas and Actium on the
west coast of Greece.

---

**Gradivus**   a name of Mars (cf. line 13).

**Getic**   the Getae lived in the north of Thrace, but ancient poets are not interested in
geographical precision.

**Polydorus**   his dreadful story is told (rather differently) in Euripides' play *Hecuba*, in
which his ghost appears. When Priam feared that Troy was doomed, he sent this, his
youngest son, with vast treasures from Troy to his guest-friend Polymestor, king of
Thrace. When the latter understood that Troy was truly doomed, he murdered Polydorus
for the treasure.

**an iron crop of weapons transfixed me**   while in Euripides' play Polydorus had been
killed and cast into the sea, in Aeneas' account he was killed by a volley of spears that
transfixed him to the ground and took root.

**my hair stood on end and my voice stuck in my throat**   Aeneas reacts to the supernatural
in this way also at 2.774 and 4.280.

**3.274–89**  Soon the cloudy peaks of Mount Leucate and Apollo's temple, **dreaded by sailors**, 275
became visible. **Hither** we wearily sailed and approached **the little city**. We threw
our anchors from the prows and beached our ships. And so, having at last, **against
all expectation**, set foot on dry land, we performed the rites of purification to
Jupiter, made the altars blaze with our offerings and **crowded the shores of** 280
**Actium with our Trojan games**. My comrades stripped off and, their bodies
slippery with oil, engaged in the wrestling-bouts inherited from their fathers. We
were glad to have avoided so many Greek cities and to have made our escape
through the middle of our enemies.

Meanwhile the sun rolled on through the great circle of the year and **icy winter** 285
roughened the waves with its north winds. On **the entrance portals** I fixed a
shield of hollow bronze which great **Abas** had carried, and I commemorated the
event with a verse:

'AENEAS DEDICATES THESE ARMS WON FROM VICTORIOUS GREEKS.'

Then I told my men to man the benches and to leave the harbour.

---

- This is the only episode in Book 3 which does not include prophecy or some
  indication of progress towards the final goal. Why has Virgil included it?

---

**dreaded by sailors**  the promontory of Leucate, crowned by the temple of Apollo, was
a dangerous landmark.

**Hither**  Virgil conflates Leucate with Actium, which is some 30 or 40 miles away. There
too (on the south side of the entrance to the Ambracian gulf – see map on p. 133) was a
temple of Apollo, rebuilt by Octavian/Augustus in honour of his victory at Actium in 31
BC. He dedicated ten captured ships there. Apollo was the god with whom he particularly
identified himself.

**the little city**  after Actium, Octavian/Augustus enlarged this town on the north side
of the straits, transforming it into a great new city called Nicopolis ('victory city'). On its
northern edge he built a new sanctuary of Apollo with a stadium and a gymnasium. It
was crowned by a victory monument on the site of the tent which Octavian had used
when he was encamped there for the battle of Actium.

**against all expectation**  because they had been sailing through Greek seas, inevitably
hostile to Trojan refugees.

**crowded the shores of Actium with our Trojan games**  Virgil is here causing Aeneas
to look forward to the games in honour of Actian Apollo which were refounded by
Octavian/Augustus, who greatly enhanced their prestige. Held every four years at the
new sanctuary, they had equal status with the Olympic games.

**icy winter**  the Trojans, having left Troy in early summer, had reached Actium before the
winter.

**the entrance portals**  of Apollo's temple. Aeneas' dedication looks forward to Octavian's
(cf. the latter's dedications to Apollo on the Palatine (8.720–2)).

**Abas**  a Greek warrior.

## City-building

Later in the book the Trojans come to Buthrotum in north-west Greece where Priam's son Helenus, who has married Hector's widow Andromache, now rules. They have built a miniature Troy. Aeneas describes it like this: 'I went forward and recognized a little Troy, a copy of Pergama [the citadel of Troy] and a dry river-bed by the name of Xanthus [one of the rivers of Troy], and I embraced the portals of a Scaean gate' (lines 349–51).

* How do you react to this re-creation of Troy?

Aeneas continues with the story of his travels, telling Dido of how he and his men eventually came to the coast of North Africa. His father Anchises had died near the end of the journey.

# 5 Dido and Aeneas

## Book 4

4.1–5   But the queen, **long since wounded with the grievous pain of love**, feeds **the wound** with her life-blood and is consumed by **a fire** deep within her. Many a thought of the **courage** of the man goes racing around in her mind, many a thought of his **noble lineage**. His **features** and his **words** stick fast in her heart and the pain of her love allows her limbs no soothing rest.                           5

> Dido tells her sister Anna that if she had not resolved after Sychaeus' death not to marry again – 'may the earth swallow me or Jupiter blast me to the underworld before I go against my conscience' (lines 24–7) – she might have yielded. Anna persuades her of the advantages of marriage with Aeneas, no doubt saying to her what she wants to hear.

4.54–89   With these words Anna fanned the flames in a heart already burning with love, gave hope to her Dido's wavering thoughts and broke the bonds of her conscience.  55
First they go to the shrines of the gods and seek divine approval at altar after altar; they sacrifice yearling sheep chosen by due ritual to **Ceres, the law-giver**, and **Phoebus** and father **Lyaeus**, above all to Juno, guardian of the marriage bond. The most beautiful Dido herself, holding the sacred dish in her right hand, pours  60
libations between the two horns of a white cow or walks solemnly before the images of the gods to their rich altars, and **keeps inaugurating the day with gifts**, and, when the breasts of the cattle are opened, she pores eagerly over them and

---

**long since wounded with the grievous pain of love**   in fact it has all happened very quickly, with divine intervention playing its part. The wording may suggest that *Dido* has the impression that her love for Aeneas has already lasted for a long time.

**the wound, a fire**   Cupid's traditional wounds are arrows (causing the wound of love) and fire (symbolic of the flames of passion). At the end of the book, Dido stabs herself and then, in Book 5 (lines 2–3), is consumed by the flames of a pyre. The metaphors become realities.

**courage, noble lineage, features, words**   hers is not simply a physical passion. She is in love with everything about him, appreciating all his outstanding qualities as a man.

**Ceres, the law-giver, Phoebus, Lyaeus**   these three gods had special connections with marriage. Ceres is the law-giver because, as goddess of agriculture, she gave men a settled life. Lyaeus is a name for Bacchus meaning 'the loosener' (of inhibitions, etc.).

**keeps inaugurating the day with gifts**   she repeats her offerings throughout the day. Her behaviour is obsessive. Why do you think that she is performing these rites?

seeks the guidance of the breathing entrails. Ah, how ignorant the minds of seers! 65
What can prayers, what can shrines avail her in her frenzy? All the time **the flame is eating the soft marrow** of her bones and the wound lives silently under her breast. The unhappy Dido is on fire and wanders all over the city in her frenzy **like a deer** pierced by an arrow which a shepherd hunting in the woods of Crete 70 has shot from afar, hitting her off her guard and leaving the winged steel in her flesh, unaware of what he has done. In her flight she wanders through the wooded glades of Mount Dicte; the deadly arrow is sticking in her **side**. Now she leads Aeneas with her through the middle of the city and shows him the wealth of 75

*This statue of a deer from the House of the Tragic Poet in Pompeii was one of a pair which stood on the edge of a water basin in the main hall. Water was fed into their hollow bodies through a pipe leading to a hole in their underside and they spouted water from their mouths into the basin.*

**Sidon** and the city that lies ready for him. She begins to speak and stops in mid-sentence. Now, as day is ending, she calls for that same banquet again, and in her madness demands to hear the tale of Troy's sufferings once more and once more hangs from his lips as he tells it. Afterwards when they have 80 parted and the dim moon subdues her light in its turn, and the setting stars are urging sleep, she grieves alone in her empty house and throws herself on the couch he has left. He is not there and they are apart, but she hears him and she sees him. Or, captivated by the boy's resemblance to his father, she keeps back **Ascanius** on her lap in the hope that she may 85 comfort a love she cannot speak of.

---

**the flame is eating the soft marrow**   I am tempted to go against the editors and translate the Latin here as 'the soft flame is eating the marrow …'. The adjective 'soft' applied to the marrow of bones is otiose: the marrow *is* soft. But to refer to the flame of love as soft as it consumes Dido is powerfully evocative.

**like a deer … side**   the correspondences between Dido and Aeneas and the deer and the shepherd of the simile are illuminating. There is strong emotional colouring too, especially in the simile's pathos and its evocation of pain. Matthew Arnold (1822–88) reworks it to memorable effect in *Sohrab and Rustum*, lines 503–6:

> most like the roar
> Of some pain'd desert-lion, who all day
> Hath trail'd the hunter's javelin in his side,
> And comes at night to die upon the sand.

**Sidon**   Virgil uses the place-names Tyre and Sidon interchangeably.

**Ascanius**   the real Ascanius is back by now.

**The towers she has begun to build do not rise**, the young men do not exercise in arms or build harbours or fortifications for safety in war. Everything has stopped, all the building, the huge threatening walls and the crane towering to the sky – all at a standstill.

> 1 What moments in this passage particularly gain your attention? What feelings towards Dido do they evoke?
>
> 2 Comment on the exact correspondences between the wounded-deer simile and the situation of Dido and Aeneas.
>
> 3 In what ways does this passage convey the destructive nature of love?

The goddesses Juno and Venus converse. Desiring, as she does, to stop the Trojans establishing themselves in Italy, Juno proposes an alliance between them and the Carthaginians. Venus assents on condition that Jupiter can be persuaded, which she knows is impossible. Dido and Aeneas are about to go hunting. Juno will interrupt their expedition with a storm which will drive them together in a cave where she will 'marry' them. Venus agrees to this.

4.129–50     Meanwhile **Aurora** rose and left the ocean and, when the sun's rays appeared, the 130
pick of the young men came out of the gates carrying **wide- and fine-meshed nets** and broad-bladed hunting spears. The African horsemen and keen-scented powerful hounds rushed up. The first men of the Carthaginians waited for the queen at her doorway as she lingered in her **chamber**, and her high-mettled steed 135
stood there, brilliant in purple and gold, champing its foaming bit. At last she came out with a great crowd pressing round her, wearing a Sidonian cloak with embroidered hem. Her quiver was of gold, her hair was knotted in a golden clasp, golden was the brooch that fastened her purple dress. And with her too there went 140
the delighted Iulus and the Trojan company. Aeneas himself, **most beautiful of**

---

**The towers she has begun to build do not rise**   these words launch a fine evocation of suspended activity. The crane simply standing there idle is an especially eloquent image (metonymy). The dynamic Dido we met in Book 1 has been eroded by her passion.

**Aurora**   goddess of dawn. This episode of the story has a joyful beginning.

**wide- and fine-meshed nets**   in a Roman hunt, nets were set up at the far end of the hunting area and the animals were driven into them and killed.

**chamber**   the word translated here is commonly used of a marriage chamber. There is a hint of Dido as a bashful bride.

**most beautiful**   compare the surpassing beauty of Dido in line 60, where the same adjective is used.

all the men, stepped forward to join her and united his band with hers. **As when Apollo** leaves his winter home of **Lycia where the river Xanthus flows**, visiting **Delos, his mother's island**, and starting up the dance anew; and round his altars mingling throngs of Cretans and **Dryopes** and painted **Agathyrsians** make an uproar; Apollo himself strides on the ridges of Cynthus shaping his flowing locks with soft foliage and entwining them with gold. His arrows sound on his **shoulders**. Aeneas moved with no less vigour, the same beauty shone forth from his noble face. 150

*Apollo. This statue is from a bronze original, probably of the fourth century BC. The god steps forward to see the effect of the arrow he has just shot. The graceful elegance and the strength of his body and his keen gaze have won much admiration. The statue is called the Apollo Belvedere because it is placed in the Belvedere courtyard of the Vatican in Rome.*

**As when Apollo … shoulders**   the simile looks back to another in Book 1 which compares Dido with Apollo's sister Diana (1.498–502). In the Book 4 simile, the spring setting and the rumbustious noise of an international festival as well as the splendid appearance of the god create a heady impression. But there is a sinister effect in the sounding of the arrows on Apollo's shoulder. Compare Homer, *Iliad* 1.45–7, where Apollo flies down to bring plague to the Greek forces at Troy. Aeneas and the arrow of love are to prove fatal to Dido.

The fact that the gods to whom Dido and Aeneas are likened are brother and sister may add a suggestion of the illicit to the sexual relationship that will inevitably develop between them.

**Lycia where the river Xanthus flows**   Apollo had a shrine in Patara in Lycia (in modern Turkey) on the river Xanthus (a different Xanthus from the one at Troy). He went to the island of Delos, right in the middle of the Aegean, when the seas became navigable.

**Delos, his mother's island**   Latona gave birth to Apollo and Diana beneath a palm tree on this island.

**Dryopes, Agathyrsians**   from northern Greece and Scythia respectively.

1 What is the feeling conveyed in the lines where everybody assembles for the hunt (129–41)?

2 In his *Voyage of the Argonauts* the Hellenistic poet Apollonius of Rhodes (third century BC) introduces Jason with the following simile when he is meeting Medea: 'She longed to see him, and he soon appeared to her, his tall figure springing into view like the dog-star Sirius coming from the ocean. The star rises beautiful and clear to behold but brings unspeakable woe to the animals. Thus Jason came to her, beautiful to look on, but his appearance aroused the torments of love' (3.956–61). In what important ways does Apollonius' simile contrast with Virgil's likening Aeneas to Apollo?

**4.151–72**

After they came to the high mountains, the trackless forests where the animals have their lairs, look! down from the ridges ran wild mountain-goats, **driven downwards** from a rocky pinnacle. **On the other side** deer went skimming across the open plains and massed their dusty ranks in flight as they left the mountains. 155
But in the midst of the valleys **the boy Ascanius** gloried in his spirited horse, galloping past the deer and the goats, and prayed longingly that, in among all these timorous creatures, he might be presented with a foaming wild boar or a tawny lion down from the mountain.

Meanwhile the sky began to rumble with a great turmoil of thunder. A cloudburst 160
followed mixed with hail, and the Tyrian huntsmen, the young men of Troy and **the grandson of Venus, of the line of Dardanus**, scattered fearfully all over the countryside, seeking shelter. **Rivers rushed down headlong from the mountains.**

**driven downwards**   by the beaters (who drive the animals into the hunting area).

**On the other side**   Austin suggests that Virgil had a painting in mind.

**the boy Ascanius**   his whole future will be threatened by what is about to happen. It is appropriate that he should be presented here as the embodiment of high-spirited youth. The slaying of a wild beast is a rite of passage into adulthood.

**the grandson of Venus, of the line of Dardanus**   why this grandiloquent circumlocution for Ascanius? Is it a Virgilian joke? The boy Ascanius, referred to with epic grandeur, scuttles fearfully for shelter in the storm.

**Rivers rushed down headlong from the mountains**   'the dry river-beds are flooded in a moment' (Austin).

Dido and the Trojan leader came to the same cave. Primeval Earth and Juno, 165
**goddess of marriage**, gave the sign; **fires blazed** and the sky was **witness** to the
marriage, and the Nymphs **cried out** on the mountain top. That day was the
first that led to death, the first that led to disaster. Dido was no longer moved by 170
thoughts of how things looked or what people said, she no longer kept her love a
furtive secret in her heart. She called it marriage and under that name she cloaked
her guilt.

1 Who has caused the storm? What does it symbolize? How might Dido's
   interpretation of it differ from yours as a reader?

2 The focus of the final three lines (170–2) is on Dido. No mention is made of
   Aeneas and his emotions. Why do you think this may be?

3 How do lines 129–72 explore the conflict between Dido's private feelings
   and her public role as queen?

The foul goddess Rumour spreads a malicious but essentially truthful
account of the love affair between Dido and Aeneas. Finally she tells Dido's
African suitor Iarbas who angrily protests to Jupiter. The god sends down his
messenger Mercury to tell Aeneas that his obligation is to an Italian future,
not to Carthage. He must set sail. Mercury flies down to deliver his message.

**goddess of marriage** but the Latin word used here also refers to the matron who was
in charge of the wedding ceremony on the bride's side.

**fires blazed** flashes of lightning, but also suggesting the marriage torches.

**witness** another suggestion of the marriage ceremony.

**cried out** the wedding song is suggested, but, while the Latin word used here can be used
of ritual cries, much more often it conveys a cry of horror or distress ('howl', 'yell'). On this
passage Deryck Williams remarks that 'the elemental powers of nature and supernatural
divinities conspire to produce a parody of a wedding, a hallucination by which the unhappy
Dido is deceived'.

Compare John Milton's memorable lines when Eve eats the apple (*Paradise Lost*, 9.782–4):
> Earth felt the wound, and nature from her seat
> Sighing through all her works gave signs of woe,
> That all was lost.

**4.259–95**    As soon as he had flown to the huts of Africa on **his winged feet**, he caught sight 260
of Aeneas establishing fortifications and building new houses. Yes, and his **sword**
was starred with yellow jasper and his cloak hung from his shoulders blazing with

**Tyrian purple**, gifts which wealthy Dido had made, interweaving the web with a subtle thread of gold. The moment Mercury saw him, he went for him. 'You there, are you laying the foundations of lofty 265 Carthage now and building a fine city **to gratify your wife**? Alas! Have you forgotten your kingdom and your destiny? The ruler of the gods himself, whose divine power makes the heavens and the earth revolve, sends me down to you from bright Olympus. It is he who instructs me to bring these 270 commands through the swift breezes. What are you planning? What do you hope to gain by wasting time on Libyan soil? If you are left unmoved by the glory of such a great destiny, have some regard for your 275 growing son **Ascanius** and the hopes that **Iulus** has as your heir. The kingdom of Italy and the Roman land are his by right.' Such were the words that **the god from Mount Cyllene** spoke. He left the sight of the mortal Aeneas in mid-speech and vanished from his eyes far off into thin air.

*This statue of Mercury by Giambologna (1529–1608) is Renaissance in period but classical in feeling. He has wings on his hat and ankles, and he holds the caduceus, a winged staff with two serpents twining round it. A personified wind blows him on his way.*

---

**his winged feet**    Mercury wears winged sandals.

**sword**    presumably the scabbard or/and the hilt, in fact. What confronts Mercury is a figure dressed in luxurious eastern attire. Earlier the African chieftain Iarbas had spoken of Aeneas as 'a second Paris with his company of eunuchs, his chin and perfumed hair bound with a Lydian turban' (lines 215–17). While the African's bitter speech is hyperbolical, Aeneas is looking very much unlike a Roman. Virgil's readers would have inevitably thought of Antony and his relationship with Cleopatra, so negatively presented in Octavian's propaganda. As Osgood puts it, Cleopatra's Alexandria would for Italians 'figure into another moral geography in which it became the anti-Rome, a place where the City's traditions … were perverted by eastern degeneracy' (p. 335). The common thread in Octavian's propaganda was Cleopatra, envisioned 'as overpowering – even emasculating – a Roman man, and so upsetting the natural order' (p. 344). The irony is that Octavian was to become pharaoh of Egypt in 30 BC.

But Aeneas was distraught at what he had seen. He was dumbfounded, his hair 280
stood on end with dread and his voice stuck in his throat. He was on fire to escape
and to leave the delightful land, stunned as he was by such a strong warning and
command from the gods. Alas! what was he to do? With what words could he find
the courage to approach the frenzied queen? **How could he begin his speech to
her?** And as **he cast his swift thoughts now one way, now the other**, darted them 285
in different directions and considered all possibilities, this struck him as the best
solution to his dilemma. He called Mnestheus and Sergestus and brave Serestus,
instructing them to get a fleet ready but to tell nobody, and to call their comrades 290
to the shore. They should prepare the tackle and make an excuse for the change of
plan. In the meantime, since **the admirable Dido** knew nothing and never imagined

Shakespeare (via Plutarch, *Life of Antony* 26) brilliantly captures the impression of
eastern luxury in Enobarbus' description of Cleopatra's barge as she sails towards her first
meeting with Antony (*Antony and Cleopatra*, 2.2.201–9):

> The barge she sat in, like a burnished throne
> Burned on the water. The poop was beaten gold;
> Purple the sails, and so perfumèd that
> The winds were lovesick with them. The oars were silver,
> Which to the tune of flutes kept stroke, and made
> The water which they beat to follow faster,
> As amorous of their strokes. For her own person,
> It beggared all description: she did lie
> In her pavilion – cloth of gold, of tissue – ...

**Tyrian purple**   the Phoenicians were famous for their manufacture of purple cloth. Their
Tyrian dye, which produced a glowing purple colour, was made from an extract from a
vein of the whelk (a shellfish) and was very expensive, with some 12,000 whelks being
necessary to produce 1.5 grams of fluid.

**to gratify your wife**   the Latin word is 'uxorius' (English 'uxorious'). Mercury has added
this taunt to the rebuke that Jupiter told him to deliver. Again, there is a suggestion of
Antony under the spell of Cleopatra.

**Ascanius, Iulus**   Aeneas' son is referred to by his two different names, emphasizing his
position at the head of the Julian line, to which Julius Caesar and Octavian belonged. It
may be thought that part of his function in the poem is to serve as a symbol of the future,
its promise and its obligations.

**the god from Mount Cyllene**   Mercury was supposedly born on this mountain in Arcadia
in southern Greece.

**How could he begin his speech to her?**   Aeneas is seen as an orator trying to select his
opening words.

**he cast his swift thoughts now one way, now the other**   Tennyson reproduced this in his
'This way and that dividing the swift mind' (*Morte d'Arthur*).

**the admirable Dido**   we are following Aeneas' thought-processes here. It is *his* judgement
that Dido is admirable. Though he longs to leave, he still shows a sincere appreciation of
her virtues.

the breaking of so great a love, he himself would look for ways of approaching her and try to find the kindest time to speak, the right way to handle things. His men obeyed his orders **happily** and all speedily carried out his commands. 295

---

1 What has happened to Aeneas during his time in Carthage?

2 How is the theme of city-founding treated in this passage?

3 How justified is the criticism Mercury utters against Aeneas? How much sympathy, if any, do you feel towards the Trojan hero?

4 Sum up Aeneas' reaction to Mercury's appearance and speech.

5 Would there ever have been a right time to tell Dido? Give reasons for your answer.

---

**4.296–330**  But the queen – who could deceive a lover? – had a presentiment of his trickery and, fearful even when all was safe, at once caught on that there was trouble to come. That same unholy Rumour brought to the woman, already in a frenzy, the news that the fleet was being fitted out and a voyage planned. Lost to reason and inflamed with passion, she raved all over the city like a **bacchant** roused by the  300 shaking of **the holy symbols** when she hears the Bacchic cry, the **triennial rites** excite her and **Cithaeron** calls her by night with its shouting. At last she takes the initiative and accosts him with these words:

'You traitor, did you really hope that you could cover up such a great wrong and  305 leave my country without saying anything? Does neither our love hold you here nor **the pledge your right hand once gave me** nor Dido who will perish in a cruel death? More than that, are you busy with your fleet in the season of winter and hurrying to go over the deep when the north winds are at their worst, cruel  310 man? What! If you were not making for other people's land and an unknown

---

**happily**  we know that Aeneas is on fire to leave. His men are happy at the prospect too.

**bacchant**  an ecstatic follower of Bacchus. The simile evokes the terrifying world of Euripides' play *Bacchae*, in which the women of Thebes are maddened by the god to the extent that they tear a man, the son of one of them, to pieces.

**the holy symbols**  the emblems of the god, brandished in ecstasy.

**triennial rites**  according to the Roman system of counting, 'triennial' events happened every other year.

**Cithaeron**  the mountain near Thebes, the city where Bacchus was born. It was the location for the mutilation in *Bacchae* referred to above.

**the pledge your right hand once gave me**  is Dido referring back to the 'marriage' in the cave, or to an oath that she imagines Aeneas swore? He certainly responded to Dido's passion but, so far as we can tell from the poem, he made no commitment. What do you think of his behaviour?

home, and ancient Troy were still standing, **would you be making for Troy** over the swelling sea in your ships? Is it me you are running away from? By these tears and your right hand I pray you – since I have left myself nothing else now in my misery – by our union, by the marriage we have begun, if I have deserved well of you in any way or if anything about me was dear to you, pity a house that is falling and change this decision of yours, I beg you – if there is any place left for prayers. Because of *you* the tribes of Libya and the Numidian kings hate me and the Tyrians are my enemies. Yes, because of you my honour has been quenched, my former reputation too, by which alone I was making my way to the stars. To what fate do you abandon me on the point of death – my *guest*, since that name alone is left over from the name of husband? Why do I linger here? Is it until my brother Pygmalion razes the walls of my city or Gaetulian Iarbas leads me captive? At least if I had taken in my arms a child born from you before you fled, if some **darling little Aeneas** were playing in my palace who would bring you back to me through his likeness in spite of everything, I would not feel utterly **cheated and desolate**.'

---

1   What does the simile of the bacchant (lines 301–3) tell us about what has happened to Dido?

2   Is Dido addressing Aeneas more as a ruler denouncing a broken alliance or as a cheated lover?

3   Trace Dido's emotions through the course of her speech. Do you agree with T. E. Page that it is 'an appeal which would move a stone'?

---

**4.331–61**   She had spoken. As Jupiter had commanded, **he held his gaze steadfast** and with a great struggle he kept his love hidden in his heart. **At length he said a few words:**

---

**would you be making for Troy**   the implication is that Aeneas would not risk a voyage on the winter seas even to go home. It is beyond reason that he is doing so to voyage into the unknown.

**darling little Aeneas**   the common Latin word for little is *parvus*; its diminutive is *parvulus*, translated here as 'darling little'. It is the only diminutive in the *Aeneid* and comes across with considerable emotional power.

**cheated and desolate**   literally, 'captured and deserted'. Dido refers to herself with words appropriate to a sacked city (such as Troy).

**he held his gaze steadfast**   a kind of stage direction; again we are in the world of Greek tragedy.

**At length**   there has been a pause since Dido stopped speaking. We are made to focus on the time (described in lines 331–2) during which Aeneas struggles to master his feelings.

**he said a few words**   Aeneas' speech, his only one in this exchange, is actually the same length as Dido's, but the poet says that it was 'a few words'. As you read it, you may wish to consider why this may be.

'I shall never deny, o queen, that you have earned my gratitude for all the countless services that you can list in words, and I shall never forget the memory of **Elissa** 335 as long as I have memory of myself and breath rules these limbs. **Let me speak a few words to meet the case. I did not hope to keep my flight a secret from you** – never imagine that – and I never held out the marriage torch or entered into that contract. If the fates were allowing me to lead my life as I wanted and to 340 arrange all that grieves me to my own liking, my first concern would be to look after the city of Troy and what remains of my own dear people, Priam's lofty palace **would still be there**, and I would have founded a reborn Pergama for the conquered with my own hands. But as things stand, it is the great country of Italy, 345 of Italy that **Apollo of Gryneum and the oracle of Lycia** have told me to make for. That is my love, that is my fatherland. If you, a Phoenician, delight in the citadel of Carthage and the sight of a city in Libya, why, tell me, do you begrudge Trojans a settled future in the land of **Ausonia**? We too have the right to look for a 350 foreign kingdom. Every time the night covers the earth with her watery shadows, every time the fiery stars arise, **the troubled ghost of my father Anchises gives me warning** in my sleep and fills me with terror. The thought comes to me of the boy Ascanius and the wrong I am doing to someone I love in cheating him of the 355 kingdom of Hesperia and the lands that are his by fate. Now even the messenger of the gods, sent by Jupiter himself – I swear it by your life and by mine – has brought down his commands through the swift breezes. Yes, with my own eyes and in the clear light of day I saw him entering the walls. With my own ears I drank in his words. Stop inflaming both of us with your complaints. I make for 360 Italy, but **not of my own free will**.'

---

**Elissa**  Dido's original Phoenician name.

**Let me speak a few words to meet the case**  Aeneas talks as if he is in a law court.

**I did not hope to keep my flight a secret from you**  Aeneas doubtless thinks he is being sincere when he says this, but it is hard to take him altogether at his word. What is your response to this statement?

**would still be there**  i.e. would have been reconstructed by me.

**Apollo of Gryneum and the oracle of Lycia**  Apollo had a temple at Gryneum in Asia Minor (modern Turkey). See the note at line 143 (p. 73) for Apollo's connection with Lycia. We have not heard anything about these oracles before.

**Ausonia**  Italy.

**the troubled ghost of my father Anchises gives me warning**  this is the first time we have heard of this too (see two notes above). It makes psychological sense. Aeneas' guilty conscience is disturbing his sleep and invading his dreams. It is appropriate that it is his father, still thought of by him as the head of the family, who is pushing him to act on his obligations to that family instead of taking his own pleasure.

**not of my own free will**  how true is this?

1. How much evidence (if any) is there in this passage that Aeneas really does love Dido?

2. What use is made of the city-building theme in this passage?

3. Aeneas' speech has divided the critics. Austin reacts to T. E. Page's decidedly extreme comment that 'not all Virgil's art can make the figure of Aeneas here appear other than despicable', by saying, 'It is unfair and untrue.' It may be that the truth lies somewhere between these two views. Trace the arguments that Aeneas uses. What are your feelings about what he says? Which arguments, even if true, would have been especially hurtful to Dido?

**4.362–92**    All the time he was saying these words, **she was turned** away from him but still watching him, darting glances this way and that. With expressionless eyes she looked over every part of him, and blazing with passion, she spoke thus:

'**No goddess was your mother** and Dardanus was not the founder of your line, 365 you traitor, but rugged **Caucasus** begat you on its hard rocks and **Hyrcanian** tigers gave you suck. Why do I need to pretend? What greater crisis will there be to make me hold back now? Did he sigh when I wept? Did he turn his eyes on me? Did he yield and shed tears or pity the woman who loves him? No. **What shall I say first,** 370 **what second?** Now, now neither mighty Juno nor father Jupiter, the son of Saturn, looks on these things with just eyes. I cannot safely put my trust in anything. I took him in when he was cast out destitute on my shore and in my madness I gave him a share in my kingdom. I found the fleet he had lost, I saved his comrades 375 from death. Alas! I am being driven by the fires of frenzy. Now **he tells me of** the **prophet** Apollo, now of the Lycian oracle, now of the messenger of the gods sent

---

**she was turned away ...**    another stage direction.

**No goddess was your mother**    this passage looks back to *Iliad* 16.33–5, where Patroclus reproaches Achilles, saying, 'Pitiless man, so your father was not the horseman Peleus and your mother was not [the goddess] Thetis, but the grey sea and high rocks bore you, so harsh is your spirit.' Another famous imitation of the Homer passage comes at Catullus 64.154–6, where Ariadne denounces the absent Theseus who has deserted her.

**Caucasus**    the Caucasus mountains were famous for their hard cliffs.

**Hyrcanian**    the region around the Caspian sea, including Hyrcania at its south-east end, was considered particularly barbarous and savage.

**What shall I say first, what second?**    i.e. everything is equally appalling.

**he tells me of**    in her frenzy, Dido's language becomes disjointed. This is most effective in Latin but does not work in English and I have supplied these words to complete the sense. She mocks Aeneas' words at lines 345, 346 and 356–7.

**prophet**    Dido uses the word 'augur', a distinctly Roman term, referring to one who observes and interprets the behaviour of birds, and more generally a seer or a prophet.

by Jupiter himself bringing dread commands through the air. **Indeed!** So the gods above are troubled about *this*! *This* worries them and troubles their calm! I do not 380 keep you here and I do not argue against what you have said. Go, seek Italy on the winds, make for your kingdom over the waves! I hope, indeed I hope, if the pious deities have any power, that you will drain the cup of punishment on the rocks in mid-sea, calling the name Dido again and again. Though I shall be far from you, I shall pursue you **with dark flames** and, when cold death takes my breath from 385 my body, my shade will be with you everywhere. Ruthless man, you will pay the penalty. I shall hear of it, and the report will come to me deep among the dead.'

With these words she broke off her speech, turned away from him as he looked at her, and, sick with despair, went fleeing from the air of day, leaving him deeply 390 uncertain in his fear and rehearsing many things to say. Her maids supported her as she fainted, carried her to **her marble chamber** and placed her on her bed.

---

1   What use is made of body language and eye contact (or lack of it) here?

2   Trace the emotions and arguments which make up Dido's speech. What may have been going through Aeneas' mind as he listened to it?

3   A foreign queen out of control will have brought Cleopatra to mind. What admirable qualities (if any) can you identify in the Dido of this passage? What do you feel about her here?

---

4.393–415    But **pious** Aeneas, although he longed to calm her by comforting her in her sorrow and to assuage her bitterness with his words, even so, with many a sigh and 395 **shaken to the depths of his heart by his great love, carried out the orders of the gods** and went back to his fleet. Then indeed **the Trojans worked with a will** and

---

**Indeed!**   savagely ironical, as are the next two exclamations.

**with dark flames**   the reference is to the murky torches of the avenging Furies, but, as Servius points out, there is a hint at the flames of Dido's funeral pyre.

**her marble chamber**   the cold stone contrasts with her frenzied emotion and her feverish body. Dido will never leave her palace again; this is the last time that Aeneas sees her.

**pious**   this epithet (adjective) is used of Aeneas 20 times in the poem. We have not heard it so far in Book 4. (It came last at 1.378.) Now that he is acting in accordance with his destiny this epithet can be restored to him. There is a sense in which Virgil is here emptying the word 'pious' of any positive or negative associations. He is just telling us the fundamental truth about the man we now see.

**shaken to the depths of his heart by his great love**   Virgil assures us of this, but an authorial statement may not carry as great a weight as a character's words or deeds. What do you feel about this? We see into Dido's heart in a way that is almost completely denied to us in the case of Aeneas.

**carried out the orders of the gods**   Aeneas shows himself to be a true Stoic.

**the Trojans worked with a will**   as Austin neatly puts it, they work like Trojans.

---

dragged the tall ships down all along the shore. Shiny with pitch, the vessels went afloat. From the woods they carried timber still unfashioned, oars still sprouting leaves, in their eagerness to get away. You could have seen them rushing on from every part of the city. And **just as when ants**, mindful of winter, plunder a huge heap of wheat and store it in their home: **a black column goes over the plain** and they gather in their booty through the grass along a narrow track. Some push huge grains of wheat, straining with their shoulders. Others keep the column together and punish the stragglers. **The whole path seethes with activity.** What were your feelings then, **Dido**, when you saw this! What sighs did you breathe when you looked out from the top of **your citadel** at the shore seething along all its length and saw the whole sea a mass of confusion before your eyes! **Relentless Love**, is there no limit to which you do not force the human heart? She was forced to resort to tears once more, once more to try to move him with prayers and to humble her proud spirit to supplication, in case she left anything undone and died when there was no need.

400

405

410

415

---

**just as when ants …**   A. S. Pease suggests that perhaps the comparison to ants 'suggests not only the industry of the Trojans at this time but also that, at the distance from which Dido viewed them, they seem scarcely distinguishable one from another. In fact, though many individual Trojans are named in the *Aeneid*, the number to whom any distinct individuality attaches is small.' It is interesting that the simile Virgil uses elsewhere in the poem to suggest a happily cooperative community, that of bees in a sunlit and flowery countryside (1.430–6, 6.707–9), is starkly transformed here into a description of efficient ants who, effortfully provident with their thoughts on winter, summon up, in part by Virgil's use of military vocabulary, a picture of Fascistic discipline for Dido and for us to behold. It is in this bleak light that we are asked at this moment to view the destiny of Rome. Do you agree with my assessment here?

**a black column goes over the plain**   a quotation from Ennius (239–169 BC), the father of Roman epic poetry, who applied the words to elephants. For those who recognized Virgil's source, there would have been something grotesque and comic about his transformation of elephants to ants.

**The whole path seethes with activity**   the expression is reminiscent of Virgil's summation of the labouring bees at *Georgics* 4.169 and *Aeneid* 1.436.

**Dido**   a wonderful moment. Virgil addresses Dido in sympathetic apostrophe, the literary device by which an author turns away from his audience to speak to one of his characters.

**your citadel**   where her palace is.

**Relentless Love**   a fine effect. The poet moves from his address to Dido to talk to Amor, the god of love (the name means 'love': hence my translation). One senses how deeply Virgil is caught up in his story.

1 How do lines 259–415 direct our emotions towards both Aeneas and Dido?

2 Are the differences between Dido and Aeneas, in behaviour, speech and emotions, differences that Virgil is associating with their genders?

3 Our modern world-view is very different from the Roman one. Virgil portrays Aeneas as obeying the orders of the gods (line 396). How might a modern author represent the external constraints to which he bows?

4 What impression do you get of the Trojans here?

Dido sends Anna down to the harbour to plead with Aeneas, but her sister's appeal falls on deaf ears.

### Aeneas responds to Anna's appeal

After Anna has appealed to Aeneas, Virgil tells us that:

*he is moved by no tears. He hears nothing she says in a yielding spirit. The fates block the way, and the god stops the man's kindly ears [or stops the man's ears, leaving them undisturbed]. And just as when the north winds of the Alps, blowing now from this side, now from that, battle with each other to uproot an oak, a tree mighty with the strength of years, there is the sound of cracking, and, as the trunk is shaken, the leaves on high strew the ground; but the tree itself holds firmly to the rocks, stretching as far down to Tartarus with its roots as it reaches to the winds of heaven with its top – in just that way the hero is buffeted on this side and on that by constant appeals, and feels the pain of love in all his mighty breast. His purpose remains unmoved. Tears pour down, but in vain. (4.438–49)*

1 What does the Alpine-oak simile tell us about Aeneas?

2 In the final line we are not told whose tears are pouring down. Aeneas', Anna's, Dido's? Or is it all three? Or should we ask? What do you feel is the effect created here?

**Cleopatra and Dido**

In his *Odes* (1.37), Virgil's friend and contemporary Horace celebrated the suicide of Cleopatra in 30 BC ('Now is the time for drinking, now is the time for uncontrolled dancing …'). He says that it was wrong to celebrate while the queen in her madness was plotting Rome's ruin with her gang of vile perverts (lines 1–12). But her frenzy has been curbed by her defeat at the battle of Actium by Octavian who has pursued her to Egypt in order to put her in chains. But 'she, seeking to die more nobly, did not tremble at the sword in womanish fear and did not reach some hidden shore with her swift fleet. She had the courage to look upon her ruined palace with a calm face and to handle fierce snakes so that her body could drink up their black poison. Once resolved on death she was the more defiant, scorning – you can be sure of it – to be taken to Rome as a private person in the galleys of savage Liburnians for a proud triumph. She was no humble woman' (lines 21–32).

- Horace's poem in fact veers round, ending with a tribute to Cleopatra. It is hard to believe that Virgil did not wish his readers to identify Dido with Cleopatra at least to some extent. How sympathetic to Dido does he seem to be? If you believe that he *is* sympathetic, what do you think Octavian, by now the most powerful man in the western world, would have felt about the attitude of these two poets, whom he knew and counted among his circle?

Dido now wishes to die. Terrible omens torment her and invade her sleep.

4.465–73    In her dreams savage Aeneas drives her in her frenzy and she always seems to be left alone and solitary, **always to be travelling on a long road without a companion,** looking for her Tyrians in a desert land. She was like **Pentheus** in his madness when he sees the columns of the Furies and a double sun and a two-fold Thebes    470

---

**always to be travelling on a long road without a companion**   Austin quotes Coleridge's *Ancient Mariner* (lines 446–51):

> Like one, that on a lonesome road
> Doth walk in fear and dread
> And having once turned round, walks on,
> And turns no more his head;
> Because he knows, a frightful fiend
> Doth close behind him tread.

What associations does the imagery of Dido's dream evoke?

**Pentheus**   we are now given further detail from Euripides' play, *Bacchae*. Because Pentheus tries to deny Dionysus his worship, the god drives him mad, causing him to hallucinate on stage and thus to see a double sun and a two-fold vision of his city of Thebes. Pentheus then goes to the mountains where the bacchants, led by his mother, tear him to pieces: this happens off stage, though we later see his dismembered body.

*Cleopatra.*

### Cleopatra

| | |
|---|---|
| 52 BC | Cleopatra succeeds her father Ptolemy Auletes on the throne of Egypt, sharing it with two younger brothers, to whom she was nominally married. |
| 48–47 | Supports Julius Caesar in the Alexandrian war, becoming his mistress and having a child by him (Caesarion). |
| 46 | Follows Caesar to Rome. |
| 44 | Returns to Egypt after Caesar's assassination. |
| 41 | Meets Mark Antony at Tarsus and starts a liaison with him. Antony makes an agreement with Octavian and marries his sister Octavia. Antony's affair with Cleopatra is interrupted. |
| 37 | The affair is revived. Cleopatra and Antony live together in imperial magnificence at Alexandria. |
| 33 | The agreement between Antony and Octavian expires. |
| 32 | Antony divorces Octavia. Octavian declares war on Cleopatra. |
| 31 | The battle of Actium. Octavian defeats Antony and Cleopatra. |
| 30 | First Antony and then Cleopatra commit suicide, the latter partly to avoid being paraded in Octavian's triumph. |

appearing before him, or like Agamemnon's son Orestes when he is **tormented upon the stage** as he flees his mother who is armed with torches and black snakes while the avenging Furies sit at the doors.

Pretending that she is making use of a sorceress's spells either to win Aeneas back or to put an end to her passion for him, Dido persuades her sister Anna to build a pyre on which the arms and clothes he has left behind can be incinerated. Anna does what she is asked. In a night-time soliloquy the sleepless Dido explores the options open to her. She resolves that it is better to die. She concludes by acknowledging that she has not kept her pledge to stay faithful to Sychaeus after his death (4.552).

**tormented upon the stage**  Orestes was instructed by Apollo to kill his mother in vengeance for her murder of his father. Aeschylus' play, *Libation Bearers*, tells of how he carries out Apollo's commands, but his matricide rouses the Furies, who avenge such murders. Unseen by the audience, they chase him off the stage at the end of the tragedy, and they actually appear in *Furies*, the play that continues the story, and pursue him to Athens. Their appearance was so alarming that it is asserted in the ancient *Life of Aeschylus* that at the first performance a woman in the audience gave premature birth in her terror. Torches and snakes were traditionally their weapons. In the Aeschylus plays, Clytemnestra is not herself a Fury, but she is of course the cause of their pursuit of Orestes and so it is not inappropriate that she should be assimilated to them.

**4.553–83**  Such were the lamentations that kept bursting from her heart. As for Aeneas, now that he was determined to go and everything was now duly prepared, **he was** 555 **sleeping** on the lofty stern of his ship. To him there appeared, **in a dream**, the form of the god coming a second time and looking the same as before, and he seemed to give him a second warning in these words. He was like Mercury in every respect, in his voice, his complexion, his golden hair and the grace of his youthful body.

'Son of a goddess, can you sleep at such a perilous time? Don't you see what dangers 560 surround you at this moment, you madman, and **don't you hear the favourable west winds blowing? Resolved on death, she is pondering some trickery in her heart**, some terrible crime, stirring the shifting tides of her anger. Will you not 565 flee from here in haste while hasty flight is still a possibility? Soon you will see a turmoil of ships on the sea and fierce fire-brands blazing, soon you'll see the shore seething with flames if dawn finds you lingering in this land. Up! Up! No more delay. Women are always fickle and changeable.' With these words he melted away 570 into the black night.

Here at last we have an explicit reference to tragedy, but we have already found a number of evocations of the genre in the poem. What does its presence in the *Aeneid* signify? In 1915 Richard Heinze made use of the terms Aristotle employs in his discussion of tragedy in the *Poetics*, viewing Dido as a tragic protagonist who undergoes a sudden 'reversal' as she falls from her dream of happiness to meet her death. Does this make any sense to you? You will need to come back to this question at the end of Book 4. Can you think of any other possible significances of Virgil's incorporation of tragedy?

Finally, it must be acknowledged that Virgil's source may not have been the Aeschylus plays but one or more tragedies in Latin. Ennius and a number of others had written dramas on some phases of the Orestes myth in that language. However, the previous lines about Pentheus so unmistakably refer to Euripides' *Bacchae* that it is hard to disbelieve that here too Virgil is looking back to the Greek original.

**he was sleeping**  Aeneas' conscience is now easy. There is a clear contrast here with the insomniac Dido.

**in a dream**  this is not an actual visit from Mercury. Aeneas later tells his men that a god has come to see him again (lines 574–6) but the truth is not so clear-cut. Virgil stresses the apparition's *likeness* to Mercury.

**don't you hear the favourable west winds blowing?**  'while Aeneas has been asleep, a miraculous favouring west wind has sprung up – the winter storms are over – and he is still delaying' (Austin).

**Resolved on death**  i.e. what has she got to lose?

**she is pondering some trickery in her heart**  there is no problem about telling who 'she' is! While it is true that Dido later contemplates an all-out attack on the departing Trojans, at lines 592–4, this does seem to be a momentary impulse. In the following line (595) she says, 'What am I saying? Or where am I? What madness is changing my resolve?' The apparition is stating what is tendentious as if it were factual.

Then indeed, terrified by the sudden apparition, Aeneas abruptly shook off sleep and roused his companions to instant action. 'Men, wake up this moment and sit at the benches. Spread the sails – and get a move on. A god, yes, a god sent down from high heaven spurs us on a second time to speed our flight and cut the  575 twisted cables. We follow you, o blessed god, **whoever you are**, and once more perform your bidding with joy. O, be with us, give us your kindly help and bring us favourable stars in the sky.'

He spoke and snatched his sword like lightning from its sheath and **struck the**  580 **mooring cables with the drawn blade**. The same excitement gripped them all at once: they hurried and scurried. Suddenly the shore was empty. The sea could not be seen for ships. Bending to their task, they churned up the foam and swept the blue waters with their oars.

> •   Comment on the apparition's words: 'Women are always fickle and
>     changeable.' Whose views are being expressed?

> Dido watches the Trojan fleet move away. Her frenetic emotions carry her this
> way and that, but eventually she launches into a terrible curse.

4.607–29   'O **Sun**, whose fiery rays survey all the works of earth, and you **Juno, mediator** and witness of my sufferings, and you, **Hecate**, whose name is howled by night at the city crossroads, and avenging Furies, and gods of dying Elissa, listen to me  610 now, turn your divine power upon my wrongs as I have deserved from you, and hear my prayers. **If it is inevitable** for that vile creature to come to harbour and

---

**whoever you are**   a religious formula, not in fact expressing any doubt about Mercury's identity.

**struck the mooring cables with the drawn blade**   a moment of enormous symbolic importance. Aeneas 'cuts loose' not only from Africa but from Dido. At the same time, he dooms Dido to death. She will kill herself with one of his swords.

**Sun**   the sun sees everything: nothing can be hidden from it. Dido calls upon it as a witness of Aeneas' treachery.

**Juno, mediator**   Dido cannot fully understand the extent of the role that Juno has played in her liaison with Aeneas. The reader may feel that the word 'go-between' is as appropriate as 'mediator'.

**Hecate**   the goddess Diana is the moon in the sky, the huntress on earth and Hecate in the underworld. Associations of witchcraft and horror make her an appropriate goddess for a woman determined upon suicide to invoke.

**If it is inevitable …**   Dido's curse is modelled on Polyphemus' curse upon Odysseus at *Odyssey* 9.532–5. As Williams remarks, all her curses on Aeneas came true in one way or another. 'He was harassed in warfare by Turnus and his Rutulians; he left the Trojan camp and the embrace of Iulus to seek help from Evander; he saw the death of many of his

to sail to land, if that is what the fates of Jupiter demand and the outcome cannot be altered, at least let him be harried in war by the arms of a bold people, exiled 615 from his territory and torn away from the embrace of Iulus, and let him beg for help, and look upon the shameful deaths of his own people. And when he has surrendered to the terms of an unequal peace, may he not enjoy his kingdom or the light of life that he longs for. No, may he fall before his time and lie unburied 620 on the open shore. This is my prayer, these are the final words I pour forth with my lifeblood.

'And then you, my Tyrians, must harry the whole line of his descendants with your hatred. This is the offering you must make to my ashes. Let there be no love between our peoples and no treaties. Arise, **unknown avenger**, from my bones, to 625 pursue the Trojan settlers with fire and the sword, now, one day, whenever there is strength to do it. I pray that shore may fight with shore, sea with sea, arms with arms. Let them fight, they and **their sons' sons!**'

---

1 What factors cause Dido's curse to make so strong an impression?

2 Contrast the vision of the Trojans' future here with that offered by Jupiter in Book 1.

3 Dido's speech looks forward to the Punic wars, during which Hannibal almost brought Rome to her knees. What is the effect of this projection into the future?

---

men (notably Pallas); he accepted peace terms more favourable to the Italians than the Trojans (12.834–5); and [after the action of the poem] he did not rule his people for long (three years), but (according to one version of the legend) was drowned in the Numicus or (according to another) killed in battle and his body not recovered.'

The English king Charles I was confronted by these terrible lines when he opened his Virgil in the 1640s. He was taking the *Sortes Vergilianae*. To do this, you open your Virgil; the passage you touch at random with your finger is the oracular response. Charles was beheaded in 1649.

**unknown avenger**   this will be the Carthaginian general Hannibal, who came close to destroying Rome in 217 and 216 BC. Dido calls out to him across the centuries with a passionate immediacy.

**their sons' sons**   something extraordinary happens in the Latin at the end of the last line of Dido's great curse. There is one syllable too many to fit the metre of a hexameter and no convincing way of eliminating it. The line simply goes on for too long. Austin comments: 'Dido seems to leave the two peoples locked for ever in their enmity. And would not the Roman reader have thought also of those more recent struggles that had appeared unending, the civil wars?'

---

**4.642–705**   Shivering, frantic in her terrible design, rolling her bloodshot eyes, her trembling cheeks blotched with stains, and pale at the thought of death so near, Dido burst 645 into the inner courtyard of her palace and in her frenzy climbed up the lofty pyre and unsheathed a Trojan sword, a gift she had asked for, but not for such a purpose. Here, after she saw the Trojan clothing and the familiar bed, she paused a little in tearful thought and fell on the bed and spoke these final words: 650

'Sweet things that once were his, sweet as long as god and the fates allowed it, take this my spirit and free me from this pain. **I have lived my life** and completed the course that fortune had given me, and now **the great spirit** of what I am shall go beneath the earth. I have established a glorious city; I have seen my own walls built; 655 avenging my husband **I exacted punishment** from my brother who was my enemy – **happy, ah! too happy, if only the Trojan ships had never touched our shores.**'

She spoke, buried her face in the bed, and said, 'We shall die unavenged but let us die. This, this is the way I choose to go to join the shades. Let the cruel **Trojan** 660 **drink in the sight of this fire from the high seas** and take with him the omen of my death.'

She had spoken, and **as she spoke her companions saw that she had fallen upon her sword**, the weapon foaming with blood, her hands bespattered. Shouts hit 665 the high hall's roof; Rumour rushes wildly through the stricken city. The palace

---

**I have lived my life**   Austin suggests that this may not necessarily mean 'my life is done'. Dido could be saying that she has lived a full life. Her assertions have the simple dignity of inscriptions on tombstones.

**the great spirit**   ghosts were supposedly larger than life: compare Creusa's ghost (2.773, p. 64). But surely there must also be a reference to greatness of character.

**I exacted punishment**   she sailed away with Pygmalion's ships, his gold and a sizeable part of his population.

**happy, ah! too happy, if only the Trojan ships had never touched our shores**   the wording here is strongly reminiscent of the thoughts of Medea at Apollonius of Rhodes, *Voyage of the Argonauts* 3.774–7, 4.32–3 and of Ariadne (abandoned by Theseus) at Catullus 64.171–2.

**Trojan**   the Latin word used literally means 'descended from Dardanus'. Dido cannot bring herself to name Aeneas.

**drink in the sight of this fire from the high seas**   as indeed Aeneas will do at the start of Book 5 (lines 3–7). He cannot know what has happened but he and his men feel a grim foreboding.

**as she spoke her companions saw that she had fallen upon her sword**   Williams comments: 'Like a Greek tragedian, Virgil does not describe the death stroke, only the fact that it has occurred.'

resounds with laments, groans and the shrieks of women, and **the heaven echoes with loud sounds of lamentation**. It was just as if **all Carthage were falling, or ancient Tyre**, the enemy within the walls, and flames were rolling in a frenzy over the roofs of men and gods. 670

Her sister heard and was out of her mind with panic. Utterly terrified, she ran trembling through the middle of the crowd, bloodying her face with her nails and bruising her breasts with her fists, and called upon the dying woman by name:

'So was *this* what it was all for, my sister? Was it a trick when you sought my help? *This* was what your pyre was for, was it, and the fire and the altars? What should I complain of first, now that you have deserted me? Did you think that your sister was unworthy to join you in your death? You should have called me to the same fate. The sword should have taken off both of us in the same agony, at the same hour. And, more than that, did these hands of mine build the pyre, this voice call upon our ancestral gods, only so that when you laid yourself down here, cruel woman, I should be somewhere else? **You have destroyed** yourself and me, my sister, and your people and **the fathers from Sidon** and your city. **Let me** wash her wound in water and, **if there is any last breath still lingering, let me catch it with my lips.**' 675

680

685

---

**the heaven echoes with loud sounds of lamentation**  the tragic episode is given cosmic reverberations. What is happening here will affect the history of the world.

**all Carthage were falling, or ancient Tyre**  we have Appian's grim description of the seven-day-long sack of Carthage by the Romans in 146 BC (Appian 8.127–32). The Roman general is said to have been reduced to tears, and to have quoted Homer on the fall of cities (8.132): 'The day will come when sacred Troy will be destroyed and with it Priam and the people of Priam with his fine ash spear.' (*Iliad* 6.448–9)

As for Tyre, Arrian gives a detailed description of its seven-month siege by Alexander in 332 BC and the grisly aftermath in which the Macedonians set fire to the city and massacred 8,000 inhabitants (*Anabasis* 2.18–24).

The two similes look into the future. Dido's curse and her suicide will lead to the annihilation of her city. This is a strikingly inverted instance of the city-building motif. Austin comments that the sacking of a city was 'the most dreadful scene of horror that an ancient writer could imagine'. We have, of course, been given an intensely powerful description of the sack of Troy in Book 2.

**You have destroyed …**  Anna is presumably thinking of the defencelessness of Carthage against Pygmalion and the African tribes when the queen is dead rather than the threat of a more momentous destruction. However, she certainly speaks the truth. Dido has brought eventual doom on her people and her city: see the previous note.

**the fathers from Sidon**  i.e. the Carthaginian elders.

**Let me**  she addresses the crowd.

**if there is any last breath still lingering, let me catch it with my lips**  the soul was contained in the last breath of a dying person; the closest relation would try to catch it.

---

As she said these words, she had climbed the steps to the top and, embracing her dying sister in her arms, she groaned as she caressed her and tried to dry the black blood with her dress. Dido attempted once more to lift her heavy eyes, but failed. The wound fixed in her breast **hissed**. Three times she raised herself, leaning upon 690 her elbow. Three times she fell back on the bed, and with her wandering eyes she sought the light in the high heaven and groaned when she had found it.

*Iris. This is from an illustration in a famous early manuscript of the* Aeneid *in the Vatican Library, dating from the fifth or sixth century AD.*

Then all-powerful Juno, pitying her long agony and her difficult death, sent **Iris** down from Olympus **to set her struggling spirit free and** 695 **loose her close-locked limbs.** For because she was not dying at her fated time or by a death she had deserved, but wretchedly before her day, set on fire by a sudden frenzy, **Proserpina had not yet taken a golden lock from her head** and forfeited her life to Stygian **Orcus.** And so Iris flew down through the sky with dew upon 700 her saffron wings, trailing a thousand different colours as the sun shone on her, and she stood above Dido's head, saying: 'In obedience to my orders I take this lock as a sacred offering to Dis and I free you from your body.'

So she spoke and she cut the lock with her right hand; and together with it all the warmth passed from her and her life departed into the winds. 705

---

**hissed** 'the word accurately expresses the whistling sound with which breath escapes from a pierced lung' (J. W. Mackail).

**Iris** the messenger of Juno or Jupiter, the goddess of the rainbow.

**to set her struggling spirit free and loose her close-locked limbs** why is Juno choosing to do this now? How does this information reflect on Juno's treatment of Dido earlier?

**Proserpina had not yet taken a golden lock from her head** Keith Maclennan writes, 'The idea that Proserpina took a lock of hair from a dying person at the moment of death was unfamiliar enough to readers in late antiquity for some to think Virgil had invented it, though a scholar was able to point to an instance in a Euripides play (*Alcestis* 74ff.). It seems to follow that Virgil is taking advantage of an obscure or rarely-held belief to mark with great delicacy an important point in his narrative.'

**Orcus** a synonym for Dis or Pluto (king of the underworld).

---

1 How do you respond to Dido at these supreme moments of her tragedy? Heinze referred to her 'truly Roman heroism'. What can you find to support and what to go against this judgement?

2 Does Virgil's sympathetic treatment of the ruler of Rome's bitter enemy Carthage surprise you?

3 What is the effect of the descent of Iris at the end? Do you feel that her appearance proves an effective conclusion to the book?

## A passionate reaction to Dido's tragedy

The French composer Hector Berlioz (1803–69) who, in his great opera *The Trojans*, set the story of Book 4 (and of Book 2) to music, writes memorably of his early response to Virgil:

*One day, I remember, I was disturbed from the outset of the lesson by the line: 'But the queen, long since wounded with the grievous pain of love …'. Somehow or other I struggled on till we came to the great turning-point of the drama. But when I reached the scene in which Dido expires on the funeral pyre, surrounded by the gifts and weapons of the perfidious Aeneas, and pours forth on the bed – 'that bed with all its memories' – the bitter stream of her life-blood, and I had to pronounce the despairing utterances of the dying queen, 'three times raising herself upon her elbow, three times falling back', to describe her wound and the disastrous love that convulsed her to the depth of her being, the cries of her sister and her nurse and her distracted women, and that agony so terrible that the gods themselves are moved to pity and send Iris to end it, my lips trembled and the words came with difficulty, indistinctly. At last, at the line 'She sought the light in the high heaven and groaned when she had found it', at that sublime image I was seized with a nervous shuddering and stopped dead. I could not have read another word. It was one of the occasions when I was most sensible of my father's unfailing goodness. Seeing how confused and embarrassed I was by such an emotion, but pretending not to have noticed anything, he rose abruptly and shut the book. 'That will do, my boy,' he said, 'I'm tired.' I rushed away, out of sight of everybody, to indulge my Virgilian grief.* (translation by David Cairns)

# 6 Aeneas goes down to the underworld

**Book 5**

> The Trojans are sailing for Italy but a violent storm causes them to go back to Sicily where Aeneas' father Anchises had died the year before. On the anniversary of Anchises' death Aeneas proclaims a solemn sacrifice at his tomb, which is followed on the ninth day by contests in rowing, running, boxing and archery. We include the account of the foot race.

**5.286–361**

After **this contest** was over, pious Aeneas moved to a grassy plain surrounded on all sides by woods on a circle of hills. In the middle of the valley there was a circular theatre and hither the hero went in the middle of a crowd of many thousands and 290 sat on a platform. Here he set up prizes for any who might wish to compete **in a foot race**, sharpening their spirit with rewards. Trojans came together from all sides with Sicilians among them, Nisus and Euryalus at the forefront, Euryalus 295 standing out in the youthful bloom of his beauty, **Nisus in his pious love of the boy**. Then followed Diores, a prince of Priam's noble line, and next came Salius and Patron together, of whom the one was an **Acarnanian**, the other of **Arcadian** blood, a **Tegean** by birth. Then there were two young Sicilians, Helymus and 300 Panopes, woodmen and attendants on old **Acestes**; there were many others too whose fame is hidden in darkness.

Then Aeneas spoke these words in the middle of them: 'Listen attentively to what I say and hear me with cheerful hearts. None of this number will go away without 305 a prize from me. To everyone I shall give two Cretan arrows to take away, their steel tips polished and gleaming, and a two-bladed axe embossed with silver. These marks of honour will be the same for all. The first three will receive prizes

---

**this contest**   the boat race.

**in a foot race**   the whole sequence of games looks back to the games Achilles puts on in honour of Patroclus in *Iliad* 23. Homer's foot race, the model here, is at 23.740–97.

**Nisus in his pious love of the boy**   Nisus is the older of the two.

**Acarnanian, Arcadian, Tegean**   they were Greeks. Presumably they joined the Trojans at Buthrotum (3.293–505). The Arcadian presence may look forward to Evander (see the note on 6.96–7, p. 100).

**Acestes**   the Sicilian king, of Trojan lineage.

---

and their heads will be bound with yellow-green foliage of the olive. The winner 310
will take a horse with splendid trappings, the second an **Amazonian** quiver full
of **Thracian** arrows, attached to a broad shoulder belt studded with gold, and the
clasp that fastens it is a polished gem. The man in third place will go away content
with this Argive helmet.'

When he had said these things, they took their places and the moment they heard 315
the signal, they left the starting-point and dashed along the course, streaming
forward **like a cloud**. As soon as they came in sight of the finish, away went Nisus
first, shooting forward in front of all the other figures, swifter than the winds and
the wings of lightning. Closest behind him, but behind by a long way, followed 320
Salius. Then after a gap came Euryalus in third position, and Helymus followed
him. Then just behind him, look! Diores flew, **grazing heel with heel** and pressing
on his shoulder. And if there had been more of the course left to run, he would 325
have slipped by him and gained a position or **left the issue in doubt**. And now
they were almost at the end of the course and were nearing the finishing-point
in exhaustion when the unlucky **Nisus slid in some slippery blood**, where it
happened to have been shed at the sacrifice of some bullocks, soaking the ground 330
and the green grass above it. As he trod on this spot, the young man, exhilarated
now at the thought of victory, could not hold his footing but stumbled and fell
flat on his face in the filthy dung and the blood of the sacrifice. But he did not
forget Euryalus or his love for him – not he. For rising on the slippery ground, 335
he moved in the way of Salius who went head over heels and lay flat on the firm
sand. Euryalus shot forward and, victorious thanks to his friend, took first place
and flew on amid enthusiastic applause and cheers. After him came Helymus and
then Diores, now the winner of the third prize.

At this point Salius filled the huge theatre with loud shouts as he appealed to the 340
whole audience and to **the fathers watching at the front**. He demanded that the
prize snatched from him by cheating should be given back to him. The good-

---

**Amazonian, Thracian**  the Amazons and the Thracians had fought on the Trojan side in
the Trojan war.

**like a cloud**  'the point of the comparison is that the rapidly moving massed runners
are like the rapidly moving mass of a storm cloud as it comes across the sky' (Deryck
Williams).

**grazing heel with heel**  anatomically impossible, but the meaning comes across clearly.

**left the issue in doubt**  i.e. a photo-finish would have been necessary, so to speak.

**Nisus slid in some slippery blood**  the accident is modelled on *Iliad* 23.774–7, where Ajax
slips and falls in the dung left by sacrificed animals. Nisus' disgraceful cheating is Virgil's
invention.

**the fathers watching at the front**  Virgil is probably thinking of Roman senators (often
referred to as fathers), who were allocated front seats at the theatre or in the circus (Livy
1.35.8).

---

will felt towards Euryalus argued in favour of him **as did his modest tears** and his manly spirit, all the more pleasing in that it presented itself in so beautiful a figure. Diores supported him and shouted in a loud voice: he had gained a prize-  345
winning place but had won the last prize all for nothing if the distinction of victory were restored to Salius. Then father Aeneas said, 'Your prizes will definitely still be yours, my lads. No one is changing the order of the prize-winners. Let me be allowed to show pity for the bad luck of a friend who was not to blame.' With  350
these words he gave Salius the vast hide of a **Gaetulian** lion, heavy with shaggy hair and gilded claws. **At this point Nisus said,** 'If the losers get such splendid prizes and you show pity for people who fall, what in all fairness will you give to  355
Nisus? I would have gained first prize by my merits if I had not been the victim of the same bad fortune as Salius.' And as he said these words, he displayed his face and his body, befouled with wet dung. The excellent father **smiled** at him and ordered that a shield should be brought out, the handiwork of **Didymaon, taken
down by the Greeks** from a sacred portal of Neptune. He gave this splendid gift  360
to the noble youth.

---

1   What is the tone of this passage? Does it strike you as different from that of what you have read of the *Aeneid* so far?

2   Why do you think that Virgil included these sporting scenes in his poem?

3   How does Aeneas come over here?

4   What view of homosexual love is presented here?

5   It is clear that Euryalus wins sympathy because he is so beautiful. What do you feel about this? Is it understandable?

---

**as did his modest tears**   Euryalus does not make a great fuss about the matter like Salius and Diores.

**Gaetulian**   the Gaetuli were a tribe in north-west Africa.

**At this point Nisus said …**   after his shameful foul, Nisus' speech is outrageous.

**smiled**   a replay of the great moment in *Iliad* 23 when, after a similar argument following the chariot race, Achilles smiles for the only time in that poem (23.555). The same is true of Aeneas in the *Aeneid*. (The Latin word used here could mean 'laughed'.) What does this tell us about the nature of both poems?

Williams sums up this scene with fine responsiveness: 'Virgil's brief description gives a lively picture of the chief persons involved in the dispute – Salius filled with excited indignation, and loudly protesting; Euryalus silent, winning people's sympathy by his evident fear of the protest being upheld; Diores vehemently opposing Salius' objection, in case he should lose his third prize; Aeneas benevolent and tactful, meeting the situation by awarding an extra prize to Salius; finally Nisus, covered with mud, urging with a theatrical gesture his own very doubtful claim, and Aeneas smilingly accepting it.'

**Didymaon**   a figure otherwise unknown.

**taken down by the Greeks**   we do not know how Aeneas acquired this shield.

The games conclude with an equestrian display by the Trojan boys. This is the ceremony which Iulus later introduced to Alba Longa and it became a Roman tradition, called 'the Trojan game'. Meanwhile Juno sends down Iris to incite the dispirited women of Troy to burn the ships so that they can wander no more. In response to Aeneas' prayer, Jupiter quenches the fires with a thunderstorm and almost all of the ships are saved. A vision of his father Anchises appears to Aeneas in the night, telling him to come down to the underworld to meet him and hear his destiny. A city is founded in Sicily for those who cannot face going on to Italy. Neptune promises Venus that the Trojans' voyage there will be a safe one, though one life will have to be sacrificed. The book ends with the sad story of the helmsman Palinurus.

5.835–71    And now dewy Night had almost reached **the half-way mark of her journey through the sky**; the sailors, stretched out on the hard benches under the oars, were relaxing their bodies in quiet rest: when Sleep, slipping down lightly from the stars of heaven, sundered the shadowy air and parted the darkness, seeking    840
you, Palinurus, bringing you disastrous sleep, you, a guiltless man; and the god sat on the high stern, looking like **Phorbas**, and poured these soft words from his lips:

'Palinurus, son of **Iasius**, the sea is carrying the ships along on its own, the winds breathe steadily, this is the time for sleep. Lay down your head and steal a rest    845
from labour. I shall take over your task for you for a short while myself.'

**Scarcely raising his eyes**, Palinurus said to him: 'Do you tell *me* of all men to forget what I know about the sea's calm face and its tranquil waves, *me* to put faith in **this demon**? For how could I entrust Aeneas to the treachery of winds and    850
weather when I have so often been deceived by a clear sky?'

He said these words and clung fast to the tiller, never slackening his hold and fixing his eyes up on the stars. But look! the god shook over both his temples a branch dripping with the dew of **Lethe**, made drowsy with the power of **Styx**,    855
and despite all his efforts, closed his swimming eyes. Scarcely had sleep begun to

---

**the half-way mark of her journey through the sky**   Night drives a chariot.

**Phorbas**   a fellow Trojan.

**Iasius**   son of Jupiter and a founder of the Trojan race. Palinurus was one of his descendants.

**Scarcely raising his eyes**   because he is concentrating so much on his task.

**this demon**   the sea.

**Lethe**   the river of forgetfulness in the underworld.

**Styx**   Styx is the river of death; Sleep is the brother of Death (6.278); and what is happening will prove fatal to Palinurus.

relax the limbs of the unsuspecting man when, looming over him, the god tore off part of the stern and flung him **and the tiller too** headless into the waves of the sea, calling vainly on his companions again and again. As for the god, he rose 860 on his wings and flew away to the thin air above. The fleet sailed on just as fast, speeding safely over the sea, and went forward without alarm in accordance with the promises of father Neptune.

And now as the fleet voyaged on it was approaching the rocks of **the Sirens**, in former times perilous and white with the bones of many men – at this time the 865 rocks in the ceaseless surf were booming hoarsely afar – when father Aeneas sensed that his ship was drifting aimlessly without a helmsman and he himself steered her amid the waves of night. With many a sigh and sick at heart at his friend's misfortune, he said: 'O Palinurus, you trusted too much in a calm sky and 870 sea. **You will lie naked on an unknown shore.**'

---

1   What impression do you get of Palinurus from this passage?

2   What is the tone of this passage? What do you make of Aeneas' misunderstanding of Palinurus' devotion to his task?

3   Do you find this an effective conclusion to the book?

---

## Book 6

> The Trojans land at Cumae in Italy. Aeneas goes to consult the Sibyl. He asks her to grant that the Trojans may find rest in Latium (lines 66–8) and continues.

6.69–101   'Then I shall set up **a temple of solid marble to Phoebus and Diana** and festival 70 **days in Phoebus' name. A great shrine** awaits you too in our kingdom. For here I

---

**and the tiller too**   Palinurus continues to cling tightly to the tiller even after he has been drugged by Sleep. He never betrays his calling or his devoted service to Aeneas.

**the Sirens**   the tradition was that these songstresses, whose singing lured mariners to their death, had killed themselves after Odysseus (Ulysses) had sailed by them safely. Their enchanting but deadly song has been replaced by the harsh boom of sea against rocks.

**You will lie naked on an unknown shore**   these words are picked up at 6.362.

**a temple of solid marble to Phoebus and Diana**   the reference is to Octavian's building of a temple to Phoebus Apollo on the Palatine hill by his house, which was connected to it by a ramp (it was dedicated on 9 October 28 BC). On one side of the statue of Apollo stood one of his sister Diana.

**festival days in Phoebus' name**   the games of Apollo were established in 212 BC during the second Punic war (with Hannibal).

shall place your oracles, the secrets of fate told to my people, and, o gracious one, I shall ordain chosen men to serve you. Only do not trust your prophecies to leaves in case they fly away in disorder, the playthings of the winds that whirl them off. 75 **I beg you to sing them yourself.**' He brought his speech to an end.

But the priestess, not yet broken in by **Apollo**, raved wildly in the cavern, in the hope that she might shake the mighty god from her breast. He wearied her foaming 80 mouth all the more, taming her wild heart and moulding her by his pressure. And now the hundred huge mouths of the house suddenly opened of their own accord and carried the responses of the prophetess through the air:

'O you who have finally come to the end of great dangers at sea (but more grievous ones await you on land), the descendants of Dardanus shall come to the kingdom of 85 **Lavinium** (cast that fear from your heart) but they will also wish that they had not come. I see wars, terrible wars and the Tiber foaming with much blood. You will find **a Simois, a Xanthus and a Greek camp.** **Another Achilles** has already been born in

*A tunnel hewn out of the rock at Cumae leading to the Sibyl's cave. It is lit by six galleries opening to the left.*

---

**A great shrine**   the Sibylline books, the collection of the oracles of the Cumaean and other Sibyls, were moved by Augustus to the temple of Apollo on the Palatine where they were kept under the statue of the god. This happened before 19 BC, the year of Virgil's death. The Sibyl's prophecies were believed to be inspired by Apollo and were held in great reverence.

**I beg you to sing them yourself**   Helenus told Aeneas to do this at 3.457.

**Apollo**   the god who possesses her.

**Lavinium**   Aeneas' first settlement in Italy.

**a Simois, a Xanthus and a Greek camp**   Simois and Xanthus were the two rivers of Troy, and the Italian equivalents will be the Tiber and the Numicus. (Austin illustrates the evocative nature of river names in such a context by a reference to the Somme.) The equivalent of the Greek camp will be that of the Italian Turnus and his Rutulians.

**Another Achilles**   Turnus. The Trojans' greatest enemy at Troy had been Achilles, the son of the sea-goddess Thetis. Turnus was the son of the nymph Venilia.

Latium and he too is the son of a goddess. Nor will Juno ever fail to harry the 90
Trojans by her presence while all the time you will be praying for help in your dire
need to every possible Italian tribe, every possible city. The cause of such disaster
for the Trojans is again **a foreign bride**, again a marriage with a stranger. Do not
yield to these troubles but go to meet them all the more boldly along the path that 95
fortune lets you travel. The first road to safety – the last thing you expect – will be
opened up to you **by a Greek city**.'

In these words the Cumaean Sibyl sang the fearful riddles of her responses from
her shrine, booming forth from her cave as she wrapped the truth in darkness. So 100
did Apollo shake the reins as she raged, turning the goads beneath her breast.

> Aeneas now asks the Sibyl to give him guidance about how he can go down to
> the underworld to visit his father's spirit. She makes the following reply.

6.125–55    'Born of the blood of the gods, Trojan son of Anchises, the descent **by way of**
**Avernus** is easy; the door of gloomy Dis stands open night and day; but to recall
one's steps and to come out to the upper air, this is the task, this the labour. Some
few, whom impartial Jupiter loved or whose blazing virtue took them up to heaven, 130
the sons of gods – these have succeeded. Forests cover **the whole heartland of the**
**underworld** and **Cocytus** surrounds it as it slips along with its dark folds. But if
you have conceived so great a love in your heart, so great a desire to sail across the
waters of the Styx **twice** and twice to see black Tartarus, and it pleases you to yield 135
to this mad endeavour, hear what must be done first.

---

**a foreign bride**   just as Paris' abduction of the Greek Helen had caused the Trojan war,
so the planned marriage of Aeneas with the Latin princess Lavinia will prove a key factor
in the outbreak of war between the Trojans and the Italians.

**by a Greek city**   the Arcadian Evander's settlement of Pallanteum, which Aeneas will
visit in Book 8 (see p. 124).

**by way of Avernus**   by way of lake Avernus (near Cumae) where there was a fabled
entrance to the underworld. Alternatively Avernus could mean 'the underworld' by
metonymy. In that case, the Latin would mean that 'the way to Avernus is easy'.

**the whole heartland of the underworld**   or 'the area between the upper world and the
underworld'.

**Cocytus**   the river of lamentation.

**twice**   he will have to cross the river at his death. He wishes to do so now as well.

'There lies hidden in a shady tree **a branch with leaves and pliant stem of gold**, said to be sacred to **Juno of the underworld**; the whole grove covers it and shadows conceal it in the dark valleys. But it is not permitted to go beneath the hidden places of the earth before a man has plucked the golden-haired growth from the tree. Beautiful Proserpina has laid it down that this is the offering that must be brought to her. When the first branch is torn away, a second does not fail to take its place, golden too, and the shoot grows leaves of the same metal. So look upwards and track it down and when you have found it, pluck it with your hand with due solemnity. For of itself it will follow you, freely and easily, if it is you that the fates are calling. Otherwise you will not be able to win it by any force or to cut it off with hard steel. 140 145

'Moreover, **a friend of yours**, I must tell you, lies dead (alas! you do not know this) and is polluting the whole fleet with his body while you are lingering at my threshold in your search for oracles. First place him in his due resting place and hide him in a tomb. 150

'**Bring black cattle**: let these be your first appeasement offerings. In this way alone will you finally look upon the Stygian groves and the kingdom where no living man may tread.' She spoke, closed her lips and **fell silent**. 155

---

1 How does the Sibyl come across in these two passages? Does she appear different in each of them? If so, in what way?

2 What do you suppose that Aeneas is feeling as he listens to her responses? How does the Trojan mission come across in the first passage? Would there be grounds for a positive reaction from him in the second?

3 What is the overall impression you get of the underworld in the second passage?

---

**a branch with leaves and pliant stem of gold** we do not know Virgil's sources for the golden bough. As Deryck Williams says, 'it is a mysterious talisman whose significance in folk-lore cannot be defined with precision … It is a symbol of mystery, a kind of light in darkness, a kind of life in death.'

**Juno of the underworld** Proserpina, queen of the underworld.

**a friend of yours** this turns out to be Misenus, who had impiously challenged the gods to a trumpet-playing contest. The sea-god Triton proceeded to drown him. The Trojans give him a magnificent funeral. His hubristic challenge reminds us of the value of pious behaviour, and we see in Misenus' funeral the 'normal' way to get down to the underworld. Aeneas, the man of supreme piety, will break the rules.

**Bring black cattle** the Sibyl is here issuing instructions about the preparation for the journey to the underworld, not about the funeral of Misenus.

**fell silent** Austin notes, 'The sudden brevity is very Sibylline.' He refers to lines 6.54, 321, 398, 408 and 538.

---

> **Aeneas and the golden bough**
>
> Aeneas is led to the golden bough by two doves, the birds of his mother Venus. Virgil tells us that, when he sees it, he 'seizes it at once and greedily breaks it off, though it resists, and carries it to the house of the prophetess, the Sibyl' (lines 210–11).
>
> - In what way does his gaining possession of the bough fail to fit the Sibyl's prophetic words above (lines 145–8)? What do you feel may be the point of this discrepancy?

After breaking off the golden bough and performing the funeral rites for Misenus, Aeneas, together with the Sibyl, makes the preparatory sacrifices for the journey down to the shades. Virgil now invokes the gods of the underworld, asking them to allow him to tell of the journey.

**6.264–316**   You gods who have dominion over spirits, and you silent shades, and **Chaos** and   265
Phlegethon, tracts where silence spreads wide in the **darkness**, may it be right for me to speak what I have heard: may it be by your divine power that I unfold things buried deep in the darkness under the earth.

They were going, dim travellers, beneath the lonely night through the shadow, through the empty dwellings of Dis and his desolate kingdom, like people walking   270
in the woods by the niggardly light of a fitful moon when Jupiter has hidden the sky in shade and black night has taken the colour from everything. In front of the entrance hall, in the very **throat** of **Orcus**, Grief and avenging Cares have placed their beds and pale Diseases dwell there and grim Old Age and Fear and Hunger   275
that urges men to evil and foul Poverty, shapes terrible to look upon, and Death and Toil: then Sleep, the brother of Death, the soul's corrupt Pleasures, and, on the threshold opposite, death-dealing War and the Furies in their iron cells and   280
demented Discord, her snaky hair bound with bloody bands of wool.

---

**Chaos, Phlegethon, darkness**   Chaos is the parent of Night and Erebus. Phlegethon is the burning river of the underworld, here representing all its rivers. The three words bring together in a single line three very vivid and unsettling ideas of the underworld: the emptiness of Chaos, fire, and the dark.

**throat**   the Latin word used here also refers to the narrow passage leading from the front door of a Roman house to its atrium (the first main room). There is a sense in which the grim figures camping outside the house of the king of the underworld are his clients (see note on *Georgics* 2.461–2, p. 25), waiting to be received by him in a morning that will never come.

**Orcus**   a Latin deity identified with Pluto (or Dis).

In the middle an elm, shadowy and huge, stretches out the ancient arms of its branches, which, men say, swarms of false Dreams have as their home, **clinging** beneath every leaf. Here too are many monstrous shapes of different 285 wild beasts, **Centaurs** stabled at the doors and **double-formed Scyllas** and the hundred-headed Briareus and **the monster of Lerna** with its terrifying hiss, and **Chimaera** armed with flames, Gorgons and **Harpies** and the shape of **the three-bodied phantom**. Here Aeneas trembled in sudden fear and, seizing his sword, 290 turned its drawn blade to them as they came towards him; and had not his wise companion warned him that they were insubstantial creatures without a body flitting about in the unreal semblance of a shape, he would have rushed at them and slashed shadows with his sword – to no avail.

From here there goes a road which leads to the waves of Acheron, a river of 295 Tartarus. Here a whirlpool thick with mud and unfathomed in its abyss, boils up and belches all its sand into Cocytus. The grim ferryman who guards these waters and rivers is Charon, a filthy and fearsome figure with a mass of unkempt white 300 hair on his chin: his eyes are fixed and fiery. A grimy cloak hangs by a knot from his shoulders. He punts the boat with his pole and tends the sails and conveys the bodies in his rust-coloured boat. He is aged now, but a god's old age is vigorous 305 and green. The whole crowd rushed streaming to this part of the bank, **women and men**, and shapes of great-hearted heroes whose lives were over, and unwedded girls, and young men placed on the pyre before the eyes of their parents: as many as the leaves that slip and fall in the woods in the first chill of autumn, or as the 310 birds that gather together to the land from the stormy deep when the cold season of the year makes them flee over the sea and sends them to sunny lands. They were standing, begging to make the crossing first and stretching out their hands in longing for the farther bank. But the grim ferryman took now these, now those, 315 while others he pushed away, keeping them far from the sandy shore.

---

**clinging**   like bats.

**Centaurs**   half man, half horse.

**double-formed Scyllas**   maiden above, sea-monster below.

**the monster of Lerna**   the Hydra, a monster with multiple snake's heads, killed by Hercules.

**Chimaera**   a combination of fire-breathing lion, goat and serpent.

**Harpies**   birds with women's faces.

**the three-bodied phantom**   the triple-bodied Geryon, killed by Hercules. His three bodies now have no substance.

**women and men ...**   these lines (306–8) were used by Virgil at *Georgics* 4.475–7.

1   What is the effect of Virgil's invocation of the powers of the underworld (lines 264–7)?

2   How effective do you find the description of the light in lines 268–72?

3   Why do you think Virgil has included (a) the gathering of personifications at Orcus' door (lines 273–81) and (b) the elm tree and the hybrid monsters in the middle (282–9)? Do the passages work as suggestive poetry? Give your reasons for your answer.

4   What is the tone of the lines where Aeneas almost slashes at the monsters but is stopped by the Sibyl (290–4)?

5   What are the main features of the portrait of Charon (lines 298–316)? Do you find it surprising in some ways? What is your impression of him?

6   Was Virgil right to reproduce the lines from the *Georgics* at lines 306–8?

7   Comment on the two similes in lines 309–12. They have been much admired. Do you share the admiration?

The Sibyl explains to Aeneas that the spirits whom Charon is pushing away belong to the unburied. They have to flit around for a hundred years and only then can they come back. Aeneas sees Palinurus' ghost among them.

6.337–416   Look! there moving towards him was the helmsman Palinurus who had fallen from the stern on the recent voyage from Libya, pitched out into the midst of the waves while watching the stars. Aeneas recognized this sad figure, though with 340 difficulty amid the deep shadows, and was the first to speak:

'Which of the gods, Palinurus, snatched you from us and plunged you deep beneath the sea? Tell me. For Apollo, who I have never found false before, deceived me with this one response. He prophesied that you would be safe upon the sea 345 and come to the **Ausonian** shores. Is this how he keeps his promise?'

Palinurus replied: 'The oracle of Phoebus did not deceive you, son of Anchises, my captain, **nor did a god plunge me in the deep**. I was holding the rudder firmly as 350 its appointed guardian, directing the course of the ship, when it was torn away by a mighty force and as I went headlong I dragged it with me. I swear by the rough seas that I did not fear so much for myself as for your ship, in case it foundered in **those great surging waves**, stripped of its steering gear, with its helmsman

---

**Ausonian**   Italian: the Ausonians were the indigenous people of Campania.

**nor did a god plunge me in the deep**   he is unaware that this is precisely what *did* happen. He is the victim of the god Sleep. In fact, Palinurus seems to mean that he did not drown: he got to land, as we now discover.

**those great surging waves**   the sea was calm when Palinurus was pushed overboard. But I do not see any inconsistency here. The waves will have looked very different to a man swimming for his life in their midst.

flung into the sea. For three wintry nights the fierce south wind carried me over 355
the waters of the measureless sea. On the fourth dawn, lifted high on the crest
of a wave, I just managed to make out Italy. Little by little I swam to the shore. I
was already reaching safety when a cruel tribe, thinking in their ignorance that I
was booty worth having, attacked me with their swords as, weighed down by my
soaking clothes, I was trying to grab the jagged top of a high cliff with clutching 360
fingers. Now the waves hold me and the winds move me to and fro at the water's
edge. So I beg you by heaven's sweet light and air, by your father, by your hope in
Iulus as he grows, snatch me, unconquered one, from these woes. Either throw 365
earth on me (**for you can**) by returning to the harbour of Velia. Or if there is
any way, if the goddess your mother shows you one (for it is not without the full
assent of the gods that you are preparing to journey over so great a river and the
marsh of the Styx), give your right hand to a wretched man and carry me with you 370
over the waters, so that I may **at least** find a quiet resting place in death.'

He had said these words when the prophetess began to speak: 'Where, Palinurus,
does so monstrous a longing come from? Unburied as you are, will you look upon 375
the waters of the Styx and the grim river of the Furies and go to its bank without
a summons? Stop hoping that the fates of the gods can be changed by prayers.
But listen to my words and remember them. They will console you in your hard
lot. **For the neighbouring people in the cities far and wide**, driven by portents
in the sky, will appease your bones and build a burial mound and at the mound 380
they will dedicate ritual offerings every year, and **the place will have the name of
Palinurus** for all time.'

His anguish was dispelled by these words, and his grief was driven from his heart
**for a short time**. He rejoiced in the special name of the land.

So they went on with the journey they had begun and came near to the river.
When the sailor saw them from where he was on the waters of the Styx as they 385
came through the silent wood and headed for the bank, without waiting for them
to speak, he challenged them with these words:

'Whoever you are who come to our river in arms, tell me – from where you stand
– why you are here, and don't take another step. This is the place of shades, of 390

---

**for you can**   these words are in the style of a formal prayer.

**at least**   i.e. if he cannot now go ahead with the Trojan mission, may he at least find
rest in death.

**For the neighbouring people in the cities far and wide**   the people of Lucania.

**the place will have the name of Palinurus**   it is still called Punta di Palinuro (Palinurus
Point).

**for a short time**   it is characteristic of this poem that sorrow can be banished only
briefly.

Sleep and of drowsy Night. Divine law does not allow me to carry living bodies in my Stygian boat. I had no joy of it when I took Hercules on these waters when he came here, or Theseus and Pirithous, although they were the sons of gods and unconquered in might. Hercules wanted to put the **guard of Tartarus** in 395 chains with his own hands and dragged him trembling from the throne of the king himself. The other two tried to carry off our mistress from her marriage chamber.'

The **Amphrysian** prophetess spoke briefly in answer: 'There is no such scheming here. Calm down. These weapons offer no violence. Let the huge doorkeeper 400 terrify the bloodless shades, barking away in his cave for ever. Let Proserpina **remain chaste as she looks after her uncle's home**. Trojan Aeneas, famous for his piety and his feats of arms, is coming down to his father, to the lowest shades of **Erebus**. If the embodiment of such great piety does not move you at all, at 405 least recognize this branch.' (She revealed the branch which had been hidden in her robe.) The swelling anger in his heart subsided. There was no more need for words. He looked in wonder at the gift of the branch of fate, **seen after a long gap of time**, turned his dark boat and drew near to the shore. He pushed **the** 410 **other ghosts** who were sitting on the long benches out of the way and cleared the gangways. At the same time he took the huge Aeneas in his hollow boat. The vessel was made of skins and it groaned under his weight and took in a lot of water through the seams. At last Charon carried the priestess and the man safely across 415 the river and disembarked them on the ugly mud and grey-green sedge.

---

**guard of Tartarus**   Cerberus, the three-headed dog.

**Amphrysian**   a very round-about way of saying that the Sibyl is Apollo's prophetess. The god had been forced to serve as a herdsman to Admetus, king of Thessaly, by the river Amphrysus. For such Alexandrian periphrasis, see p. 31. A note of learned formality is struck, possibly ironically in view of the comic overtones of her speech.

**remain chaste as she looks after her uncle's home**   there is surely mockery here. Proserpina may be chaste, but she was in fact raped by her uncle Pluto before they married. Marriage between uncle and niece was illegal in Virgil's Rome.

**Erebus**   the underworld.

**seen after a long gap of time**   we do not know when Charon had seen the branch previously.

**the other ghosts**   it seems that Charon must be a ghost himself.

1   Brooks Otis suggests that in his encounters in the underworld Aeneas is travelling backwards through his past, exorcizing it. Palinurus represents the journey to Italy. Does such symbolism make sense to you?

2   Neither Palinurus nor Aeneas realize that the helmsman did his duty with dogged devotion and that the god Sleep was to blame. They will stay in ignorance for ever. What emotions are evoked by the Palinurus episode?

3   How are (a) Charon and (b) the Sibyl characterized in their exchange? I have suggested that some notes of comedy are struck. Do you agree?

4   How does the mention of the descents to the underworld of Hercules and of Theseus and Pirithous contribute to the passage?

5   How do the last lines (412–14) contribute to the effect of this passage?

The Sibyl drugs Cerberus and she and Aeneas slip by him. They now come to the region of the untimely dead. In the Mourning Field Aeneas sees a number of women who have died from unhappy love.

6.450–76   Phoenician Dido, her wound still fresh, was wandering among them in the great wood. As soon as the Trojan hero stood near her and recognized her dim form through the shadows, like the moon which a man sees or thinks he has seen rising through the clouds **at the month's beginning**, tears fell from his eyes and he spoke   455 to her sweetly in his love:

'**Unhappy Dido**, so the report that came to me was true then, that you were dead and had ended your life by the sword. Alas! was I the cause of your death? By the stars I swear, by the gods above, by whatever is sacred in the depths of the earth, it was **against my will** that I left your shore. But I was driven on by the   460 gods' imperious commands, which now compel me to go through these shades, through this desolate, decaying place and the deep darkness of night. And I could not believe that I was bringing you such great pain by my departure. Stop, and do   465 not take yourself away from my sight. **Who are you running away from?** This is the last word that fate allows me to speak to you.'

With these words Aeneas tried to soften the blazing anger of the grim-eyed queen and **he was shedding tears**. She had turned away from him and was keeping her eyes fixed on the ground. While he was speaking, her expression changed no more   470

---

**at the month's beginning**   i.e. it is a crescent moon: there is not much of it to see.

**Unhappy Dido**   something of a leitmotif (a running theme) from Book 4.

**against my will**   how true is this?

**Who are you running away from?**   looking back poignantly to Dido's words at 4.314.

**he was shedding tears**   the Latin could mean that 'he tried to arouse her tears'. Which translation do you think works better in the context?

than if she were hard flint or **Marpessian** rock standing there. At length she snatched herself away and fled, still his enemy, into a shady grove where her husband of long ago, Sychaeus, answered her sorrow and requited her love. Yet none the less did 475 Aeneas, stricken by her unjust doom, follow her with his eyes as she moved far away, weeping and pitying her.

---

1   How do you feel about Aeneas as he is shown here? According to Brooks Otis, the great importance of this passage, 'for the book and for the poem as a whole, is its revelation of the irrevocability of the past. Here Aeneas sees both what he has done (and did not yet realize) and what he cannot undo' (pp. 289–97). As he goes further back in his past after his encounter with Palinurus, he must accept his responsibility for Dido's death and the fact that there will be no forgiveness for it, and he must move on.

2   What are your feelings about Dido here? Why does Virgil bring her together with Sychaeus, who according to the rules of logic has no place in the Mourning Fields?

---

Aeneas now meets the ghosts of various Argive and Trojan warriors, and then he sees **Deiphobus**, a son of Priam who had married Helen after Paris' death and been hideously mutilated during the sack of Troy. He tells Aeneas what happened to him on that terrible last night. The Sibyl interrupts their talk, aware that time is moving on in the upper world.

6.539–47   'Night is coming on fast, Aeneas. We are dragging out the time weeping. This is the 540 place where the path splits in the two directions. The right-hand way which goes up to the walls of great Dis is the road we must take to Elysium. But the left-hand one sends evil men to unholy Tartarus where they meet their punishment.' Deiphobus replied: 'Do not be angry, great priestess. I shall depart. I shall return to the shades 545 and make the number complete. **Onwards**, glory of our race, onwards! **Enjoy a better fate.**' This was all he said and with these words he turned on his heel.

---

**Marpessian**   Marpessos was a mountain in Paros, famous for its marble, which had a luminous quality of surface. We look back to Dido's assertion at 4.366–7 that the Caucasus mountains begot Aeneas. In the underworld, she has found the hardness of emotion towards him that she had previously identified in him.

**Deiphobus**   'his whole body [is] mangled, his face cruelly torn, his face and both his hands, his temples disfigured, his ears ripped off, his nostrils torn with a foul wound' (lines 494–6). This hideously mutilated figure is a visual emblem of the last night of Troy. Aeneas has already come to terms with his journey (Palinurus) and with the disastrous experience of Carthage (Dido). Now he can lay to rest the ghost of Troy.

**Onwards**   'Deiphobus' words mark a crucial turning-point in the development of the sixth book; Aeneas' encounters with his past are now over, and his thoughts must turn to the future' (Deryck Williams).

**Enjoy a better fate**   Better than whose? Than Deiphobus' fate? Or than Aeneas' fate so far? Virgil leaves this open.

Aeneas and the Sibyl pass by Tartarus, where the worst sinners are punished, and the Sibyl, who has visited it, describes its horrors to her companion. They finally reach the Groves of the Blessed in Elysium and are directed to Anchises.

**6.679–721**   But father Anchises was deep in a green valley, surveying with earnest thought **the 680 imprisoned souls that were about to go to the light of the upper world**, and, as it happened, he was counting the full number of his people, reviewing his dear children, the fates and fortunes of his men, their characters and their works. When he saw Aeneas coming towards him over the grass, he eagerly stretched out both 685 of his hands, tears poured down his cheeks, and these words fell from his lips:

'Have you come at last? And has the piety your father expected from you overcome the hard toil of the journey? Am I allowed to see your face, my son, and to hear your well-known voice and make reply? This is what I kept working out in my 690 mind, this is what I kept thinking would happen as I counted the days, and my anxious hope has not misled me. Over what lands and what great seas have you travelled to meet me here! What great dangers have buffeted you! How afraid I was that the kingdom of Libya would do you some harm!'

Aeneas answered: 'It was your ghost, father, your sad ghost that **often** came to 695 me and drove me to come to the threshold of this place. **My fleet stands in the Tyrrhenian sea.** Allow me to clasp your right hand in mine, father, allow me this, and do not step back from my embrace.' As he said these words, floods of tears streamed down his cheeks. **Three times** then he tried to put his arms round 700 his neck; three times the phantom, clasped in vain, escaped his grasp, like to the weightless winds, liker still to winging sleep.

And now Aeneas saw in a valley set some way back a secluded grove with whispering woodland thickets and the river Lethe which drifted past peaceful houses. Around 705 this flitted numberless nations and communities, and it was just as when in the meadows on a clear summer day the bees settle on the many-coloured flowers and pour round the white lilies, and the whole plain resounds with their murmuring.

---

**the imprisoned souls that were about to go to the light of the upper world**   the ghosts waiting for rebirth by the river Lethe. We get more details later (713–15). The ideas here are based largely on Orphic and Pythagorean teaching about purification and rebirth. Behind it all lies the concept of human perfectibility.

**often**   the ghost of Anchises frequently appeared to Aeneas in his sleep when he was in Carthage (4.351–3, p.80), and then came to him after the burning of the ships in Sicily (5.722–41). It was during that final appearance that Anchises told his son to seek him out in the underworld.

**My fleet stands in the Tyrrhenian sea**   i.e. we have reached Italy.

**Three times …**   these lines are repeated from 2.792–4 where Aeneas tries to embrace his wife Creusa's ghost.

Aeneas **shuddered** at the sudden sight and in his incomprehension asked what the river in the distance was and what men filled the plain in such great numbers. Father Anchises then replied: 'They are the spirits to whom a second body is owed by fate. By the waters of the river Lethe they are drinking the draught that takes away their cares and gives them long forgetfulness. Indeed I have long desired to tell you who they are and to show them to you face to face, and to count this line of my descendants, so that you may rejoice with me all the more now that you have found Italy.' Aeneas replied, 'O father, are we really to think that some spirits go up to the light of heaven from here and return to clogging bodies? Why do the wretched spirits have such a terrible longing for the light?' 710 715 720

---

1   What emotions are conveyed in the scene where Aeneas meets the ghost of Anchises? What does the use of the lines from Book 2 contribute to the effect here? Don't forget about the similar language used of Orpheus and Euridice in *Georgics* 4.499–502 (p. 37).

2   What are the differences between Anchises' and Aeneas' way of looking at things?

3   How effective is the bee simile here (lines 706–9)? Where have we met it before? Do you feel that its effect is different here?

---

Anchises gives Aeneas an explanation of the soul's relationship with the body and what happens to it after death. He then points out to him the famous Romans who are waiting their turn to go up to the light of day: the kings of Alba Longa, Romulus, Augustus, the kings of Rome and the great heroes of the Roman republic. The passage is generally known as 'the pageant of heroes'. Much of it is superbly assertive, as in the following lines about Augustus.

6.791–807   This is the man, this is the one whom you so often hear promised to you, Augustus Caesar, **the son of a god**, who will establish a second golden age in Latium across the fields once reigned over by Saturn and will carry the bounds of his empire beyond **the Garamantes** and the Indians. That land will lie beyond the stars, beyond the paths of the year and the sun, where sky-bearing Atlas wheels on his shoulders the blazing star-studded vault of heaven. At the prospect of his coming even now 795

---

**shuddered**   an ancient commentator wrote that the Latin word used conveyed the meaning that Aeneas 'was startled with surprise'. 'Shuddered' seems to me to fit the context better. We see from his question to Anchises at the end of the passage that he is appalled at the idea that the spirits may want to live a second life. His vision of human existence is one of dogged toil, duty and suffering. But you may disagree. If so, why do you think that I am wrong?

**the son of a god**   Octavian received this title after his adoptive father was deified in 42 BC.

**the Garamantes**   a Tripolitanian (African) people.

the Caspian kingdoms and the Maeotian land shudder at the oracles of the gods, and the seven-fold mouths of the 800 Nile are in a turmoil. Not even Hercules traversed so much of the earth, even if he transfixed the bronze-footed stag and brought peace to the woods of Erymanthus and made Lerna tremble at his bow. Nor did the one who guides his yoked animals in triumph with reins of vine shoots, Bacchus, driving 805 his tigers down from Nysa's lofty peak. And do we still hesitate to enlarge our worth by our actions? Does fear stop us settling on Ausonian land?

*In this noble statue of Augustus from Prima Porta near Rome, now in the Vatican, the Cupid on a dolphin, supporting the leg, is a reference to the god's mother Venus, the legendary ancestress of the Julian family and thus of Augustus. The centre of the breastplate shows the recovery from the Parthians of the Roman standards lost at the battle of Carrhae (53 BC): see note on 8.726 (p. 137, Euphrates).*

the Caspian kingdoms, the Maeotian land   the areas inhabited by the Scythians and Parthians at the north-eastern boundary of the Roman empire.

the bronze-footed stag   the stag of Cerynaea in Arcadia.

Erymanthus   where the wild boar killed by Hercules lived.

Lerna   the home of the hydra.

Nysa   a mountain in India where Bacchus' worship was said to have originated.

1 Why do you think the mouths of the Nile are in a turmoil (line 800)?

2 Why do you think Virgil brings in the specific figures of Hercules and Bacchus?

3 Do you find this passage too extravagantly hyperbolical? Or is it an acceptable encomium?

4 The questions in lines 806–7 are rhetorical. What do you imagine Aeneas' response would have been?

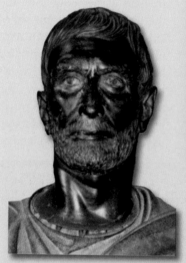

*Brutus. This moving bust dates from the late fourth century BC.*

### Brutus

In contrast with the heady triumphalism of much of the pageant of heroes, a negative or at least ambivalent note can be sounded, as in this passage about Brutus, the first consul of Rome (509 BC). He had expelled the last king of Rome, Tarquin the Proud, in vengeance for the rape of Lucretia by Tarquin's son Sextus, and thus had created the Roman republic. He was said to be the ancestor of the Brutus who assassinated Julius Caesar. Anchises says: 'Do you also wish to see the Tarquin kings and the proud spirit of the avenging Brutus and the fasces he regained? He will be the first to take the authority of consul and the cruel axes, and when his sons stir up renewed warfare he will call them to punishment for the sake of noble liberty – unhappy man, however later generations will judge his deed. His love of his fatherland will prevail and a measureless desire for praises' (6.817–23).

1 What is the effect Virgil achieves by referring to the *proud* spirit of the man who drove out Tarquin the Proud?

2 The 'fasces' were the rods which symbolized the consul's authority. What is the English word derived from the Latin one? The lictors, who attended on the consul, usually carried axes too. What does this tell us about the nature of Roman authority?

3 Tarquin's sons plotted to bring back the Tarquins. Brutus had them executed. What do you feel about his behaviour here?

4 What can you say is positive and what negative in this passage? Does one aspect dominate?

At the climax of the pageant of heroes, Anchises celebrates the greatness of the Roman mission.

6.847–900     'Others will beat out bronze so that it breathes in softer lines (yes, I am sure of it) and **will mould living features from the marble**, will plead cases more eloquently and mark out the motions of the heavens with **the rod** and predict the risings of  850 the stars. You, **O Roman**, never forget to rule the peoples of the world under your command (these will be your arts) and to **add** civilization to peace, **to spare those who submit** and fight the proud into submission.'

That was what Anchises said, and as they stood in wonder he added: 'See there  855 how **Marcellus** moves along marked out by **the rich spoils**, a victor towering over all the men. It is he who will **ride** to steady the Roman state when a great rising confounds it, flattening the Carthaginians and the rebellious Gauls, he who will hang up a third set of captured arms to father Quirinus.'

And at this point Aeneas asked a question – for at Marcellus' side he saw an  860 outstandingly handsome young man in shining armour, but his expression was unhappy and his eyes downcast: 'Who is that, father, the one who accompanies the man like that as he walks along? Is it his son, or one of his great line of descendants? What a stir there is among his companions! What a presence he has!  865 But black night hovers around his head with its sad shadow.'

---

**Others**   i.e. the Greeks.

**will mould living features from the marble**   in fact Roman portrait sculpture tends to be far more true to life ('warts and all') than the Greek equivalent.

**the rod**   i.e. the rod used in geometry.

**O Roman**   Austin writes: 'Anchises now speaks not to Aeneas alone but to each future Roman, exhorting each to his duty.' There is the further point that the father addresses his Trojan son as a Roman. What is the effect of this?

**add**   the Latin word here could more literally, and possibly more accurately, be translated 'impose'. Is civilization something that can be imposed?

**to spare those who submit**   one will inevitably remember these climactic words spoken by Aeneas' father at the central moment of the poem, when at the very end of the *Aeneid* the hero flatly goes against what he is instructed to do here.

**Marcellus**   five times a consul, Marcus Claudius Marcellus defeated the Insubrian Gauls in 222 BC and served with distinction against Hannibal in the second Punic war.

**the rich spoils**   these were awarded to a Roman general who killed the enemy general with his own hand. Marcellus killed Viridomarus, a Gallic chieftain, at Clastidium.

**ride**   the battle with the Gauls was mainly a cavalry engagement.

*Model of the mausoleum of Augustus on the northern side of the Campus Martius, in Rome. In this model the great tomb is reflected in the river Tiber.*

**Then Anchises burst into tears** and began: 'O my son, do not ask about the immense sorrow of your people. The fates will only grant the earth a glimpse of this man and will not allow him to live longer than that. You thought, you gods, that the Roman stock would be too powerful if this gift had been theirs to keep. What sounds of mourning from the people will the famous **Field of Mars** send up to **the god's** great city! What a funeral will you see, O Tiber, when you glide past the newly built tomb! No young man of the Trojan race will ever raise his Latin ancestors to such high hopes, and never in times to come will the land of Romulus feel so proud of any of her young. Alas for his piety! Alas for his old-

870

875

---

**Then Anchises burst into tears**  Anchises has done his utmost to instil in Aeneas a gung-ho vision of his Roman future. Now, asked by his son about a key figure, he bursts into tears. The Marcellus mentioned here, another Marcus Claudius, is the son of Octavia, the sister of Augustus, who married his daughter Julia, was adopted by him in 25 BC and was thus marked out as his heir, but died in 23 BC at the age of 19. There is no reason to disbelieve the story of Servius and Donatus (ancient commentators on Virgil) that Octavia burst into tears when Virgil was reading this passage to her and Augustus and reached line 882 (see front cover).

**Field of Mars**  Augustus had built a mausoleum for himself and his family on the Field of Mars (the Campus Martius) close to the Tiber in 27 BC. Its substantial ruins survive. Marcellus was the first member of the imperial family to be interred there.

**the god's**  the god is Mars, the father of Romulus, Rome's founder.

fashioned integrity and his right hand unconquered in war. No one would ever have challenged him in arms without suffering for it, whether he was on foot against his foe or digging the flanks of his foaming horse with his spurs. Alas, pitiable boy, if only you could somehow break through rough fate! You will be Marcellus. Give lilies from full hands. Let me scatter radiant flowers and heap at least these gifts on the spirit of my descendant, performing a vain task.' 885

Thus they wandered everywhere over the whole region in the wide **fields of air** and looked at each sight. After Anchises had taken his son through everything and fired his heart with the love of the glory to come, he told the man of the 890 wars which he would next have to fight, and taught him about the peoples of Laurentum and the city of Latinus, and how he could either escape or endure each labour.

**There are two gates of Sleep**, one of which is said to be made of horn and through it an easy exit is granted to true shades. The other is made of gleaming ivory but 895 the world below sends false dreams to the heavens. As he spoke in this way to his son and the Sybil too, Anchises escorted them there and sent them out by the ivory gate. Aeneas went swiftly to the ships and rejoined his comrades. Then he sailed straight along the shore to the harbour at Caieta. 900

---

1   How inspiring is the Roman mission as it is presented in lines 847–53?

2   What does the passage about the young Marcellus contribute to the poem? How effectively is sadness here communicated? Does the evocation of the Augustan Rome of the 20s BC work (lines 860–86)? If so, how?

3   We are told at line 889 that Anchises fires Aeneas' heart with love of the glory to come. Does what you have read of the pageant of heroes justify this authorial assertion?

4   We are told at lines 890–2 that Anchises gives Aeneas specific and practical military advice, but we hear no more of this in the second half of the poem. If practical military considerations are not the answer, what do you feel to be the reasons why Virgil causes Aeneas to visit his father in the underworld?

5   How effective a conclusion to the underworld episode do the gates of Sleep prove to be?

---

**fields of air**   the Elysian fields have their own solar system (lines 640–1).

**There are two gates of Sleep**   the gates come from Homer, *Odyssey* 19.562–7. Why do Aeneas and the Sibyl exit through the gate of false dreams? Of course, they are not true shades but real human beings and in that sense do not qualify for the gate made of horn. But that seems unsatisfactory as a full explanation. Are we being told that the whole underworld experience is a kind of allegory, not to be taken literally? Or that the great dream of Roman empire is a false dream? Do you have an explanation for this strange yet suggestive moment?

# 7 The Trojans in Italy

## Book 7

At the beginning of Book 7, the Trojans reach the river Tiber.

**7.25–45**  And now the sea was reddening with the rays of the sun and saffron **Aurora** was shining from the high heaven in her rosy chariot, when the winds fell and every breath was suddenly stilled, and **the oars laboured in the sluggish smoothness of the water**. And here, as he looked from his ship, Aeneas saw before him a huge forest. In the middle of this the beautiful river Tiber burst forth into the sea, 30 yellow with all the sand in its swift eddies. Around and above all sorts of birds, the natives of the river's banks and its bed, caressed the air with their singing as they flew through the woods. Aeneas ordered his companions to change course and 35 turn their prows to the land, and he approached the shadowy river **with joy in his heart**.

Come now, **Erato**! I shall set forth the kings of ancient Latium, its history, and the way things stood there when first the foreign army landed its fleet on the shores of Ausonia, and I shall recall what began the first battle. You goddess, I call upon 40 you to prompt your bard. I shall speak of terrible wars, I shall speak of armies drawn up in battle array, and kings driven by their ardour to their death, and the forces of Etruria and the whole land of Hesperia mustered for war. A grander succession of events now opens up for me. **I am embarking on the greater part** 45 **of my work.**

---

**Aurora**   the goddess of dawn. The colours evoke two of Homer's epithets for the goddess, 'rosy-fingered' and 'saffron-robed'.

**the oars laboured in the sluggish smoothness of the water**   the sea is reluctant to yield to the oars' pressure.

**with joy in his heart**   Aeneas seems to feel instinctively that he has come to the land destined for him. See Creusa's words at 2.781–2 ('You will come to … Hesperia where the … Tiber flows': cf. 5.82–3). He does not discover as a fact that the river he is entering is the Tiber until line 151. How evocative do you find the dawn picture in this passage? What mood does it convey?

**Erato**   Virgil invokes one of the nine Muses in the epic tradition established by Homer in the invocations at the start of the *Iliad* and the *Odyssey*. Erato is the Muse of love poetry. The battles of the second half of the *Aeneid* arise, like those of the *Iliad*, from a dispute over who has the right to a woman (in Homer's poem Helen, in Virgil's Lavinia).

**I am embarking on the greater part of my work**   Virgil clearly felt that in some important way the second, *Iliadic* half of his poem (see 'Introduction to the *Aeneid*', pp. 40–1) was

Latinus, the king of the Latins, has no male heir and it is planned – a plan passionately supported by his wife Amata – that his daughter Lavinia will marry Turnus, the handsome young king of the Rutulians. However, the gods show by various frightening portents that they are opposed to the match.

7.59–70    In the middle of [Latinus'] palace, in its innermost lofty courtyard, there was a laurel tree. Its foliage was sacred and it had been preserved in reverent fear for  60 many years. It is said that Latinus himself found it when he was building his first citadel, and dedicated it to **Phoebus** and named his settlers **Laurentines** after it. In the top of this there settled a thick swarm of bees – an event wondrous to relate – borne through the clear sky with their loud buzzing, and intertwining their legs  65 with each other they hung in their sudden swarm from a leafy bough. At once the prophet said, 'We see a foreigner arriving and a column of men **making for the same parts from the same parts** and lording it in the citadel's height.'  70

greater than the first. The simplest explanation is that he is dealing with warfare, the theme of the greater of Homer's epics. The subject-matter endows it with surpassing stature. In the same kind of way, Milton saw his own great epic *Paradise Lost* as superior to the poems of Homer and Virgil because his subject was the great religious story of the fall of man. Even so, he needs the help of the Muse (9.13–21):

> sad task! yet argument [topic]
> Not less but more heroic than the wrath
> Of stern Achilles on his foe pursued
> Thrice fugitive about Troy wall; or rage
> Of Turnus for Lavinia disespoused,
> Or Neptune's ire or Juno's, that so long
> Perplexed the Greek and Cytherea's son [Aeneas];
> If answerable style I can obtain
> Of my celestial patroness …

When you reach the end of the *Aeneid*, you will be asked whether you think that the second half of the poem is in fact greater.

**Phoebus**    the laurel was Apollo's emblematic tree.

**Laurentines**    the Latin word for laurel tree is *laurus*: Virgil here claims that the name of the people derives from it.

**making for the same parts from the same parts**    i.e. as the bees, who had come to the tree in the heart of the palace from a distance. The wording is in cryptic oracular vein. What do you feel about the omen? It was said that bees had swarmed on the standard of Pompey at Pharsalus and of Brutus at Philippi. Both men were defeated.

Another portent occurs when Lavinia's hair catches fire at a religious ceremony and she scatters flames throughout the palace. This is interpreted as meaning that her own fame and fate will be bright but that a great war will afflict her people (71–80). When Latinus consults the oracle of his prophetic father Faunus, a voice instructs him not to marry his daughter to a Latin. (The prohibition presumably includes the Rutulian Turnus.) His son-in-law will be a stranger who will raise the name of the Latins to the stars. The story now returns to the Trojans.

7.107–34 Aeneas and his senior leaders and beautiful Iulus laid their bodies down beneath the branches of a high tree and got a feast ready, placing **their flat wheat wafers** on the grass and then – as Jupiter himself inspired them – putting the food on top of them, heaping the wafer plates underneath with the produce of the countryside. 110
Here it so happened that, when everything else had been eaten up, the shortage of food made them begin to consume the thin wafers and to **violate** with rash hands and jaws the circles of the fateful bread, not sparing **the flat quarter-circles**, and 115
Iulus said, 'Hey, are we even eating our tables?' He was joking and that was all he said, but when his words were heard, they gave the first sign that their labours were ended. When they had fallen from his lips, his father seized upon them as the first omen, and astounded by the divine revelation, he stopped him from saying more. At once he said, 'Hail, land owed to me by the fates, and hail, you household 120
gods of Troy, who have stayed true to me! **This is our home, this our fatherland.** For such were the secrets of fate (now I remember) which **my father Anchises** left me: "My son, when you have travelled to unknown shores and your food is all eaten up so that hunger compels you to consume your tables, that is the time 125
to hope for a home in your weary heart. Remember to place your first buildings there and pile up a rampart round them." This was the hunger he spoke of, the final hunger that lay in store for us, the one that will put an end to our calamities. So come now, and at the sun's first light let us go cheerfully in different directions 130
from our harbour and explore what place this is, what men live here and where their city is. Now pour libations to Jupiter from your cups, call upon my father Anchises in your prayers, and put wine upon the tables.'

**their flat wheat wafers**   these were cakes made with wheaten flour, cheese and egg. They were often used in sacrifices.

**violate**   because of the wafers' religious significance.

**the flat quarter-circles**   they seem to look like the base of a pizza.

**This is our home, this our fatherland**   an echo of his words to Dido at 4.347.

**my father Anchises**   Aeneas misremembers. It was in fact the harpy Celaeno who had made the prophecy at 3.254–7. At times it appears that Aeneas is fulfilling his mission in a mist.

- There is optimism in these opening passages of Book 7. Are there any aspects which undermine a positive view?

Aeneas sends an embassy to Latinus asking for peace and then sets to work on building his new settlement. The king receives the embassy hospitably, assures the Trojans of his goodwill and offers his daughter in marriage to Aeneas, realizing that he is the stranger marked out by the gods. The outlook is bright.

7.286–91　But look, **the savage wife of Jupiter** was coming back from Argos, city of **Inachus**, journeying through the air in her chariot, when from afar in the sky, all the way from **Cape Pachynus** in Sicily, she caught sight of the joyful Aeneas and the Trojan fleet. She saw that they had left their ships and were now working at building a　290 home **with confidence in the location**. She stopped, pierced with bitter sorrow.

She pours out her rage against the Trojans. She has done everything to stop them, but they have still found their way to their future home.

7.308–29　'But I, the great wife of Jupiter, who could not leave any attempt untried in my misery, who did everything I possibly could, *I* am being defeated by Aeneas. But　310 if my own divine power is not strong enough, I need not hesitate to beg for any help anywhere. If I cannot control the gods in heaven, I shall set hell in motion. I shall not be allowed to keep him from his kingdom in Latium. **I accept that.** And his marriage to Lavinia is irrevocably determined by fate. **But what I *can* do is**　315 **draw out and impose delay on these great events** and wreak destruction on the

**the savage wife of Jupiter**　Juno's reactions and her speech here look straight back to her appearance in Book 1, lines 34–49. The action replay adds to the impression of Book 7 as a new start to the poem.

**Inachus**　the legendary founder of Argos.

**Cape Pachynus**　the south-east promontory of Sicily.

**with confidence in the location**　Aeneas had already started building three cities. Now at least he is confident that he is doing so in the right place.

**I accept that**　she had not accepted it in Book 1 (line 38). She *has* developed, but her malevolence still has much horror to inflict.

**But what I *can* do is draw out and impose delay on these great events**　for the fact that, though fate cannot be altered, it can be delayed, see the note on 1.22 (p. 42, the fates). Do you feel any sympathy with Juno here? Why do you think that Virgil lays such stress on her malevolence?

peoples of **both kings. Let that be the price that their subjects will pay for the bond between son-in-law and father-in-law.** Your dowry, **maiden,** will be paid in Trojan and Rutulian blood. **Bellona** is waiting to act as **matron of honour** at your wedding. Cisseus' daughter **Hecuba** was not alone in conceiving a firebrand and giving birth to **the marriage torches of Paris and Helen.** No, Venus' offspring will be the same, **a second Paris,** and **torches** will again bring death to reborn Troy.' 320

When she had said these things, the terrible goddess made for the earth; she summoned Allecto, the bringer of sorrow, from the infernal shadows where the dread Furies dwell. Grim wars and rage and treachery and foul crimes were dear to her heart. Even her father Pluto hated this monstrous creature, her own sisters in Tartarus hated her. She transformed herself in so many ways, she assumed such frightening shapes, her black form sprouted so many snakes. 325

> Juno sends this vile creature first of all to inflame Latinus' wife Amata, who is already enraged over the fact that her daughter must marry Aeneas and not Turnus, with uncontrollable passion. Amata fails to make Latinus change his decision, but then, pretending to be possessed by a Bacchic frenzy, she causes all the women of the city to leave their homes for the woods. Frenzy ('furor', line 406) has taken them over. Allecto now goes to Turnus at Ardea.

7.413–69  Here in his high halls **Turnus** was sleeping deeply in the middle of the black night. Allecto put off her fierce appearance, emptied her body of its frenzy, and transformed herself so that she looked like an old woman. She ploughed her ugly forehead with wrinkles, made her hair white, **tied it with a headband and wove a spray of olive leaves around it.** She became Calybe, the aged priestess of 415

---

**both kings** Aeneas and Latinus.

**Let that ... between son-in-law and father-in-law** there may well be a reminiscence here of the passage in the pageant of heroes referring to Julius Caesar and Pompey (6.826–36). Pompey married Caesar's daughter to cement their political union. But the two men would eventually fight a horrific civil war.

**maiden** Lavinia, whom Juno addresses in a chilling apostrophe.

**Bellona** a primitive Italian war goddess.

**matron of honour** the role assumed by Juno at Dido's 'wedding' (4.166).

**Hecuba** Priam's wife, the queen of Troy, who dreamed that she was pregnant with a firebrand before she gave birth to Paris.

**the marriage torches of Paris and Helen** which led, of course, to the burning of Troy.

**a second Paris** is the comparison of Aeneas to Paris fair? Who else has made it?

**torches** what use is made of the motif of fire in this passage?

**Turnus** this is the first appearance of Turnus in the poem.

**tied it with a headband and wove a spray of olive leaves around it** the headband and olive spray are part of her disguise as a priestess.

**Juno and her temple**, and presented herself to the young man's eyes with these 420
words.

'Turnus, are you going to see **all your many labours spent in vain** and your
expectations of kingship made over to Trojan settlers, and do nothing about it?
The king is refusing you the marriage and the dowry you have earned with your
blood and is looking for a stranger as heir to his kingdom. **Go now** and confront 425
dangers! The only thanks you get is laughter. Go, flatten the Etruscan lines, shield
the Latins with peace. This is the exact message that the all-powerful **daughter
of Saturn** herself ordered me to tell you plainly as you lie in the calm of night.
So into action with you and, with joy in your heart, get the young men to arm 430
themselves and to move out of the gates **into the fields** and torch the Phrygian
leaders who have established themselves by our beautiful river – them and their
painted ships! The mighty power of heaven commands it. If king Latinus himself
does not agree to give you your wife and to abide by his promise, let him feel it to
his cost and at last find out what it is like to cross swords with Turnus.'

At this point the young man laughed at **the seer** and began to speak in reply with 435
these words: 'The news that a fleet has sailed into Tiber's waters has not failed
to reach my ears as you suppose. Please don't dream up such terrible fears. And
queen Juno does not forget me. But it's your senility, so feeble and decayed that it 440
has lost contact with reality, mother, that troubles you with needless anxieties and
mocks your prophetic skill with false terrors when kings are taking up arms. It is
your job to look after the statues of the gods and their temples. Men will see to
matters of war and peace, for it is they who have to fight the wars.'

At these words, Allecto blazed forth in fury and a sudden trembling seized the 445
young man's limbs as he spoke, and his eyes stood fixed in their sockets – with
so many snakes did the Fury hiss, **so great was the shape she revealed**. Then, as

---

**Juno and her temple**   Juno had a temple at the historical Ardea.

**all your many labours spent in vain**   a version of the legend has Turnus helping the
Latins in war against the Etruscans.

**Go now**   sarcastic.

**daughter of Saturn**   Juno.

**into the fields**   another manuscript reading would cause this to mean 'to arms'. The
Latin words for 'fields' and 'arms' differ by only one letter.

**the seer**   she has claimed to be a seer by talking of the goddess Juno's communication
with her.

**so great was the shape she revealed**   it is clear that Allecto is now appearing as
herself.

**Rumour**

What does Allecto contribute to the poem? How effective is Virgil's portrayal of her? As well as finding out some more about the appearance of the Furies, you may wish to compare Virgil's portrait of the goddess Rumour, who spreads the news of the liaison of Dido and Aeneas (4.174–88):

*Rumour, the swiftest of all evils, goes through the great cities of Libya. She thrives on her speed, gaining strength as she moves. At first she is small through her fear but soon she rears herself to the sky and while she walks on the ground she hides her head in the clouds. She was the last offspring, so they say, of Mother Earth, who was provoked to bring her to birth by her anger against the gods [at the fact that they had destroyed her children, the Titans and Giants]. She was a sister to Coeus the Titan and Enceladus the Giant, swift of foot and speedy wing, a hideous and huge monster. For every feather on her body there is a watchful eye beneath – a wonder to relate – and she has as many tongues, as many sounding mouths, as many pricked-up ears. She flies screeching through the shadows of night midway between earth and sky, and she never closes her eyes in sweet sleep; in the light of day she sits watching either on high rooftops or on lofty towers and she terrifies great cities, as persistent a messenger of what is invented and distorted as of what is true.*

Virgil's picture is a vastly extended adaptation of Homer's personification of Strife (*Iliad* 4.443–5). Compare Shakespeare's Rumour: 'Enter Rumour painted full of tongues' (*Henry IV Part 2*, Induction).

he stammered and sought to say more, she rolled her flaming eyes and pushed him back. She raised two snakes from her locks, made her whiplashes sound, and 450 added these words from her frenzied mouth: 'Look at me. So my senility, so feeble and decayed that it has lost contact with reality, mocks me with false terrors when kings are taking up arms! Look at me now! I am here from the dwelling of the Dread Sisters. In my hand I carry war and death.'   455

With these words **she flung a torch at the young man** and fixed the brand,

---

**she flung a torch at the young man**   we here look back to the terrifying passage in which Allecto flings a snake into Amata in order to madden her (7.346–53):

> The goddess flung at her one of the snakes from her blue-black hair and slipped it into her bosom to the depths of her heart, so that, frenzied with this hellish thing, she would throw the whole house into confusion. Sliding unfelt, the snake glided between her clothes and her smooth breasts, and it was not noticed by the frenzied woman as it breathed its snaky breath into her. The huge serpent became the necklace of twisted gold round her neck, it became the hanging end of the long ribbon round her head, and it wove itself into her hair and strayed slipping over her limbs.

smoking with **black light**, deep in his heart. An overwhelming fear broke off his sleep and a sweat broke out over his whole body, soaking his bones and his limbs. Madly he shouted for arms, he searched for arms **in his bed** and throughout the house. A passion for the iron sword raged within him and the criminal madness of war. Crowning all was his rage – as when a fire of twigs, crackling loudly, is heaped up under the sides of a boiling cauldron, and the water leaps with the heat and a smoky river rages within and bubbles up high with foam, and the water now has no room for itself and the dense steam flies into the air. 460 465

And so, violating the peace, he ordered the leaders of his youthful army to march to king Latinus and bade them to prepare for war, to protect Italy and thrust the enemy from their territory.

> 1 What does the initial reaction of the dreaming Turnus to the disguised Allecto tell us about him?
>
> 2 How effective is the simile of the water boiling in the cauldron (lines 462–6)?
>
> 3 What overall impression do you have of Turnus so far? Do you think he would have reacted strongly against Aeneas even without the intervention of Juno?

Allecto sets the war in motion by bringing about a situation in which Iulus, while out hunting, shoots a pet stag much loved among the Latins. The Latin herdsmen gather for revenge. Latinus refuses to declare war but withdraws from command and shuts himself up in his palace. When he is unwilling to open the Gates of War, Juno does so. The Latins prepare for battle and at the end of Book 7, Virgil lists the Italian forces, concluding with this portrait of the Volscian warrior-maiden Camilla.

**7.803–17**   As well as these there came **Camilla**, of Volscian race, leading a troop of cavalry and squadrons brilliant in bronze armour, a warrior maiden, her woman's hands unfamiliar with **Minerva**'s distaff and wool-baskets. No, she was a girl with the spirit to endure stern warfare and to outstrip the winds with her fleetness of foot. She could have flown over the topmost blades of an unreaped crop and not have hurt the tender ears of grain as she passed, or made her way over the middle of the sea, poised on the swelling waves, and not dipped her swift feet in 805 810

---

**black light**   black either because the flame is smoky or because the light comes from the underworld.

**in his bed**   at 6.523 Deiphobus says that he kept his sword under his pillow.

**Camilla**   she seems to be entirely Virgil's invention.

**Minerva**   the goddess of handicraft among other things (as we have seen).

the waters. All the young men poured out of the houses and fields, and mothers crowded to wonder at her, following her progress with their eyes, open-mouthed with astonishment at how **royal splendour covered her smooth shoulders with purple,** how the clasp bound up her hair with gold, and how she bore a Lycian quiver in her hands as well as **the shepherds' myrtle staff with an iron blade fixed in its head.**

815

> • How do you respond to the picture of Camilla? What do you imagine is going to happen to her?

## Book 8

> Turnus gives the signal for war. A troubled Aeneas is reassured in a dream by the river-god Tiberinus that he has indeed reached his goal. The god tells him to seek help from the Arcadian king Evander. Rowing peacefully up the Tiber, Aeneas comes to Pallanteum, Evander's humble settlement on the future site of Rome. He finds the Arcadians celebrating a festival of Hercules. After being challenged by Evander's son Pallas, the Trojans are given a warm welcome and promised help. When they have feasted together, Evander explains to Aeneas why they are worshipping Hercules.

8.185–269    'It is no vain superstition or **failure to acknowledge the old gods** that has laid upon us these solemn rites, this customary feast, this altar of so great a divinity. It is because we have been saved from cruel dangers, Trojan guest, that **we pay the honour that is due and renew it each year.**

'First look now at this cliff with its overhanging rocks. See how boulders have been scattered afar, an abandoned mountain dwelling remains, and the rocks have

190

---

**royal splendour covered her smooth shoulders with purple**   the purple as well as the gold in her hair and the quiver look back to Dido's appearance before the hunt (4.137–9). Why should Virgil wish to evoke Dido at this point?

**the shepherds' myrtle staff with an iron blade fixed in its head**   this line 'brilliantly summarizes the ambiguity of Camilla, carrying the myrtle staff from the idyllic pastoral world (cf. *Eclogues* 8.16) converted to military use by its iron point' (Deryck Williams).

**failure to acknowledge the old gods**    as the worship of Hercules, a deified mortal, could possibly be construed.

**we pay the honour that is due and renew it each year**   the festival of Hercules, the day on which Aeneas arrived at the site of Rome, was held on 12 August. Octavian began his triple triumph (see note on p. 136) on 13 August 29 BC and would have been outside the walls of the city on the day before. As often in the *Aeneid*, the past reaches out into the future.

*Hercules. This colossal gilded statue is a Roman work modelled on a Greek original from the fourth century BC.*

crashed down in a mighty avalanche. Here, receding to a vast depth, was the cave, never struck by the sun's rays, in which there lived a terrifying monster, the half-human **Cacus**. The ground was always wet with fresh blood and faces of men hung fixed to its proud portals, pale with horrible decay. **Vulcan** was the father of this monster. It was his black fires that he belched forth from his mouth as he moved along with his massive bulk. To us as we prayed, as to others, time at long last brought help with the arrival of **the god**. For the mighty avenger Hercules **came this way**, proudly driving his huge bulls, the spoils from the triple-bodied Geryon whom he had conquered and killed, and the bulls were at pasture in **the valley** and the river. But Cacus, his mind wild with frenzy, wished to ensure that he left no crime or trick undared or unattempted, and stole from their pasture four bulls of outstanding size and the same number of surpassingly fine heifers. And so that there should be no hoof-prints pointing in the right direction, the rustler dragged them into the cave by the tail to reverse the signs of where they had gone and hid them in the darkness of the rock. For anyone searching there were no traces pointing to the cave. Meanwhile, when the son of **Amphitryon** was now moving the well-fed herds from the pasturage and getting ready to go away, the cattle lowed as they departed. The whole grove was filled with their complaints as they moved off from the hills bellowing. One of the cows returned the sound and mooed from deep in the vast cave, frustrating the hopes of the monster who held her prisoner. At this the black-galled anger of Hercules truly blazed up in his **frenzy**. He snatched up his arms and his heavy club

195
200
205
210
215
220

---

**Cacus**   the 'a' is long: C-*ah*-cus.

**Vulcan**   the god of fire.

**the god**   Hercules' divinity is anticipated.

**came this way**   Hercules came to the site of Rome from Spain where he had killed Geryon (see 6.289) and taken his cattle.

**the valley**   the area that became the Roman Forum Boarium.

**Amphitryon**   Hercules' mortal father: Jupiter was his true father.

**frenzy**   the good hero's frenzy will meet that of the monster.

of knotted oak in his hands and made for **the heights of the lofty mountain** at a run. Then for the first time our eyes beheld Cacus frightened and confused. At that moment he ran away more swiftly than the east wind and made for his cave. His fear gave his feet wings.

'When he had shut himself in and, bursting its chains, let fall the huge rock 225
which was **suspended by steel supports forged by his father Vulcan's art**, and strengthened the support of the doorposts with the obstacle, look! the hero from **Tiryns** was there with frenzy in his heart, and scanning every approach, he cast his eyes this way and that, grinding his teeth. Three times he went round the 230
whole of the Aventine mountain burning with anger, three times he tried the rocky entrance, but in vain, three times he sat down in the valley exhausted. A jagged pinnacle of flint stood sheer on all sides, rising on the back of the cave, a towering height to look up at, a fitting home for the nests of **birds of ill-omen**. 235
Pushing full against it from the right where it leant sloping away from the ridge towards the river on the left, he shook it, loosened it, tore it up from its lowest depths, and then suddenly he pushed it. As he pushed, the great sky thundered, the banks leapt apart and the river flowed backwards in utter terror. The cave and 240
huge palace of Cacus stood uncovered and the shadowy recesses were revealed to their depths, just as if some force were to make the earth gape open to its depths and reveal the dwellings of the underworld and uncover the pallid kingdom which 245
the gods loathe, and the monstrous abyss were to be seen from above **while the shades of the dead tremble as the light pours in**.

'So, trapped in the cave and bellowing as never before, Cacus was suddenly caught in the unexpected light of day. Hercules harried him from above with missiles, using any weapon as he attacked him with branches and rocks as big as millstones. 250
He, however – since there was no other escape from danger left to him – belched forth huge clouds of smoke from his throat – a wonder to relate – and rolled blinding darkness round his dwelling, blotting out all sight of it, and gathered a mass of smoky night deep in the cave, with fire burning amid its darkness. 255

'Hercules' rage could not endure this, and with a headlong leap he flung himself through the fire where the smoke rolled its waves most thickly and the huge cave

---

**the heights of the lofty mountain**   a highly epic way of describing one of the hills of Rome.

**suspended by steel supports forged by his father Vulcan's art**   Cacus' technology will prove useless against Hercules' brute force.

**Tiryns**   Hercules was brought up there.

**birds of ill-omen**   carrion birds who could feast on Cacus' victims. There is something primitively totemic about this ghastly pinnacle of rock.

**while the shades of the dead tremble as the light pours in**   there is a striking shift in perspective in the simile. We are now looking up from below, indeed from Cacus' viewpoint. What is the effect of the simile?

seethed with black clouds. Here he seized Cacus as he vainly belched forth fire in the shadows, clasping him into a knot, and, holding on, he throttled him till his  260
eyes started from his head and his throat was drained dry of blood. At once the doors were torn off and the dark house laid open and the stolen cattle whose theft he had denied on oath were revealed to the light of day, and the hideous corpse was dragged out by the feet. Our hearts could not have enough of gazing upon  265
his terrible eyes, his face and the shaggy bristles on his half-human chest and the mouth whose fires had been extinguished.

'From that time we have honoured Hercules with celebration and **our descendants** have happily observed this day…'

---

### Livy and Cacus

At about the same time as Virgil was writing the *Aeneid*, the historian Livy was at work on his account of the early days of Rome. It is impossible to be certain which of the two versions of the Cacus story came first. Livy's version is given below. What are the main differences between the accounts? Do you have a view on which was written first?

*They say that after Hercules had killed Geryon, he drove off his wonderfully beautiful cattle to this region, and close to the river Tiber, which he had swum across driving the herd in front of him, he found a grassy area where he could refresh the cattle with rest and abundant food and lie down himself in his exhaustion after his journey. Heavy with food and wine, he fell into a deep sleep there. Then a shepherd called Cacus who lived near that place, a man who was fierce because of his great strength, was attracted by the beauty of the cattle and wanted to steal them as his plunder. But he thought that if he drove the herd into his tent by leading them, their tracks, let alone anything else, would lead their owner there in his search; and so he dragged the cattle he stole, all of them of outstanding beauty, into his cave by their tails. When Hercules woke at daybreak, he looked over his herd and realized that some of its number were missing and went to the closest cave to see if there were footprints leading to it. When he saw that they were all pointing outwards and yet weren't leading anywhere else, in his confusion and uncertainty he began to drive his herd away from the unlucky place. As the cattle were being driven off, some of them lowed, as often happens, because they missed those who had been left behind. An answering low from those shut up in the cave made Hercules turn back. When he was coming towards the cave and Cacus tried to stop him by force, Hercules hit him with his club and he died, calling in vain upon the shepherds to help him.* (Livy 1.7)

---

**our descendants**   Evander is an old man and so this makes sense in a literal way. But it also refers to a tradition that has lasted till Virgil's time.

1  Why has Virgil included this story? What does the fact that the civilizing Hercules is carried away with frenzy when he attacks and kills the frenzied Cacus tell us about the nature of that emotion in the poem?

2  In what ways does landscape contribute to the effect of this passage?

3  A typographical reading of the poem may suggest that there is a sense in which Hercules stands for Octavian and Cacus for Mark Antony. Do you feel that there is anything in this?

After the rites of Hercules have been completed, Evander takes Aeneas on a tour of his small settlement, showing him places which will be celebrated in the city of Rome which will be built on this site.

8.347–69    From here he led him to **the Tarpeian dwelling place and the Capitol, golden now** but once bristling with woodland scrub. Even then the dread numinosity of the place struck terror into the timorous country-folk, even then they trembled at  350 the wood and the rock. 'A god,' said Evander, 'dwells in this grove, dwells on this hill with its leafy top, but which god is uncertain. My Arcadians believe that they have seen Jupiter himself, when, as he often does, he shakes his darkening **aegis** and summons the clouds. Moreover in these two towns with their ruined walls,  355 you see what is left to remind us of the men of old. **Father Janus** founded this citadel, Saturn that one. This one was called **Janiculum**, the other **Saturnia**.'

**the Tarpeian dwelling place and the Capitol**   the Capitol on the Capitoline hill, on one side of which is the precipitous Tarpeian rock, named after Tarpeia who betrayed the city to the Sabines in the early days of Rome. Traitors, such as Tarpeia, were thrown to their death over this rock.

**golden now**   the reference is to the famous gold-roofed republican temple to Jupiter Capitolinus which was restored by Augustus. The foundations of this huge building can be seen in the Capitoline museum. As K. W. Gransden remarks, this phrase and the one that follows enshrine the 'contrast between the Capitol's primitive wildness and its Augustan splendour' which is central to the structure of Book 8. As Philip Hardie expressively puts it, 'Evander's guided tour of his settlement is glossed by the narrator with references to the present-day appearance of Rome, so that, as in a double exposure, the reader sees the gilded temples of Augustan Rome superimposed on the rustic landscape'.

**aegis**   the breastplate of Jupiter (or Athena). It is called 'darkening' because Jupiter summons the storm clouds with it.

**Father Janus**   the god of door and gate at Rome, he controlled beginnings, most notably as the deity after whom the month January was named.

**Janiculum**   this is across the Tiber.

**Saturnia**   in Evander's day this stood on the Capitol.

Conversing in this way, they were approaching the house of the poor Evander 360
and everywhere they saw herds of cattle lowing, both in the Roman forum and in
the elegant **Carinae**. When they came to his dwelling, Evander said, 'Victorious
Hercules stooped to enter this doorway. This palace was big enough for him. **Have
the courage, my guest, to scorn riches**, and like Hercules make yourself worthy of 365
godhead. Do not enter my humble realm in a harsh spirit.' He spoke, and led huge
Aeneas beneath the roof of his small house, and he set him on a bed of strewn
leaves covered with the hide of a Libyan bear. Night fell and covered the earth with
its dark wings.

---

1   Discuss the ways in which past and present (from Virgil's perspective)
    interpenetrate in this passage. What do you feel that Virgil is aiming to
    achieve by this? Is he successful?

2   What does Evander's reminiscence of Hercules contribute to this passage?

---

Venus now asks her husband Vulcan to make a new set of armour for Aeneas
('arms must be made for a spirited *man*', line 441) and he and his Cyclopes set
about the task. Evander tells Aeneas to join with the Etruscans. He is too old
to fight himself, but he entrusts his son Pallas to Aeneas' care. Venus now flies
down to Aeneas with the armour, and he gazes at the wondrous shield.

---

**Carinae**   in Virgil's time the quarter of the Carinae, on the west of the Esquiline hill, was
a very fashionable area. Pompey, Antony and Quintus Cicero (the brother of the famous
Cicero) had had houses there.

**Have the courage, my guest, to scorn riches ...**   these are famous lines, twice quoted
by the Stoic philosopher Seneca (*Moral Letters* 18.12, 31.11). The poet John Dryden,
who translated the *Aeneid*, waxed lyrical on the celebrated sentiment: 'I am lost in the
admiration of it. I contemn the world when I think of it, and myself when I translate it.'
The attack on luxury could be aimed in part at Antony and Cleopatra (as well as Dido and
Aeneas), but in fact many wealthy people in Augustan Rome had a luxurious lifestyle.
Efforts to curb this, e.g. by Julius Caesar, were unsuccessful.

Evander's house is close to the site of Augustus' on the Palatine hill. The latter's house
was modest by the standards of the leading Romans of his day, and we know that he
too was concerned to restrain extravagance. What do you think Virgil is up to here?
Compare Horace, *Odes* 3.24.25–9: 'O whoever wishes to put an end to impious slaughter
and the madness of civil conflict, if he wants "Father of Cities" to be inscribed on his
statues, let him have the courage to rein in unbridled licence, and be famous among
future generations.'

**Mezentius**

Evander tells Aeneas how the Etruscans have thrown out their brutish king Mezentius (who is now fighting alongside Turnus) and are looking for a foreign leader, as an oracle requires. They will serve enthusiastically under Aeneas. Evander tells him of Mezentius' hideous tyranny (8.481–93):

*This city [the Etruscan city of Argylla] flourished for many years but then fell under the proud rule of King Mezentius, which was imposed by savage violence. Why should I tell of his unspeakable murders, of the tyrant's cruel and wild actions? May the gods reserve such things for the man himself and his descendants. Why, he would even join dead bodies to living ones, binding them hand to hand and face to face, his own form of torture, and kill them like this in a drawn-out death as they oozed in putrefying pus in that grim embrace. But at last his shattered citizens armed themselves and surrounded him as he raged unspeakably in his palace, they butchered his followers and threw fire on his roof. He slipped away amid the slaughter and took refuge on Rutulian soil, where he is defended by the army of Turnus, his host.*

1 How does the characterization of Mezentius fit into the symbolic scheme of the *Aeneid*? What are we to make of Turnus' defence of him?
2 In his last moments, at the end of Book 10, Mezentius makes it clear how much he loves his son Lausus. Why might Virgil invite a measure of sympathy for this bloody tyrant?

8.626–731 On the shield the god of fire, not unaware of the prophecies, not without knowledge of the ages to come, had fashioned the story of Italy and the triumphs of the Romans, on it were the whole line of future generations descended from Ascanius and the wars they fought in due order. He had fashioned the mother wolf lying in the green 630 cave of **Mars** and twin boys around her teats, playing as they hung there and sucked at her without fear while she bent back her smooth neck and **licked them by turns** and moulded their limbs with her tongue. Close by this he had added Rome and 635 the outrageous **rape of the Sabine women** in the midst of the audience at the circus when the great games were held, and the sudden outbreak of a new war between

---

**Mars**   the father of Romulus and Remus. The cave was held to be on the Lupercal.

**licked them by turns**   obviously it would have been impossible to portray this. A number of the pictures come to life in the same way. What is the effect of this?

**rape of the Sabine women**   Romulus' city did not contain enough women and so he invited the Sabines to some Roman games. While the men were distracted, the Romans kidnapped the women. This led to warfare between the two peoples but a reconciliation soon took place (lines 639–41).

the people of Romulus and the aged **Tatius** and his severe town of **Cures**. Next, the same kings, their conflict now laid aside, were standing in arms before the altar 640 of Jupiter, holding libation vessels in their hands as they ratified a treaty with the sacrifice of a pig. Close to this, swift four-horse chariots had torn **Mettus** apart (but you, Alban, should have stood by your word!) and **Tullus** was dragging the body of the liar through a wood while the brambles were dripping with the dew of 645 his blood. There too was **Porsenna**, ordering the Romans to admit the banished Tarquin and pressing the city hard with a great siege. The sons of Aeneas were rushing to take up steel for liberty's sake. **You could see a convincing portrayal** of a man making angry threats because **Cocles** had the courage to tear the bridge 650 down and **Cloelia** had broken her chains and was swimming the river.

*The wolf with Romulus and Remus.*
*A coin from the third century BC.*

---

**Tatius, Cures**   Tatius was king of the Sabines and Cures was his capital, a town noted for the severity and simplicity of its way of life.

**Mettus, Tullus**   Mettus Fufetius of Alba promised to help the Roman king Tullus Hostilius against the people of Fidenae but went over to the enemy. As a punishment for his double loyalties, he was tied to two chariots and torn apart, as is portrayed on this part of the shield.

**Porsenna**   the king of the Etruscans, otherwise known as Lars Porsenna, who attempted to restore Tarquin to the kingship of Rome.

**You could see a convincing portrayal …**   in a number of the pictures we are reminded that the shield is a work of art.

**Cocles**   Horatius Cocles held the bridge (the pons Sublicius) against the Etruscans until it could be cut down. He then leapt into the Tiber and swam to safety.

**Cloelia**   after Porsenna had made peace with Rome, he took hostages, one of whom was Cloelia. She escaped and swam the Tiber. The Romans sent her back but Porsenna was so impressed by her courage that he freed her.

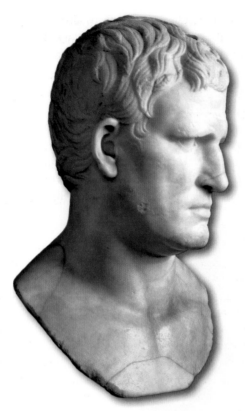

At the top of the shield **Manlius** was standing before the temple as he guarded the Tarpeian citadel and held the lofty Capitol. **The palace** was new, bristling with the thatch of Romulus, and here a goose of silver was flying through **a colonnade of gold**, giving warning that the Gauls were on the threshold. The Gauls were there in the thickets on the point of gaining the citadel, defended by the shadows and the gift of dark night. Their long hair was of gold, of gold too their clothes. They shone in their striped cloaks, and their milk-white necks were circled with gold. Each of them brandished two Gallic javelins in their hand and long shields protected their bodies.

Here the god had hammered out the **dancing Salii** and the naked **Luperci**, the wooden **helmets** with their wool tufts and the **shields** which fell from the sky, and chaste matrons were leading sacred processions through the city **in their cushioned carriages**.

*Agrippa. Until his death in 12 BC, he was Augustus'*
*greatest general. A close friend of the emperor, he was*
*laid to rest in the famous mausoleum.*

**Manlius**   the Gauls attacked Rome in 390 BC. Manlius was alerted to their hidden ascent of the Capitol by the honking of the sacred geese of Juno, which the Romans had piously refrained from killing even at a time of extreme food shortage.

**The palace ... a colonnade of gold**   these lines and the ones about the Gauls that follow are particularly good indications of the fantastically elaborate metal-work which Virgil is making us imagine in his description of the shield.

**dancing Salii**   dancing priests who turned away danger and malign influences.

**Luperci**   they ran naked along the Sacred Way in what may have been a purification or fertility rite.

**helmets, shields**   cult symbols of the Salii, not the Luperci. K. W. Gransden points out that 'the image of a magic shield appears on Aeneas' shield, which has itself descended from heaven'.

**in their cushioned carriages**   the right of Roman matrons to ride in such carriages was of long standing. It was a reward for patriotism. When Camillus had vowed to build a temple to Apollo after the fall of Veii to the Gauls in 396 BC, he could not collect enough money until the matrons donated their jewellery.

At a distance from here, he added the abodes of Tartarus also, the high gates of Dis, the punishments of criminals, and you, **Catiline**, hanging on a threatening rock and trembling at the faces of the Furies, and, in a place apart, the pious ones and **Cato** holding sway over them. 670

Spreading widely **between these scenes** there ran the likeness of the sea wrought in gold, but the water foamed with white waves, and around it a circle of dolphins, gleaming in silver, swept the seas with their tails and cut through the tide. In the middle the **brazen** fleets which fought **the battle of Actium** were visible, and you 675 could see the whole of **Leucate** seething with war's array and the waves ablaze with gold. On this side Augustus Caesar was leading the Italians into battle with **the senators** and the people, the household gods of Troy and the great gods, as he

---

**Catiline** leader of a conspiracy against the republic in 63 BC. The truth of the matter is rather more complex than Virgil's presentation suggests. There was plenty wrong with the republic which the ruling classes were prepared to do little or nothing to put right. Cicero had crushed Catiline, and it may be that Virgil, who does not mention him anywhere in the poem, is paying a tribute to the famous politician and lawyer. Since Cicero had rejoiced at the murder of Julius Caesar, the adoptive father of Augustus, it may have seemed impolitic to pay a more direct tribute to him in an Augustan poem.

**Cato** on the other hand, Virgil does pay tribute here to one of Caesar's great republican enemies with this climactic and laudatory reference to Cato, a Stoic and an uncompromising man of principle.

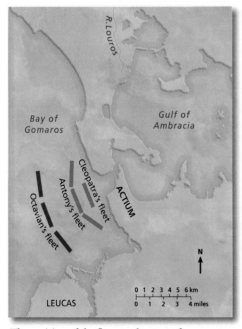

*The position of the fleets at the start of the battle of Actium.*

**between these scenes** the scenes of history occupy the upper part of the shield (line 652) and those set in the underworld the lower (666). The central position is given to the battle of Actium.

**brazen** referring to the bronze beaks of the warships, used for ramming.

**the battle of Actium** the battle was fought on 2 September 31 BC. Gransden gives a summary of the basic situation: 'Antony's fleet of around 230 ships was anchored in the gulf of Ambracia; he had no wish to leave shelter and engage the superior navy of Augustus (around 400 ships), but faced with the alternative of abandoning his entire fleet and attempting a retreat by land he decided to fight his way out of the gulf (691) and make a run for it, in the hope of saving Cleopatra's sixty ships which had sails as well as oars (708) and carried valuable treasure (685)'.

**Leucate** the promontory (not visible on the map) on the south of the island of Leucas.

**the senators** in fact the two consuls and over three hundred senators had left Rome in 32 BC to join Antony.

stood on the lofty stern of his ship. His exultant brow shot forth a double flame 680
and **his father's star appeared above his head**. In a different part was **Agrippa**,
high-towering too as he led his fleet in battle array with the favour of the winds
and the gods. His temples gleamed, beaked with **the naval crown**, a proud token
of warfare. On this side was Antony, with his barbarian wealth and **different** 685
**sorts of armour**, returning **triumphant** from the nations of the Dawn and the
Indian Ocean and bringing with him Egypt and the might of the East and furthest
**Bactra**, and – the sin of it! – **his Egyptian wife. All rushed together** and the whole
sea foamed, churned up by the tug of the oars and the three-pronged beaks. **They** 690
**made for the high sea.** You would believe that **the Cyclades** had been torn up and
were swimming on the sea or that tall mountains were clashing with mountains,
so vast were the towered ships in which the men moved to the fight. Flaming tow
and a shower of iron-tipped weapons flew from their hands, and the fields of 695

---

**his father's star appeared above his head**   the comet known as the Julian star appeared
when Octavian was celebrating the funeral games in honour of his adoptive father Julius
Caesar. It was generally understood as a sign of Caesar's apotheosis. Octavian put a star
on the head of the statue of Caesar which was dedicated in the forum soon afterwards,
and later a star was shown on his own helmet. Where else in the poem have we seen fire
upon heads? What appears to be its significance? See also Romulus at 6.779–80: 'Do you
see how twin crests stand upon his head and the father of the gods himself already marks
him out with the honour of his own emblem [the thunderbolt]?'

**Agrippa**   Marcus Vipsanius Agrippa, who effectively won the battle for Octavian/
Augustus and later married his daughter.

**the naval crown**   this was a golden crown adorned with representations of beaked ships,
awarded to Agrippa after his defeat of Sextus Pompey at Naulochus in 36 BC.

**different sorts of armour**   a united Italy faces a motley collection of orientals in line with
Octavian/Augustus' racial stereotyping. He had declared war on Cleopatra, not Antony,
thus camouflaging the fact that by doing so he was launching a civil war.

**triumphant**   a decidedly hyperbolical estimate of Antony's unsuccessful campaign
against the Parthians. Why do you think Virgil has included this tribute?

**Bactra**   the capital of Bactria in what is now northern Afghanistan and southern
Turkestan.

**his Egyptian wife**   the Augustan poets never use the name Cleopatra. Virgil uses the
expression 'the sin of it' because a full Roman marriage would only exist if both parties
were Roman citizens or had received a special grant of the right to marry. For the
sympathetic conclusion to Horace's poem about her (*Odes* 1.37), see p. 85.

**All rushed together ...**   we now move on to another picture on the shield showing the
actual fighting.

**They made for the high sea**   Antony and Cleopatra are trying to break out of the gulf:
see above on line 675 (the battle of Actium) and the map on p. 133.

**the Cyclades**   an archipelago of numerous small islands in the southern Aegean.

Neptune **turned red** with fresh blood. In the middle the queen summoned her forces with **the rattle** of her fathers and even now she did not look back at **the two asps** behind her. Monstrous shapes of gods of every kind and the barking **Anubis** held their weapons against Neptune and **Venus** and **Minerva**. Engraved in iron, 700 Mars raged in the middle of the fighting, and the grim Furies flew down from the sky, and Discord stalked rejoicing in her torn clothing, followed by **Bellona** with her bloody whip. **As he watched this sight, Actian Apollo** was stretching out his bow from above. In terror at that, all of Egypt and India, every Arab, all the 705 **Sabaeans** turned to flee. The queen herself was to be seen calling the winds and spreading her sail, just on the point of slackening and releasing the ropes. The god of fire had portrayed her amid the slaughter **pale at the death to come**, carried 710

*Gods fight alongside Roman soldiers in a sea battle.*

---

**turned red**   another of the pictures appears to change as Aeneas looks at it.

**the rattle**   used in the worship of the Egyptian goddess Isis.

**the two asps**   by whose poison Cleopatra killed herself. The historians write of a single snake. It may be that Virgil has two asps to match the double flame shooting from Augustus' head. Compare also the two snakes on Allecto's head at 7.450.

**Anubis**   this Egyptian god was portrayed with a dog's head.

**Venus**   the mother of Aeneas and hence the grandmother of Iulus and ancestress of the Julian house.

**Minerva**   presumably in her guise as the warrior goddess.

**Bellona**   a primitive Italian war goddess (cf. 7.319 on p. 120).

**As he watched this sight, Actian Apollo**   we have a picture of Apollo looking at a picture. For 'Actian Apollo', see the note on 3.276 (p. 68, the little city).

**Sabaeans**   they lived in what is now Yemen in Arabia.

**pale at the death to come**   compare Dido at 4.644.

*Mark Antony. This basalt head dates from 40–30 BC.*

along by the waves and **the north-west wind**. Facing her was the Nile, his great body possessed by grief, **opening his folds** and calling the vanquished with all of his robes into his blue-green breast and the hiding-places of his river.

But Caesar, riding into the walls of Rome **in triple triumph**, was solemnizing his immortal vow to the 715 gods of Italy to build **three hundred** great temples throughout the city. The streets echoed with joy and games and applause; **in all the temples** was a chorus of matrons, at all of them were **altars**; in front of the altars slaughtered bullocks strewed the ground. He himself, 720 sitting at **the snow-white threshold of white-gleaming Apollo**, reviewed the gifts of the peoples and **fastened them to the lofty portals**. The conquered nations moved forward in a long procession, as diverse in the languages

---

**the north-west wind**  the right wind to blow what remained of the fleet to Egypt.

**opening his folds**  the hiding-places of the river and the folds of the robe worn by the river-god. The anthropomorphism is finely handled here.

**in triple triumph**  Augustus' triple triumph, which lasted three days, celebrated (*a*) the battle of Actium, (*b*) the Dalmatian war and (*c*) the Alexandrian war. For the significance of the timing, see note on 8.189.

**three hundred**  three hundred stands for an indefinitely large number. Augustus claimed to have built 12 temples (*Res Gestae* 19) and to have restored 82 (*Res Gestae* 20).

**in all the temples …**  what is now described is a national thanksgiving (*supplicatio*).

**altars**  obviously there were altars at the temples. The meaning here is that Vulcan had portrayed them on the shield.

**the snow-white threshold of white-gleaming Apollo**  the temple of Apollo on the Palatine hill had been started in 36 BC and was dedicated in 28 BC. It was a building project that was intensely personal to Augustus, built when his house on the Palatine was hit by lightning (Suetonius, *Augustus* 29.3) and connected to it by a ramp. It was the most notable statement of the identification with Apollo that played an important part in Augustus' propaganda. But there are problems with the picture. The temple was incomplete in 29 BC, the year of the triple triumph, and in any event triumphal processions normally ended on the Capitol. At the climax of the description of the shield – and of Book 8 – Virgil seems to go against history to make the setting of his final picture a temple that was Augustus' own very significant creation.

**fastened them to the lofty portals**  compare Aeneas' action at 3.287.

as in their clothing and their arms. Here **Mulciber** had portrayed the race of the Nomads and the Africans with their loose-flowing robes, here **the Leleges and the Cares** and the arrow-bearing **Geloni**. **Euphrates** was in the procession, his waters gentler now, and **the Morini** who dwell on the edge of the earth, and **the two-horned Rhine**, and the untamed **Dahae** and **Araxes chafing at his bridge**. 725

Such were the sights on the shield of Vulcan, the gift of his mother, and he wondered at them, and, though he knew nothing of the events, he rejoiced at the pictures as he raised onto his shoulders the glory and the fate of his descendants. 730

---

1   How far do the pictures of Roman history on the top part of the shield (lines 626–66) convey an optimistic impression? How significant is it that, while Aeneas rejoices as he lifts the shield onto his shoulders, we are also told that he knew nothing of the events?

2   What, if any, is the symbolism of Aeneas' lifting the shield on his shoulders (the up-motif)? What does it look back to in the poem?

3   Why do you think that Virgil includes the scenes from the underworld (lines 667–70)?

4   Would it be just to refer to the final pictures on the shield, the battle of Actium and the triple triumph (lines 671–728), as naked propaganda, or are there some questioning, unsettling features? If so, what are they, and how far do they undermine the positive assertiveness?

5   How do you feel about the use of propaganda for political purposes?

---

**Mulciber**   the old title of Vulcan.

**the Leleges and the Cares**   from Asia Minor.

**Geloni**   from Scythia.

**Euphrates**   the river flows through Baghdad in modern Iraq. A picture of its god amid relatively peaceful waters was clearly carried in the procession. A gently flowing Euphrates means 'a more submissive Parthia' and Virgil may be thinking of the return of the legionary standards captured by the Parthians at the battle of Carrhae in 53 BC. This became an increasingly large element of Augustan propaganda during the 20s BC. The standards were returned in 20 BC, the year before Virgil's death. The moment of their handing over is portrayed as the centrepiece on the breastplate of Augustus of the statue on p. 111.

**the Morini**   a tribe in Belgica.

**the two-horned Rhine**   two-horned either because river-gods were often depicted with the heads of bulls or because the Rhine has two main estuaries, the Waal and the Lek.

**Dahae**   Scythian nomads.

**Araxes chafing at his bridge**   Alexander the Great had built a bridge over this river in Armenia but it had been swept away. Augustus built a new bridge. Is there any significance in the fact that the description of the shield concludes with an untamed tribe and a resentful river?

# 8 Aeneas and Turnus

**Book 9**

> Juno sends Iris to Turnus to tell him to attack the Trojan camp in Aeneas' absence. Staying within the camp in accordance with Aeneas' instructions, the Trojans are in a situation of appalling danger. Nisus and Euryalus, whom we encountered in Book 5 (see pp. 94–6), plan to break out through the enemy lines in order to reach Aeneas and inform him of the terrible situation. Going through Turnus' camp at night, they slaughter many of the sleeping Rutulians. Euryalus takes some **medallions** and **a gold-studded belt** from one of his victims and puts on the **beautifully plumed helmet** of the sleeping Messapus.

**9.367–449**  In the meantime, while the rest of the [Latin] forces were waiting in fighting order on the plain, horsemen who had been sent ahead from the Latin city arrived bringing a reply to King Turnus, three hundred of them, all with shields and led 370 by Volcens. They were already getting close to the camp and coming up to its walls when they spotted these men at a distance moving along on the left-hand path; and the helmet which Euryalus had now forgotten betrayed him as it gleamed with the reflection of the moonbeams amid the glimmering shadows of the night. The sighting was not disregarded. From his column Volcens shouted, 'Halt, you 375 men! What is the reason for your journey? Who are you? Why are you armed? Where are you going?' They offered no reply but hurried in flight into the woods, trusting to the night. The horsemen rushed to cut them off at the **well-known** junctions of the paths on this side and that, and they encircled every way out 380 with guards. **The wood spread wide**, bristling with thickets and dark holm-oaks and overgrown everywhere with dense brambles. Here and there a path could be made out along concealed tracks. The shadows of the branches and the weight of his booty hampered Euryalus and fear gave him false directions along the paths. 385

---

**medallions, a gold-studded belt, beautifully plumed helmet**  Nisus and Euryalus are on a mission to bring back Aeneas, but they are side-tracked by their horrific slaughter of helpless victims and Euryalus' appetite for flashy spoils. The helmet will prove his undoing. An equally ill-omened item of booty is the sword-belt that Turnus takes from the dead Pallas (10.495–505). The grisly night slaughter is based on that wreaked amid the allies of Troy by the Greek Diomedes and Odysseus in Homer, *Iliad* 10.

**well-known**  to the Rutulian horsemen, not, of course, to the Trojans.

**The wood spread wide ...**  'Woods are places of perplexity and error... Here the dark spaces of the [deceptive wood] (392) are the setting for a failure of reason' (Philip Hardie).

**Nisus got clear,** and now, without thinking about what he was doing, he had escaped from the enemy and the area which was later called Alban after the name Alba – at that time King Latinus had his high cattle enclosures there – when he stopped and looked back in vain for his absent friend: 'Unhappy Euryalus, where  390
have I left you? Where shall I look for you?' He retraced all his confused journey through the deceptive wood, scanning his footprints and going back over them, wandering amid the silent thickets. He heard the horses, he heard the uproar and the signals of pursuit. And after a short time had passed, the sound of shouting  395
reached his ears and he saw Euryalus, now in the grasp of the whole crowd of the enemy, overwhelmed as he was by the deceitful nature of the place and the night and by the sudden confused onrush, and now trying everything in a vain attempt to escape.

What was he to do? What strength could he summon, what arms could he seize to dare to rescue the young man? Should he rush to certain death in the midst of  400
the enemy's swords and hurry to the wounds that would make his end a fine one? Quickly he drew back his arm and hurled his spear, looking up at **the moon** on high, and he prayed to her in these words: 'You, goddess, be present and help me in this labour, you glory of the stars, Latona's daughter, guardian of the woods.  405
If ever my father Hyrtacus brought any gifts to your altars for my sake, if ever I myself brought them increase with my own hunting and hung offerings from your round shrine or fixed them to your sacred gables, let me throw that gang into confusion, and **direct my weapons through the air**.'

After he had said these words, he threw his spear, straining in every limb. As it flew,  410
the weapon cut through the shadows of the night and hit the back of Sulmo who had turned away, and there the head broke off and the splintered wood pierced his vital parts. He rolled over, vomiting a stream of warm blood from his chest as death made him cold and his sides heaved with long convulsive gasps. They  415
peered round in different directions. Made the more fierce by this, Nisus – look at him! – poised another weapon high up, by his ear. While they scurried in alarm, the spear went hissing through both of Tagus' temples, pierced his brain, and, hot now, stuck there. Fierce Volcens raged but could not see the man who had shot  420
the spear anywhere or work out where he should fling himself in his fury. 'But meanwhile **you** will pay me the penalty for **both men** in your hot blood,' he said.

---

**Nisus got clear ...**   he could have performed his patriotic duty and gone on to see Aeneas. His love for Euryalus drives him back to danger and death. What do you think of his behaviour here?

**the moon**   the goddess of the moon is Diana, who is also the goddess of hunting on earth.

**direct my weapons through the air**   gods in Homer do this.

**you**   i.e. Euryalus. Since Volcens cannot see Nisus, he will take his revenge on Euryalus.

**both men**   i.e. Sulmo and Tagus.

At the same time he advanced upon Euryalus with drawn sword. Then indeed, **out of his mind in utter terror**, Nisus shouted out. No longer could he hide himself in the shadows or endure such great anguish. 'It was me! Me! I did it and I am here. Turn your weapons upon me, you Rutulians! The whole crime was my doing. He did not dare the deed nor could he have. I call this heaven to witness and the all-seeing stars. His only crime was to love his unhappy friend too well.' 430

**Those were his words**, but the sword, driven in with strength, passed through the boy's ribs and burst open his white breast. Euryalus rolled over in death, and blood spread over his beautiful limbs, his neck dropped and fell on his shoulders – **as when a purple flower**, cut by the plough, droops in death, or poppies drop their 435 heads on their weary necks when weighed down by a chance shower. But Nisus rushed into their midst and made for Volcens alone among them all. Volcens was all he thought of. His enemies formed up around **him** and grappled with Nisus, 440 pushing him away from whichever side he attacked. With equal vigour Nisus pressed on, whirling his sword like lightning, until he came face to face with the Rutulian and buried it in his mouth as his enemy shouted, robbing him of his soul as he died himself. Then, pierced through and through, **he flung himself on top of his lifeless friend**, and found his final rest there in the peace of death. 445

**O fortunate pair!** If my poetry has any power, no day will ever take you from the memory of time, as long as **the house of Aeneas** dwells nearby the Capitol's immovable rock and **the Father of Rome** holds sway.

425

---

out of his mind in utter terror   Nisus is presumably terrified for Euryalus, not for himself.

Those were his words ...   'the powerlessness of speech is a constant theme of the *Aeneid*' (Philip Hardie). Can you think of any other examples?

as when a purple flower ...   the first simile is based on one in a poem by Catullus in which the poet says that his girlfriend no longer has any regard for his love, 'which has fallen through her badness like a flower at the edge of a meadow after it has been touched by the passing plough' (Catullus 11.21–4). The second is from the description in the *Iliad* of the death of Gorgythion, who dropped his head to one side 'like a poppy in a garden, bent by the weight of its seed and the showers of spring' (8.306–7). Compare the simile applied to the corpse of the young Pallas at 11.68–71 (p. 146). What is the effect of the similes applied here to Euryalus?

him   i.e. Volcens; his men are trying to defend him from Nisus' frenzied assault.

he flung himself on top of his lifeless friend   the lovers are united in death.

O fortunate pair!   'Virgil reserves for this young couple the most emphatic authorial intervention in the epic and the only explicit reference to the power of his own poetry' (Philip Hardie). Even if these minor characters are fortunate in the immortality that Virgil has given them, their deaths seem particularly futile.

the house of Aeneas   i.e. the Roman people, Aeneas' descendants.

the Father of Rome   is this Jupiter, or the Roman emperor?

1  How far do you admire Nisus and Euryalus? Look back to the foot race in Book 5.

2  Hardie remarks that 'despite their bravery and strength of arm [Nisus and Euryalus] are destroyed on the threshold of adult manhood because of a lingering immaturity. The night in which [they] run amok and then die may also symbolize their failure to emerge into the full daylight of the adult male hero (real men fight during the day).' Do you agree with Hardie's assessment of this episode?

3  A number of scholars have identified a homoerotic sensibility in Virgil's poetry. Do you feel that they are right to do so?

The Rutulians make a full-scale attack on the Trojan camp. Virgil calls upon the Muse to tell of the slaughter wrought by Turnus. Many fall on both sides.

9.590–644    Then it is said that Ascanius shot a swift arrow in war for the first time – **previously he had only terrified wild beasts in flight** – **bringing low strong Numanus** with his hand. His family name was Remulus and he had recently joined in marriage with the younger sister of Turnus. He was moving in front of the first line, yelling   595
indiscriminate insults in pride of heart at his new royal status, and **loudly boasting his mighty prowess**:

'Are you not ashamed to be cooped up again behind your ramparts in a siege – you **twice-captured** Phrygians – and to use walls to shelter you from death? **Look at** these men who back their demands to win our brides for themselves   600
with warfare! What god, what madness drove you to Italy? You will find no **sons of Atreus** here, no **Ulysses with his tricky words**. We are a hard race by descent,

---

**previously he had only terrified wild beasts in flight**  we are referred back to the Ascanius of the Carthaginian hunt (4.156–9). 'Hitherto we have seen Ascanius the hunter-boy … this is his first act of violence in war. Hunting is a training for war, but the successful hunter does not always make a good warrior' (Philip Hardie). Ascanius appears to develop successfully in this way.

**bringing low strong Numanus**  we are told before we hear Numanus' taunts (598–620) that Ascanius killed him.

**loudly boasting his mighty prowess**  Hardie calls him 'a puffed-up boaster to be deflated by Ascanius' arrow'.

**twice-captured**  once by the Greeks, once now.

**Look at …**  Numanus turns to his own side to make this mocking taunt.

**sons of Atreus**  Agamemnon and Menelaus, the Greek commanders-in-chief at Troy.

**Ulysses with his tricky words**  the Greeks won the Trojan war through a trick devised by Ulysses (the wooden horse). Numanus means that the hardy Rutulians will not have to resort to such a shift.

and we begin by taking our sons down to the rivers and hardening them in the water's cruel cold. When they grow to boyhood, they tire out the woods by night 605 with long watches at the hunt. Their sport is to handle horses and shoot arrows from the bow. But when they grow up **they endure hard toil** and become inured to frugal living, either taming the earth with hoes or shaking towns in warfare. All our life is worn down with weapons, **we goad our bullocks' backs with a reversed** 610 **spear**, and sluggish old age does not weaken the strength of our spirit or diminish our energy. We press down our grey hair with the helmet, and always delight to bring in new spoils and live on what we seize. **Your clothes are dyed in saffron** and gleaming purple. Idleness is your delight, your pleasure is the enjoyment 615 of the dance, and **your tunics have long sleeves** and your bonnets ribbons. O you Phrygian women – for that, not Phrygian men, is what you truly are – go over lofty **Dindyma** where the double pipe provides music for the devotees. The tambourines are calling you and the **Berecynthian** boxwood pipe of the mother of Ida. Leave **arms to men** and give up the iron sword.' 620

Ascanius could not endure his bragging words as he delivered his fearsome abuse, and turning to face him, he tautened the bow on the bowstring of horse sinew, drew his arms apart and took his stand, first calling upon Jupiter in suppliant prayer:

'Almighty Jupiter, give your assent to my bold undertaking. I myself shall bring 625 yearly offerings to you at your temple, and I shall set before your altar a white bullock with gilded horns, **which holds its head as high as its mother**, one ready to butt with its horns and scatter the sand with its hooves.'

The father heard him, and thundered on the left from a clear part of the sky, and 630 the fateful bow sounded together with the thunder. The arrow he had drawn back

---

**they endure hard toil** ...   Hardie refers to the 'Roman fantasy of the Italian farmer-soldier of early days, hard-working and uncorrupted by the wealth of the city ...'. How far are the ideas in this sentence familiar to you from the *Georgics*?

**we goad our bullocks' backs with a reversed spear**   i.e. they have a weapon in their hands even when engaged in agriculture.

**Your clothes are dyed in saffron**   see Iarbas' abuse at 4.215–17 (p. 76, sword). Turnus will speak in these terms at 12.99–100.

**your tunics have long sleeves**   the male Roman tunic had short sleeves: long sleeves were for foreigners and women.

**Dindyma, Berecynthian**   Dindyma and Berecynthus were mountains close to Mount Ida behind Troy, sacred to the Great Mother Cybele. Extreme worshippers of the goddess castrated themselves.

**arms to men**   one of the poem's eleven direct repetitions (with varying case and number in the word for 'man') of its opening words. This instance is deeply ironical. Numanus uses the words just before Ascanius becomes a man when he kills him with his weapon.

**which holds its head as high as its mother**   i.e. of a suitable age for sacrifice.

flew with a terrifying hiss and went through the head of Remulus and pierced his hollow temples with its iron point. 'Come on now, make fun of courageous men with your proud words. This is the answer that the twice-captured Phrygians 635 return to the Rutulians.' That was all Ascanius said. The Trojans shouted in support and roared for joy, their spirits rising to the skies.

Then, as it so happened, Apollo, the god whose hair is never cut, was sitting on a cloud, looking down from a tract of the sky at the Ausonian battle lines and **the** 640 **city**, and he addressed the victorious Iulus with these words: '**A blessing on your first act of prowess, boy!** This is the path that leads to the stars, **you son of gods who will father them too**. All the wars which fate decrees will come shall justly cease beneath the race of **Assaracus**, and **Troy cannot contain you.**'

---

1 How is Numanus characterized in this passage?
2 Is his abuse of the Trojans in any way justified?
3 What does this passage tell us about Ascanius? How do you react to him here?

---

Apollo darts down to the Trojan camp, disguises himself and tells Ascanius to keep out of the fighting in future. Two Trojan strongmen now throw open the gates of the camp and challenge the enemy to enter. The Rutulians attack, and Turnus finds himself alone inside the camp when the gates are closed. Intent on personal triumph, he fails to let in the rest of his army. After killing many Trojans, he plunges from the rampart into the Tiber and rejoins his army.

---

**the city**   i.e. the Trojan camp.

**A blessing on your first act of prowess, boy!**   David West translates this, 'You have become a man, young Iulus, and we salute you!' This far from literal translation conveys the meaning most effectively. But Apollo's praise does not fully reflect the poem's realities. As we shall see, he soon tells Iulus to keep out of the fighting.

**you son of gods who will father them too**   Ascanius is the grandson of Venus and will number Julius Caesar and Augustus among his descendants.

**Assaracus**   a Trojan ancestor.

**Troy cannot contain you**   this may look back to Philip of Macedon's words to his adolescent son Alexander after he had broken in the horse Bucephalus: 'Macedonia cannot contain you' (Plutarch, *Life of Alexander* 6.5). Ascanius is now too big for Troy.

## Book 10

Book 10 begins with a council of the gods on Olympus. The goddesses Venus and Juno speak passionately in support of the Trojans and Rutulians respectively, but Jupiter refuses to take sides.

**10.100–17**  Then the almighty father, who has supreme power over the universe, began to speak, and while he spoke, the lofty house of the gods fell silent, the earth trembled to her base, the high heaven was silent; then the Zephyrs were hushed and the sea mastered and calmed its waters.

'So take these words of mind to your hearts and fix them there. Since it is not 105 allowed that the Ausonians should be joined with the Trojans in an agreement and your dissent can find no end, I shall make no distinction in the fortune which each man will have today, or the hope which each pursues, be he Trojan or Rutulian, whether the camp is blockaded because of the fates of the Italians or sinful error 110 on the part of the Trojans and misleading prophecies they have received. And I do not exempt the Rutulians. Each man's endeavours will bring him his suffering and his success. King Jupiter is impartial to all. The fates will find a way.'

Swearing by the rivers of **his Stygian brother**, by the banks and black whirlpools of the waters that flow headlong with pitch, he nodded and **with his nod he made** 115 **all of Olympus shake**. This was the end of the conference. Then Jupiter rose from his golden throne, and the heavenly gods surrounded him and escorted him to the threshold.

> • What is your feeling about Jupiter leaving the matter for the fates to decide?

Aeneas now sails back to the beleaguered Trojan camp with Etruscan forces as well as Arcadians under the command of Evander's young son Pallas. When they land, battle breaks out with many successes on both sides. Then Turnus and Pallas meet in single combat.

**10.474–509**  Pallas flung his spear with great strength and snatched his flashing sword from 475 its hollow scabbard. In its flight it struck where the top covering of the shoulder rises up, forced its way through the layers of the shield and at last actually grazed

---

**his Stygian brother ...**   Pluto. An oath by the Styx was inviolable for the gods (6.324).

**with his nod he made all of Olympus shake**   this looks back to the famous Olympus-shaking nod of Zeus, the Greek equivalent of Jupiter, at Homer, *Iliad* 1.528–30.

the great body of Turnus. At this Turnus took his time in balancing the shaft of his spear, tipped with sharp steel, then threw it at Pallas and said these words: 'See whether my weapon is the one that pierces more keenly.' He had spoken. With quivering impact the spear went through the middle of Pallas' shield, with all its layers of iron and bronze, overlaid and encircled with so many folds of bull hide, and pierced the barrier of his breastplate and his mighty chest. Pallas snatched the **warm** spear from the wound, but in vain. His blood and his life followed by one and the same path. He collapsed onto his wound – his armour clattered about him – and as he died he bit the soil of his enemies with his bleeding mouth. Standing over him, Turnus said, 'Remember these words of mine, Arcadians, and take them back to Evander. I send Pallas back to him as **he has deserved to receive him**. Whatever honour there is in a tomb, whatever comfort lies in the act of burial, I freely grant him. His hospitality to Aeneas will cost him dear.' And, after saying these words, he pressed his left foot down on the lifeless body, snatching the huge weight of the sword-belt and the tale of sin engraved on it – **a band of young men foully slain on a single wedding night** and their bloody marriage chambers, which **Clonus, son of Eurytus**, had embossed in abundant gold. Now Turnus exulted in this spoil and took joy in the winning of it. O minds of men, so ignorant of fate and the destiny to come, and of how to keep within bounds when uplifted by good fortune! A time will come for Turnus when he would pay a great price not to have touched Pallas, when he would hate these spoils and this day. But his companions crowded round Pallas, set him on his shield with many groans and tears and carried him back. **O you who will prove a sorrow** as well as a great glory to your father when you return to him, this same day first gave you to war and took you from it. Yet in spite of that you left huge heaps of Rutulian dead.

480
485
490
495
500
505

---

- How do you feel about Turnus in this passage? Spoiling one's victim of his arms is in the noble Homeric tradition, but does Turnus go too far? How much, if anything, can be said in his favour?

---

**warm**   i.e. warmed with Pallas' blood.

**he has deserved to receive him**   i.e. because Evander had allied with the Trojans.

**a band of young men foully slain on a single wedding night**   the 'tale of sin' is that of the 50 daughters of Danaus who, with one exception, killed the 50 sons of Aegyptus on their wedding night. Danaus instigated the slaughter because an oracle had declared he would be slain by his son-in-law. The subject of a blood-stained wedding is hideously appropriate to Turnus, who is fighting to get Lavinia back.

**Clonus, son of Eurytus**   we know nothing of him.

**O you who will prove a sorrow ...**   what is the effect of the apostrophe (see p. 83, Dido) here?

**In frenzied anger Aeneas rages** over the battlefield, seeking vengeance for Pallas in a succession of violent killings. Juno removes Turnus from the fighting by causing him to pursue a phantom Aeneas onto a ship. His salvation can only be temporary. Book 10 concludes with Aeneas' killing of the brutish former king of the Etruscans, Mezentius (see p. 130) and his youthful son Lausus. The death of the latter causes Aeneas' battle frenzy to give way to sorrow and revulsion.

## Book 11

Near the start of Book 11 Aeneas makes arrangements for Pallas' body to be taken back to his father Evander.

11.59–99   When Aeneas had made this lament for Pallas, he ordered the pitiable body to be lifted up, and sent a thousand men, the pick of the whole army, to attend his 60 funeral rites and share in the father's tears, small consolation for a vast sorrow but a debt to be paid to the father in his wretchedness. Others energetically wove a soft bier of wicker-work with arbutus shoots and twigs of the oak tree and shaded **the** 65 **couch** they had made with a covering of leaves. Here they placed the young man high on his rustic bed, **like a flower** plucked by a girl's fingers, a soft violet or a drooping hyacinth; its brightness and beauty have not left it yet, but mother earth 70 no longer nourishes it and gives it strength.

Then Aeneas carried out two robes, stiff with gold and purple, which Sidonian Dido

---

**In frenzied anger Aeneas rages**   what do you feel about the fact that the man of piety falls into a frenzied rage?

**the couch**   this, of course, is the bier.

**like a flower**   for the simile here, compare the flower simile at the death of Euryalus (9.435–7) as well as lines 39–47 of Catullus 62, a marriage poem: 'As a flower grows hidden in an enclosed garden, unknown to the flock, uprooted by no plough; the breezes caress it, the sun strengthens it, the rain supports its growth; many boys desire it, many girls too: when that same flower has been plucked by a slender fingernail and sheds its petals, no boys desire it, no girls either: so it is with regard to a girl: as long as she remains untouched, for so long she is dear to her folk; when she has polluted her body and lost the flower of her chastity, she is no longer welcome to boys or dear to girls.' K. W. Gransden remarks: 'The erotic poignancy of Virgil's transformation of Catullus' lines derives from its central motif, that of virginity lost, not to marriage, as it should be ... but to death. Once the precious flower of virginity is plucked, an irreversible change occurs: in the case of Pallas or Euryalus, the ultimate transformation by the sterile bridegroom, death. The untimely deaths of these young men mean that they will now never achieve full manhood, marriage and children: the body of Pallas, its erotic beauty not yet faded, lies like a tableau before the reader.' What do *you* feel about the effect of these similes?

---

had once **made** for him with her own hands, delighting in the toil as **she interwove** 75
**the web with a subtle thread of gold.** Sadly he put one of these on the young
man as a final tribute and with its covering he veiled those locks of hair, soon to
burn on the pyre. He also piled up many prizes from the battle on **the Laurentian
fields** and ordered that the spoils should be borne in a long procession. To these
he added the horses and the weapons which he had taken from the enemy. He had 80
also bound behind their backs the hands of **those whom he intended to send as
funeral offerings to the shades below,** sprinkling the flames with the blood of the
slain; and he ordered that the leaders themselves should carry **tree trunks adorned
with the enemy's arms** and that the names of the slain foes should be inscribed on
them. Unhappy **Acoetes,** enfeebled by old age, was led along, now bruising his chest 85
with his fists, now tearing his face with his nails. He collapsed and lay stretched
out all his length on the ground. Behind him went Pallas' warhorse Aethon, **his
trappings laid aside,** weeping and wetting his face with big tears. Others carried 90
Pallas' spear and his helmet, for his conqueror **Turnus had the rest.** Then there
followed a sad troop of Trojans and all the Etruscans and the Arcadians **with their
arms reversed.** After the whole procession of his comrades had gone a long way

---

**had ... made ... she interwove the web with a subtle thread of gold**   the line is repeated
from 4.264, where it is used of a cloak Dido has made for Aeneas. Why do you think Virgil
makes a robe woven by Dido a pall for Pallas?

**the Laurentian fields**   the area south of the Tiber where the fighting has been taking
place.

**those whom he intended to send as funeral offerings to the shades below**   Aeneas had
expressed this hideous intention at 10.519. He shows himself no less capable of impious
action than Turnus or Homer's Achilles, who selected 12 prisoners, bound their hands
behind them and later sacrificed them on Patroclus' pyre (*Iliad* 21.27, 23.175). After
referring to Achilles' human sacrifice as 'a horrifying act of barbarity', Deryck Williams
remarks, 'Nothing would have been easier than for Virgil to omit this ghastly act ... in his
reworking of the story; therefore the fact that he has included it must be accorded its full
significance. The anger and passion for vengeance which overwhelms Aeneas is terrible
enough to cause even such an act of savagery as this.' Williams continues by referring to
the report in Suetonius (*Life of Augustus* 15) that Octavian offered human sacrifice to the
shade of Julius Caesar. What are your feelings about Aeneas at this point?

**tree trunks adorned with the enemy's arms**   these are Pallas' own trophies.

**Acoetes**   Pallas' squire.

**his trappings laid aside**   in mourning. The weeping warhorse is taken from the *Iliad*
where Achilles' horses weep for Patroclus (17.426–7). Suetonius (*Life of Julius Caesar* 81)
says that Caesar's horses wept at the prospect of his death. Some critics have thought the
passage about Aethon frigid and unconvincing. What do you feel?

**Turnus had the rest**   i.e. the sword-belt he stripped from Pallas, which will cost him his
life.

**with their arms reversed**   in mourning. Reversed arms were a feature of Roman military
funerals.

forward, Aeneas stopped and added these words with a deep sigh: '**The same grim** 95 **fates** of war call me away from here to weep other tears. **Hail for ever, mighty Pallas, and for ever farewell.**' He said no more, but turned towards the lofty walls of his camp and walked back to it.

A 12-day truce is arranged for the burial of the dead. Pallas' funeral procession arrives at Evander's city to the lamentations of his father.

### Evander's message to Aeneas

At the end of his speech of lamentation, Evander sends Aeneas a message, saying to the Trojans who have escorted the body of Pallas: 'Go, fix these commands in your memories and take them back to your king. The reason I prolong a life that I hate now that I have lost Pallas is your right hand, which you see owes Turnus as a gift both to son and to father. This is the only field open for the exercise of your valour and your fortune. I do not seek joy in life – that would not be right. All I ask is to take the news to my son among the shades below' (11.176–81).

- What does Evander mean by 'your right hand' (line 178) and by 'the news' (line 181)?

Latinus expresses his determination to make peace with the Trojans. Turnus, now back with the Latin army, will not allow this to happen but says that he is prepared to meet Aeneas in single combat. However, when Aeneas moves to the attack, general fighting breaks out again. The warrior maiden Camilla has her **aristeia**. An Etruscan warrior called Arruns shadows her, waiting for the moment to attack her.

11.768–84   It so happened that Chloreus, sacred to **Mount Cybelus** and for a long time a priest, was shining resplendent from afar in his Trojan arms and was urging on 770 his foaming horse which was **caparisoned with a coat of bronze scales** joined together with gold to form plumage. He himself, glorious in foreign **browns** and

---

**The same grim fates …**   'One of the shortest of Aeneas' speeches and one of the most touching', in the words of Gransden. There is deep pessimism here.

**Hail … farewell**   a Roman formula which brings gravestone inscriptions to mind.

**aristeia**   a Greek word referring to the sequence of a warrior's feats on the battlefield which show that warrior at the height of his or her prowess.

**Mount Cybelus**   the mountain of the goddess Cybele.

**caparisoned with a coat of bronze scales**   the horse wore a kind of coat of mail which gave an impression of plumage.

**browns**   the colour came from cinnabar dye from Spain.

purples, was shooting **Gortynian** arrows from his **Lycian** bow. The bow on his shoulders was golden, golden too the priest's plumed helmet. Then he had fastened 775 his saffron cape with its rustling folds of linen in a knot with a yellow-gold brooch, and his tunic and foreign trousers were embroidered with the needle. Whether it was so that she could fasten his Trojan armour up in the temple or so that she could flaunt herself in captured gold when she went hunting, the maiden blindly 780 followed him alone among all the fighters and, off her guard as she moved through the whole army, she burned with a woman's lust for booty and spoils, and then at last Arruns seized his moment and flung his spear from where he was hiding …

---

1   How does the appearance of Chloreus fit into the poem thematically?
2   What impression do you get of Camilla here? Does her behaviour remind you of anything earlier in the chapter?
3   Why do you think Virgil refers to 'a *woman*'s lust for booty and spoils' (line 782)?

---

Camilla dies, another young victim of the Roman mission, and Arruns is killed in reprisal. Eventually nightfall ends the battle.

## Book 12

Book 12 begins with Turnus renewing his offer to fight Aeneas in single combat despite the persuasion of Latinus and Amata, who says that she will never live to see Aeneas married to Lavinia.

12.64–71   As Lavinia heard these words of her mother, her burning cheeks were bathed in 65 tears. A deep blush glowed and suffused her hot face. **As when someone stains Indian ivory with blood-red dye**, or when many a white lily shines red amid a bed of roses, such were the colours the maiden showed in her face. Turnus' love 70 made him frantic and he fixed his gaze on the maiden. He burned all the more for the fight …

---

•   How does Lavinia come across here? Do you agree with Williams's assessment that she 'is not strongly characterized by Virgil: she never speaks and is merely a part of the plot'?

---

**Gortynian, Lycian**   Gortyna in Crete and Lycia were both associated with bows.

**As when someone stains Indian ivory with blood-red dye**   the simile is taken from *Iliad* 4.141–7, where the blood on the wounded Menelaus is likened to the staining of ivory by rich red dye.

Turnus arms himself for the fight with Aeneas and shouts the following lines.

12.97–106 'Grant that I may lay his body flat and with my strong hand tear off and pull to pieces the breastplate of the effeminate Phrygian, and befoul in the dust his hair, crimped with hot curling tongs and drenched with myrrh.' Such was the frenzy 100 driving him on, and as he blazed with passion, sparks flew from all over his face and fire glittered in his eager eyes – **just as when a bull** summons up terrifying bellows when he prepares himself for battle and tries to throw his anger into his horns as he crashes against the trunk of a tree, and challenges the winds with his 105 blows or paws the flying sand as he rehearses for battle.

Both sides take up positions to watch the fight between the Trojan and Rutulian leaders. It is obvious to everyone that Turnus will lose, and his sister, the immortal river nymph Juturna, causes the Rutulians to violate the truce made to bring about the single combat. General fighting breaks out again and Aeneas is wounded by an arrow from an unknown hand. Cured through the intervention of his mother Venus, Aeneas arms for battle and speaks to his son Ascanius.

12.433–40

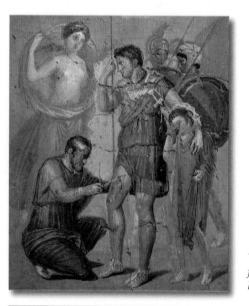

He clasped Ascanius in a mailed embrace and, lightly kissing him through his helmet, he said: '**From me, my boy, learn** courage and true endurance of hardship, 435

*The wounded Aeneas. In this wall painting from Pompeii a doctor treats the hero while his son Ascanius stands beside him.*

Grant ...   Turnus is addressing his spear.

just as when a bull ...   compare the very similar lines at *Georgics* 3.232–4 (p. 27).

From me, my boy, learn ...   the situation looks back to Hector's prayer for his son Astyanax at *Iliad* 6.476–81, though there Hector famously takes off his helmet (line 472). The words look back to those of Ajax to his son Eurysaces in Sophocles, *Ajax* 550–1: 'My son, may you be luckier than your father but otherwise the same.'

but learn fortune from others. Now my right hand will defend you in war and will lead you amid great rewards. You must make sure, when later your years have matured to manhood, that you remember, and as your mind looks back on the examples set by your kinsmen, may your father Aeneas and your uncle Hector 440 rouse your spirit.'

> • What impression do you get of the relationship between Aeneas and his son in this poem?

Aeneas and Turnus engage in indiscriminate slaughter.

12.505–28    Aeneas met the Rutulian Sucro (this was the first battle to stop the Trojans as they rushed forward) and caught him in the side with no great delay and drove his pitiless sword through his ribs, the fence of his chest where death comes most swiftly. Turnus flung Amycus and his brother **Diores** from their horses, met them 510 on foot and struck the one with his long spear as he advanced, the other with his sword, **cut off both of their heads, hung them** from his chariot and carried them along dripping with blood. Aeneas sent to death Talos and Tanais and brave Cethegus, the three of them in a single onslaught, and sad Onites, of **Echionian** 515 name, the son of Peridia. Turnus killed the brothers sent from Lycia and Apollo's fields, and young Menoetes who hated war – though little good it did him. He was an Arcadian who had practised his skill around the rivers of Lerna, rich in fish, and had lived there in a humble home. He knew nothing of the gifts of the powerful and his father sowed his crops on hired land. And like fires launched in 520 different parts of a dry wood, its thickets rustling with laurel, or as when foaming rivers rush roaring down from the high mountains and run into the sea, each one 525 leaving devastation in its wake – with no less fury did the two of them, Aeneas and Turnus, rush over the battlefield. Now, now waves of anger surged within them, their unconquerable hearts were at bursting point as, with all their might and main, they now moved to deadly combat.

> • On the basis of this passage, what are the characteristics of Virgil as a war poet? Are you impressed by this element in his work?

---

**Diores**   he had competed in the foot race in Book 5.

**cut off both of their heads, hung them ...**   we may remember the grim adornments of Cacus' cave (8.196–7).

**Echionian**   i.e. Theban, descended from Echion, one of the original Thebans.

**A flashback in Homer at the moment of the hero's death**

In his wonderful evocation of the fulfilled and contented home life of Menoetes at the moment of his death, Virgil imitates Homer, who frequently gives poignant glimpses of a hero's earlier existence in a different world as he dies. In *Iliad* 11.240–7, for example, Agamemnon struck the Thracian Iphidamas 'in the neck with his sword and loosened his limbs. So he fell on the spot and slept the sleep of bronze, the pitiable man, helping his countrymen far from the youthful wife he had won. He got no benefit from marrying her though he had given many bride-gifts. He gave a hundred cattle on the spot, and promised for later a thousand beasts – goats and sheep together – which he had in his huge flocks. But then indeed the son of Atreus stripped him and went bearing his fine armour through the press of the Achaeans.'

- What do such vignettes contribute to the poetry of war?

Aeneas now attacks the Latin city. Turnus rushes there to fight the Trojan in single combat.

12.697–727    But father Aeneas, hearing Turnus' name, left the walls and the lofty citadel and cast aside all delay, broke off every task, exultant with joy and thundering terribly 700 in his armour – as vast as **Athos**, as vast as **Eryx** or as huge father **Appenninus** himself when he roars amid his waving oak trees and rejoices as he raises his snowy summit to heaven. Now indeed the Rutulians and the Trojans and all the Italians eagerly turned their eyes, both those who were defending the high walls 705 and those who had taken off their armour from their shoulders to pound at the bottom of them with the battering ram. **Latinus himself** was dumbfounded that these huge men, born in different parts of the world, had come together and were settling the matter with the sword. And as soon as the warriors had reached an 710 empty part of the open plain, they flung their spears from a distance and rushed forward to battle with their shields and sounding bronze. The earth groaned. Then with their swords they redoubled their blows as they fell thick and fast.

---

**Athos**   Mount Athos in north-east Greece.

**Eryx**   a mountain in north-west Sicily.

**Appenninus**   the Apennines, the main mountain range of Italy, personified here as the father of Italy. What impression of Aeneas do you take from this simile?

**Latinus himself …**   Deryck Williams remarks, 'By presenting the situation as seen through the eyes of Latinus Virgil achieves a momentary detachment from the personality of the two main contestants, giving a sense of history and of the universal importance of the event.' What other features of this passage contribute to this sense of the universal importance of the fight between Aeneas and Turnus?

Chance and courage mingled together. And just as when on huge **Sila** or on the   715
top of **Taburnus two bulls** rush into deadly battle brow to brow, the cowmen fall
back in panic, the whole herd stands silent in fear, and the heifers low quietly as
they wait to see which will be lord of the forest, which all the herds will follow;
they inflict wounds on each other with great violence, they gouge each other with   720
thrusting horns and they bathe their necks and shoulders in streams of blood,
and the whole forest echoes back their bellowing – in the same way Trojan Aeneas
and the **Daunian** hero clashed with their shields and a great crashing filled the
sky. **Jupiter himself held up two scales** in equal balance and put in the different   725
fates of the two of them to see whom the struggle would doom and on which side
death would sink down with its weight.

> Turnus' sword shatters into fragments and Aeneas' spear sticks fast in the
> stump of an oleander. Juturna gives Turnus another sword and Venus gives
> Aeneas his spear back. Again they face each other, ready for the fight. The
> scene now shifts to Olympus.

**12.791–842**   Meanwhile [Jupiter], the king of all-powerful Olympus, spoke to Juno as she
watched the fighting from a golden cloud: 'What will be the end of this now, my
wife? What is left for you now at the last? You yourself know, and you admit that
you know, that Aeneas is claimed by heaven as **a native hero of the land** and that   795
the fates are raising him to the stars. What are you planning? What are you hoping
to achieve as you stay on in the chilling clouds? Was it right that **a god should be
profaned by a wound from a mortal hand** or that a missing sword should be

---

**Sila**   the Sila range is in Bruttium in south Italy.

**Taburnus**   this mountain is in Samnite territory (north of Lucania).

**two bulls**   compare *Georgics* 3.220–3 (p. 26), material reworked in this simile. What do
you feel about Virgil's reuse of an earlier poem?

**Daunian**   Daunus was Turnus' father.

**Jupiter himself held up two scales …**   as Achilles and Hector, the two protagonists of
the *Iliad*, are about to fight, 'the father [Zeus = Roman Jupiter] lifted up the golden
scales and placed in them two fates of death with its long sorrow, one of them that of
Achilles and the other that of Hector, tamer of horses. Taking the scales by the middle,
he dragged them up. Hector's day of doom sank down, and he went to Hades …' (*Iliad*
22.209–13). Virgil is clearly modelling what he writes here on Homer, but he reduces
Homer's five lines to three. It may be that there is something perfunctory about this
nod to Homer. The key difference in the treatment is that Homer tells us that Hector is
doomed (by sinking, his fate gets closer to the underworld) while Virgil does not let us
know that Turnus will die. Why might this be?

**a native hero of the land**   i.e. a deified national hero such as those invoked at *Georgics*
1.498.

**a god should be profaned by a wound from a mortal hand**   Aeneas, who was to be
deified, had, as we have seen, been wounded by an arrow earlier in the book.

restored to Turnus – for what could Juturna achieve without you? – and that the conquered should find new strength? Now at last you must stop. Be moved by my prayer. Do not let this terrible sorrow consume you in silent grief, and may your sweet lips speak no more of the woeful cares with which you visit me so often. The final moment has come. You were able to harry the Trojans on land and sea, to kindle a monstrous war, **to deface a happy home** and confound a wedding with sorrow. I forbid you to go further.' 800 805

So spoke Jupiter. So, with downcast eyes, spoke the goddess, the daughter of Saturn, in reply: 'It was because I knew that this was your will, great Jupiter, that I have reluctantly left Turnus and the earth; and you would not be seeing me sitting alone on my seat in the air suffering whatever I have to suffer – but I would be standing, circled with flames, right by the line of battle and I would be dragging the Trojans into the deadly fight. I did urge Juturna – I admit it – to come to the help of her unhappy brother and I agreed that she could dare still more to save his life, but not that she should **draw the bow or shoot the arrow**. I swear that by the implacable source of the river Styx, **the one religious sanction that is granted to the gods above**. And now I yield, yes I do, and I leave the conflict in disgust.' 810 815

*Jupiter. This famous bronze, dating from about 450 BC and found in the sea off the west coast of Greece in 1928, shows the god poised to throw his thunderbolt.*

**to deface a happy home**  i.e. because of Juno, the proposed marriage between Aeneas and Lavinia has involved terrible bloodshed.

**draw the bow or shoot the arrow**  the identity of the person who shot the bow was unknown, but the shooting certainly took place in the disruption caused by Juturna.

**the one religious sanction that is granted to the gods above**  an oath by the Styx was inviolable for the gods (6.324).

But this I beg of you **for the sake of Latium and the dignity of your people**: it is 820
forbidden by no law of fate. When they now establish peace through this happy
marriage – so be it! – when they make their laws and treaties together, do not
order the Latins, who are native here, to change their old name or become Trojans
and be called **Teucrians,** or bid the men to change their language or alter their 825
dress. Let Latium exist, let there be **Alban kings** from one generation to the next.
Let the power of the Roman stock be based on Italian courage. Troy has fallen. Let
her stay fallen together with her name.'

Smiling upon her, the creator of men and of the universe replied: 'You are the 830
sister of Jupiter and the second child of Saturn, **such great waves of passion
surge in your heart.** But come, calm the frenzy that was roused so pointlessly. I
grant what you wish. You have won me over and I willingly give in to you. The
Ausonians shall keep the language of their fathers and **their way of life** and their
name shall be as it is now. **Mixed in stock only,** the Trojans will sink down. I shall 835
add the custom and rites of worship and make them all Latins with one tongue.
From them a race shall arise mixed with Ausonian blood, which you shall see
surpass men, surpass the gods in piety, and no people shall celebrate your worship 840
as much as they shall.' Juno assented to this and reversed her purpose with joy. As
she did do, she left the cloud and departed from heaven.

---

> 1 How well balanced is the deal struck between Jupiter and Juno?
>
> 2 W. R. Johnson suggests that Juno feels joy (line 841) 'because she knows
>    that, since Dido's curse is still operative, the suffering of the Trojans cannot
>    be revoked by her temporary acquiescence to Jupiter's command, that there
>    will be other times and other places for her to attempt what she wants to
>    accomplish' (pp. 126–7). Are you at all persuaded by this?

---

**for the sake of Latium and the dignity of your people**   Jupiter's father Saturn had once
reigned in Latium, and Latinus was descended from him.

**Teucrians**   i.e. Trojans, descended from Teucer, an ancestor of the Trojan kings.

**Alban kings**   Ascanius founded Alba Longa and he and his successors ruled there for 300
years until Romulus founded Rome.

**such great waves of passion surge in your heart**   i.e. like her father Saturn, Juno is
prone to violent passions.

**their way of life**   Juno has not asked that the Latin way of life should be preserved.
Jupiter gives her more than she has requested.

**Mixed in stock only**   i.e. their only contribution will be physical union with the Italians.
But in fact Jupiter goes on to imply, rather elusively, that some features of Trojan religion
will be preserved. The household gods brought by Aeneas from Troy are of great
importance in the poem, being referred to 20 times. The temple restored by Augustus on
the Velian hill in Rome contained a shrine for them.

12.843–952    When this was done, the father himself considered something else in his heart
and prepared to send **Juturna** from her warrior brother's side. There are twin   845
horrors called the Dread Ones by name. The goddess of the dead of night bore
them in one and the same birth as hellish **Megaera**, wreathed them like her with
coils of snakes and gave them wings as swift as the wind. These attend the throne
of Jupiter on the threshold of the king when he is in angry mood, and they whet   850
the fears of suffering mortals, if ever the king of the gods is wreaking ghastly
death or diseases, or terrifying guilty cities with war. Jupiter sent one of these
swiftly down from the heights of heaven and ordered her to confront Juturna as
an omen. She flew to earth, borne by a swift whirlwind. Just like an arrow shot   855
from the bowstring through the clouds, one that a **Parthian** has let fly, a Parthian
or a **Cydonian**, an arrow armed with the gall of cruel poison, a weapon for which
there is no cure, and it leaps unseen as it hisses through the swift shadows – so
did the daughter of Night speed down on her way to the earth. After she saw the   860
battle lines of the Trojans and the columns of Turnus, she suddenly shrank into
the shape of a small bird, **the bird** that sometimes sings its ominous song amid
the shadows late at night as it sits on tombs or deserted rooftops. Taking on this   865
form, the horror flew and flew again at Turnus' face, screeching and battering his
helmet with her wings. A strange numbness loosened his limbs in dread. **His hair
stood on end in horror and his voice stuck in his throat.**

But when his unhappy sister Juturna recognized the whirring of the Dread One's
wings from a distance, she loosened her hair and tore at it, **bloodying her face**   870
**with her nails and bruising her breasts with her fists**: 'What help can your sister
bring you now, Turnus? What remains for me now after all I have endured? With
what art can I prolong your life? Can I confront such a monstrous portent? Now,
now I leave the battle. Do not make me more frightened than I already am, you   875
hellish birds. I recognize the beating of your wings, that deadly sound. I cannot

---

Juturna   she is still supporting Turnus.

Megaera   one of the Furies.

Parthian, Cydonian   the Parthians and Cydonians from Crete were famous archers.

the bird …   we now discover that the bird is an owl.

His hair stood on end in horror and his voice stuck in his throat   twice previously this
had been Aeneas' experience: 2.774, 4.280.

bloodying her face with her nails and bruising her breasts with her fists   the line is used
of Dido's sister Anna during the Carthaginian queen's final moments (4.673).

mistake the proud commands of **great-hearted** Jupiter. **Is this his recompense for my virginity?** Why did he give me eternal life? Why did he take away the possibility of death? Then I could have ended this terrible agony for certain now. 880 I could have gone through the shades at my unhappy brother's side. Is *this* what immortality means for me? Will anything of mine be sweet for me without you, my brother? Can any chasm gape deep enough for me, and send me down to the lowest of the shades, goddess though I am?' So saying, the goddess covered her 885 head in a **green** veil with many a moan and hid herself in her deep stream.

Aeneas pressed on against him and brandished his spear, huge like a tree, and spoke these words from his cruel heart: 'So what is the reason for delay now? Why Turnus, do you draw back now? We must fight it out, not in a race but hand to 890 hand with cruel arms. **Transform yourself into every shape**, summon up all your powers of courage or skill. Choose to make for the lofty stars on wings or to hide yourself in a hole in the hollow ground.' Shaking his head, Turnus replied, 'It is not your hot words that terrify me, you fierce man; it is the gods who terrify me 895 and Jupiter, my enemy.' He said no more but, looking round, he saw a huge rock, a huge and ancient rock which happened to be lying on the plain, set as a boundary stone on the land to resolve disputes about the fields. Scarcely could twice six picked men lift it onto their necks, **men of such physique as the earth now brings** 900 **forth**. The hero picked it up in his trembling hands and flung it at his enemy, stretching up high as he ran at speed. But he did not know himself as he ran or as he moved or as he lifted the huge rock in his hands or threw it. His knees gave way, 905 his blood turned cold and froze. Then the stone itself, thrown by the man through the empty space, did not cover the whole distance between them or drive its blow home. And **just as in a dream**, when drowsy sleep has pressed our eyes closed at

---

**great-hearted**   presumably spat out with bitter irony.

**Is this his recompense for my virginity?**   she had been raped by Jupiter and made an immortal river nymph in consequence.

**green**   the suitable colour for a river deity.

**Transform yourself into every shape ...**   mockingly, Aeneas suggests that Turnus should imitate Proteus and change into various shapes, so that he can fly away like a bird or hide in the ground like a mole.

**men of such physique as the earth now brings forth**   the idea of a man lifting a great stone which today's men would not have the strength to is based on *Iliad* 12.447–9, where Hector on his own has no problem in swinging a rock which two excellent men of the poet's day could not easily lever onto a wagon; and also on *Iliad* 5.302–4, where Diomedes swings a boulder which two of today's men could not lift. What is your response to Virgil's hyperbole here (*twelve* men)?

**just as in a dream ...**   an adaptation of a climactic simile in the *Iliad* when Hector runs away from Achilles: 'as in a dream the man in pursuit cannot catch the man running away: the one cannot escape nor the other catch him' (22.199–200).

night, we seem to want to run on further in our eagerness, but it is no good, we 910
feel weak and collapse in the midst of our efforts; our tongue has no power, our
familiar strength fails our body, and we can utter no sound or words – so it was
with Turnus. However courageously he sought a way, the terrible goddess denied
him success. Then his breast was in a turmoil of different emotions. He looked 915
at the Rutulians and the city, he faltered in his fear, and trembled because death
was imminent. He did not see where he could escape or where he could attack his
enemy. He did not see his chariot anywhere or his sister the charioteer.

As he faltered, Aeneas brandished his fateful spear, saw a favourable chance, 920
and with all his force he flung it from afar. Never do rocks hurled by a siege-
engine roar so loudly against city walls, nor do such crashing sounds burst from
thunderbolts. Like a black whirlpool the spear flew bearing terrible destruction,
and it pierced the edge of his breastplate and the outside of the circles of his 925
seven-layered shield. With a hiss it went through the middle of his thigh. At this
blow huge Turnus fell to the ground, his knee buckling. The Rutulians started
up with a groan. The whole mountain boomed back around them and the high
woods re-echoed the sound far and wide. He lifted his eyes and stretched out 930
his right hand, begging **in humble supplication**: 'I have earned it, and I do not
ask for mercy,' he said. 'Make use of your fortune. If any concern for a wretched
parent can touch your heart at all, I beg you – for you too had such a parent in
your father Anchises – **pity Daunus in his old age**, and **give me** or, if you choose, 935
my lifeless body **to my people**. You have conquered, and the Ausonians have seen
me stretch out my hands to my conqueror. Lavinia is yours to marry. Do not push
your hatred further.'

Aeneas stood there fierce in his arms shifting his gaze, and he restrained his hand.
And as he paused, Turnus' speech had begun to affect him more and more, when 940
the ill-omened sword-belt high on his shoulder caught his eye, shining with its
familiar studs, the sword-belt of the boy Pallas whom Turnus had wounded and
laid low in defeat – and now he was wearing his enemy's insignia on his shoulders.

---

**in humble supplication**   at 6.853 (p. 113) the ghost of Aeneas' father told his son that he
should spare his enemies in this situation.

**pity Daunus in his old age**   in the last book of the *Iliad* Priam begs Achilles to give him
the corpse of his son Hector by invoking the feelings of Achilles' own father (24.486–92):
cf. 22.419–20.

**give me … to my people**   as Hector had unsuccessfully asked of Achilles at *Iliad* 22.340–3.
Achilles does give the corpse back in Book 24. We never discover what happens to the
corpse of Turnus.

After Aeneas had gazed at those spoils which brought back his cruel grief to his 945
mind, on fire with frenzy and terrible in his wrath, he shouted: 'You are wearing
the spoils of one of my own. Are you to be snatched away from me? It is Pallas,
Pallas who sacrifices you with this stroke and exacts the penalty in your guilty
blood!' Saying this, he buried his sword in the breast of his enemy, boiling with 950
rage. But Turnus' limbs were loosened in the chill of death **and with a groan his
life fled complaining to the underworld.**

---

1  Trace your feelings about Turnus and Aeneas through the course of this
   passage. Do your sympathies incline to one side?

2  How 'satisfactory' is the end of the poem? How optimistic or pessimistic do
   you find it?

3  Do you find this a thrilling climax to the poem? Can you see at all what
   Virgil meant when he said at 7.45 that he was embarking on the greater
   part of his work when he started the second half of his poem?

---

**and with a groan his life fled complaining to the underworld**  the final focus of the
poem is on Turnus. The concluding line is also used at the death of Camilla (11.893),
another victim of the Roman mission. It is a Latin version of Homer's lines at the deaths
of Patroclus and Hector (*Iliad* 16.856–7, 22.362–3).

# Recommended reading

An excellent account of where Virgil scholarship stood at the end of the twentieth century can be found in **Philip Hardie**, *Virgil* (*Greece & Rome*, New Surveys in the Classics, no. 28; Oxford, 1998). Important work has been done on the *Georgics* since then, the most recent book being **Christopher Nappa**, *Reading after Actium: Vergil's* Georgics, *Octavian, and Rome* (Michigan, 2005). The other poems have not undergone any radical reappraisal. Still to be recommended are **Jasper Griffin**, *Virgil* (Oxford and London, 1988); **K. W. Gransden**, *Virgil: The Aeneid* (Landmarks of World Literature; Cambridge, 1990); and the classic **W. A. Camps**, *An Introduction to Virgil's* Aeneid (Oxford, 1969). *The Cambridge Companion to Virgil*, edited by **Charles Martindale** (Cambridge, 1997), is particularly strong on the reception of the poet in the modern world.

For the historical background, **Josiah Osgood**, *Caesar's Legacy: Civil War and the Emergence of the Roman Empire* (Cambridge, 2006), provides an excellent modern account, as well as including lively and illuminating responses to the *Eclogues* and *Georgics*. Also valuable is **Martin Goodman** with the assistance of **Jane Sherwood**, *The Roman World, 44 BC–AD 180* (London, 1997). For the topography of Rome, **Amanda Claridge**, *Rome* (Oxford Archaeological Guides; Oxford, 1998), is invaluable.

## Translations

For approachability, the Penguin Classics translations are the ones to go for: **Guy Lee** for the *Eclogues* (1984), **L. P. Wilkinson** for the *Georgics* (1982), and **David West** for the *Aeneid* (1991). John Dryden's translation of the *Aeneid* is a classic of English poetry and is available with an introduction by myself (Wordsworth, 1997).

The Loeb edition of the poems, which sets an English translation on the page facing the Latin, is admirable and has recently been revised: *Virgil* (2 vols.), translation by **H. Rushton Fairclough**, revised by **C. P. Goold** (Cambridge, Mass., and London, 1999).

## Commentaries

The following commentaries have proved very helpful in the writing of this book, and it is perfectly possible for the Latinless reader to gain a lot from their introductions and notes.

*Eclogues*: **R. Coleman** (Cambridge, 1977); **W. Clausen** (Oxford, 1994).

*Georgics*: **R. F. Thomas** (Cambridge, 1988); **R. A. B. Mynors** (Oxford, 1990).

*Aeneid*: Books 1, 2, 4 and 6 are available in commentaries by **R. G. Austin** (Oxford, 1971, 1964, 1955, 1977 respectively), Books 3 and 5 in commentaries by **R. D. Williams** (London, 1962, 1960). Books 7 and 8 are edited together by **C. J. Fordyce** (Glasgow and Oxford, 1977), and Books 8, 9 and 11 are published in admirable editions by Cambridge University Press, Books 8 and 11 by **K. W. Gransden** (1976 and 1991), Book 9 (particularly outstanding) by **P. R. Hardie** (1994).

**R. D. Williams** has edited the *Eclogues* and *Georgics* together (London, 1979) as well as the whole of the *Aeneid* (London, 1973).

## Authors referred to in the text but not mentioned above

**H. Dahlmann**, 'Der Bienenstaat in Vergils Georgica', *Abh. der Mainzer Akad. der Wiss.* (Geistesklasse no. 10, 1954), 547–62.

**J. Griffin**, 'The Fourth *Georgic*, Virgil and Rome', *Greece and Rome*, 26 (1979), 61–80.

**R. Heinze**, *Virgil's Epic Technique*, tr. H. and D. Harvey and F. Robertson (Bristol, 1933).

**W. R. Johnson**, *Darkness Visible: A Study of Vergil's Aeneid* (Berkeley, Los Angeles, and London, 1976).

**J. W. Mackail** (ed.), *The Aeneid* (Oxford, 1930).

**K. Maclennan**, *Aeneid 4* (Bristol, 2007).

**B. Otis**, *Virgil: A Study in Civilized Poetry* (Oxford, 1964).

**T. E. Page**, *The Aeneid* (London, 1894, 1900).

**T. E. Page**, *Bucolics and Georgics* (London, 1898).

**A. S. Pease**, *Publi Vergilii Maronis Aeneidos Liber Quartus* (Cambridge, Mass., 1935).

**M. S. Spurr**, 'Agriculture and the *Georgics*', Greece and Rome, 33 (1986), 164–87.